JEWISH PERSPECTIVES

JEWISH PERSPECTIVES

25 Years of Modern Jewish Writing

A Jewish Quarterly Anthology

Selected and Edited by
Jacob Sonntag

SECKER & WARBURG
LONDON

First published in England 1980 by
Martin Secker & Warburg Limited
54 Poland Street, London W1V 3DF
in association with the
Jewish Literary Trust Limited.

Copyright © 1980 by The Jewish Quarterly, London

All translations from the Yiddish and
German in this volume are by Jacob Sonntag,
for which the copyright is held by The
Jewish Quarterly, London.

SBN: 436 47790 4

This volume is dedicated to the memory
of the late Sylvia Shine, by the Barnett
Shine Charitable Foundation.

Printed in Great Britain by
Willmer Brothers Limited
Rock Ferry, Merseyside

CONTENTS

Editor's Note	viii
IN PERSPECTIVE	1
J. L. Talmon: *European History as the Seedbed of the Holocaust*	1
Hyam Maccoby: *The Disputation*	32
Meir Wiener: *Diogo Pires*	43
Chaim Sloves: *Baruch of Amsterdam*	46
Lionel Kochan: *Judaism for the Intellectual*	51
ON BEING ENGLISH AND JEWISH	65
Alexander Baron: '*Jewish Preoccupations...*'	66
Brian Glanville: '*At a Deeper Level one is and remains Jewish*'	72
Frederic Raphael: '*Something to be Serious About...*'	75
Gerda Charles: '*I Believe...*'	78
Wolf Mankowitz: '*I have a very Strong Sense of Origin*'	81
Dannie Abse: '*Jews are bound to each other...*'	83
Michael Hamburger: '*How my Jewishness was brought Home to me*'	87
Emanuel Litvinoff: *A Jewish Writer in England*	89
ASPECTS OF LITERATURE	103
David Daiches: *Some Aspects of Anglo-American Jewish Fiction*	103
Renee Winegarten: *Writing About Jews*	112

Rafael Scharf: *Recollections of a Bookworm*   124
Barnet Litvinoff: *Chaim Superman Gazes Down on his Night Perfect People*   138

ASPECTS OF ISRAEL   145
J. B. Segal: *The Arab Image in Israeli Fiction*   145
Shimon Ballas: *The Israeli Image in Arab Literature*   159
Erwin I. J. Rosenthal: *Judaism in the Jewish State*   172

ART AND ARTISTS   179
Charles Spencer: *Towards a Definition of Jewish Art*   179
Josef Herman: *The Modern Artist in Modern Society*   191
Gabriel Josipovici: *Absence and Echo*   198

THE WORLD OF YESTERDAY   203
Harry Zohn: *Heinrich Heine: a Reassessment*   204
Lothar Kahn: *Lion Feuchtwanger: Jewish Novelist of Our Time*   223
Alfred Werner: *Beer-Hofmann: Last of the Great Viennese*   234
Richard Beer-Hofmann: *Poem*   242
Nelly Sachs: *Poems*   244

RESISTANCE AND SURVIVAL   247
Anonymous: '*... as a Hidden Spring Underground ...*'   248
Joseph Kirman: *I'll Speak to You Frankly, my Child ...*   251
Jacob Gordon, Yitzhak Katzenelson, Selma Meerbaum-Eisinger, Pavel Friedmann, David Sfard, Antoni Slonimski: *Poems*   254

THE 'BLACK YEARS' OF THE STALINIST TERROR   267
C. Abramsky: *The 'Golden Age' of Soviet Yiddish Literature that was Brutally Destroyed*   267
Ch. Shmeruk: *Jewish Culture in Historical Perspective*   273

SOVIET-YIDDISH POETRY   283
Peretz Markish, Shmuel Halkin, David Hofshteyn   284

CONTEXT AND CONTINUITY	293
Y. L. Peretz: *The Golden Chain*	293
Josef Herman: *'Peretzism' and Yiddish*	304
Sh. Anski: *The Trial: a Chassidic Folktale*	309
Jacob Glatstein, Avram N. Stencil, Moishe Teyf: *Poems*	318

EDITOR'S NOTE

Jewish Perspectives is designed to give the reader a taste of what *The Jewish Quarterly*, the only Anglo-Jewish literary and art magazine, has in store for him. That magazine has recently completed 25 years of publication.

To present in one volume a selection of material culled, for the most part, from nearly one hundred past issues, was no easy task. In deciding on what to include and what to leave out, I was guided not so much by what would be considered 'the best' in terms of literature as by the subject matter dealt with over the years. I was struck by the timelessness and topicality of the recurrent themes.

There is the ongoing debate between Judaism and Christianity or, if you like, between Judaism and the world at large. Hyam Maccoby's reconstruction of a medieval 'disputation', of which an extract appears in this volume, touches upon the dividing line between the two world religions. But there is also a dividing line within Jewry itself between reasoned argument and blind fanaticism as manifest, for instance, in the excommunication of Baruch Spinoza by the Amsterdam 'Kahal' some 300 years ago and by the tension between the intellectuals and the religious establishment in our own day. This is illustrated by an extract from a play, 'Baruch of Amsterdam', and an essay by Lionel Kochan.

Messianic longing, so eloquently expressed in Peretz's poetic drama, 'The Golden Chain', has been a constant trend in Jewish history: it emphasizes the belief in continuity and a better future that will bring an end to suffering not only of the Jewish people but of mankind as a whole. '*The world, it must be redeemed... Let there be Sabbath, Sabbath eternal!*' Rabbi Shloime exclaims. The extract from this play was published in the very first issue of *The Jewish Quarterly*, in 1953.

To what extent is this age-old Jewish tradition discernible in the work of our contemporary writers? In their answers to an enquiry, *'On being English and Jewish'*, some of the writers show an acute awareness of their Jewishness, though not without qualifications. Yet they all admit that the Nazi Holocaust has greatly affected their outlook and influenced their work, becoming even an obsession with some.

Of the mass of material on the subject of the Holocaust, published over the years in this magazine, I limited myself in this selection to literary documents which miraculously survived their authors; they bear witness to man's capacity to resist evil and to maintain human dignity even in the shadow of certain death. This tragic chapter of recent Jewish history has also inspired Yiddish poets among the survivors, and others 'who were not there'. Since only very little of this poetry is available in English translation elsewhere, I felt justified in concentrating on these translations in particular.

An anthology of this kind should be modelled on an average, representative issue of the magazine from which it was culled. Some of its regular features will indeed be found in this selection ('Aspects of Literature', 'Aspects of Israel', 'Art and Artists' etc.). Others, such as the book section, a major feature in a regular issue, had to be disregarded, as had scholarly essays of a specialized nature, the latter mainly on account of their length. Interested readers will be able to avail themselves of a full index of the first 25 volumes of *The Jewish Quarterly*, now in preparation, which will be obtainable in due course.

For different reasons, another regular feature, Anglo-Jewish Poetry, has been omitted. Since many of the poems, first published in the magazine, have subsequently been included in several collections and anthologies, there was no point in reprinting them again here. *The Jewish Quarterly* itself, in two Special Editions, presented brief anthologies of Anglo-Jewish Poetry – in 1956 and 1966, respectively.

I would like to think that the present volume is not only a celebration of an achievement past but that, in itself, it will contribute towards a greater awareness of the Jewish cultural tradition. I would like to thank all those who made this publication possible: the writers who have in the past contributed to the magazine and thereby had a share in its accomplishment not less than those who are represented herein. Thanks are also due to Mr Tom Rosenthal, of Secker & Warburg, who encouraged me to embark upon my self-imposed task of compiling this selection; to Mr Thomas Yoseloff, who showed sufficient faith in *The Jewish Quarterly* in its early days by publishing the first anthology (*Caravan, A Jewish Quarterly Omnibus*) as far back as 1961; to Frank Cass, of Vallentine Mitchell, who published a second anthology, *Jewish Writing Today*, in 1974; to Mr Pierre Gildesgame for his generous contribution, enabling us to include the eight pages of art reproductions; and to the Honorary Officers of the Jewish Literary Trust, who secured the publication when it faced a critical stage; and to all those who, in various ways and at various times, have come to its rescue. They all may derive some satisfaction from the fact that their trust has not been misplaced and their efforts have not been in vain.

October 1979 J.S.

IN PERSPECTIVE

European History as the Seedbed of the Holocaust

J. L. TALMON

To the historian and psychologist the Nazi Holocaust poses questions beyond merely recording man's inhumanity against man. Beyond the facts he looks for an answer to the motives behind the emotions, to the 'reasoning' beyond reasons, which made possible the active participation of tens of thousands in the crime of total murder, and of other tens of thousands to acquiesce in the 'consensus of silence'.

In the following paper, presented at a Yad Va-Shem symposium on 19 April 1973, the thirtieth anniversary of the Warsaw Ghetto Uprising, J. L. Talmon, Professor of Modern History at the Hebrew University, Jerusalem, traces the roots of the ideology that led up to Hitler's 'Final Solution', and comes to the conclusion that they are to be found in the whole trend of European history from its dawn throughout the ages up to the present time. By rejecting the Jewish legacy of a messianic age of equality for all there developed the cult of the personality and of an elite which divided mankind into superior and inferior races, making the latter the carriers of all evil which have to be destroyed in order to 'save mankind'.

Never since the dawn of history had the world witnessed such a campaign of extermination as that carried out by Hitler's Germany. This was not an explosion of religious fanaticism; not a wave of pogroms, the work of incited mobs running amok or led by a ringleader; not the riots of a soldiery gone wild or drunk with victory and wine; not the fear-wrought psychosis of revolution or civil war that rises and subsides like a whirlwind. It was none of these. An entire nation was handed over by a 'legitimate' government to murderers organized by the authorities and trained to hunt and kill, with one single provision, that every one, *the entire nation*, be murdered – men and women, old and young, healthy and sick and paralysed, *everyone*, without any chance of even one of those condemned to extermination escaping his fate.

After they had suffered hunger, torture, degradation and humiliation inflicted on them by their tormentors to break them down, to rob them of the last shred of human dignity, and to deprive them of any strength to resist and perhaps of any desire to live, the victims were seized by the agencies of the state and brought from the four corners of Hitlerite Europe to the death camps, to be killed, individually or in groups, by the murderers' bullets over the graves dug by the victims themselves, or in slaughterhouses constructed especially for human beings. For the condemned there was no judge to whom to appeal for redress of injustice; no government from which to ask protection and punishment for the murders; no neighbour on whose gate to knock and ask for shelter; no God to whom to pray for mercy.

It is in all this that this last campaign of extermination differs from all the other massacres, mass killings and bloodshed perpetrated throughout history, such as the annihilation of defeated tribes in ancient times or in the African jungle, the slaughter of conquered peoples by the Mongols, the crusade of extermination against the Albigensians in the 13th century, the horrors of St Bartholomew's Night and of the wars of religion in the 16th and the 17th centuries, the Chmielnicki pogroms in 1648, and peasants' uprisings and their suppression in rivers of blood, even the massacres of Greeks and Armenians at the hands of the Turks.

The Holocaust visited on the Jews is different from all these earlier massacres in its conscious and explicit planning, in its systematic execution, in the absence of any emotional element in the remorselessly applied decision to exterminate *everyone*, but *everyone*; in the exclusion of any possibility that someone, when his turn came to be liquidated, might escape his fate by surrendering, by joining the victors and collaborating with them, by converting to the victors' faith, or by selling himself into slavery in order to save his life.

There is no doubt that even had the Final Solution not been formally decreed, tens of thousands of Jews would have perished in the war by the sword, from hunger, through epidemics, by all kinds of strange deaths. Millions of Jews would have suffered torments of hunger, infernal torture and all the degradation and humiliation possible at the hands of Nazis and their helpers. I myself heard Chaim Weizmann's sombre prediction at the beginning of the hostilities that 'in this war, we shall lose a million Jews'. Ze'ev Jabotinsky, some time before the outbreak of the war, sounded the warning that the Jews of Central and Eastern Europe must soon expect a St Bartholomew's Night. Yet no one thought, or could have thought, of an Auschwitz.

Are we dealing here with a regression to the most primitive barbarism or with the nihilism of a later, sophisticated generation? With the outbreak of sadism or with the rabid frenzy of a perverse idealism which offers release, legitimacy and even glamour to the instincts of aggression and cruelty? What made this unprecedented deviation from the norm possible at all? The immediate and simple answer is, Hitler. There is certainly no need, nor any reason, to belittle Hitler's direct responsibility. Without him, the decision to proceed with the Final Solution would never have been taken. This answer is, however, entirely unsatisfactory. Hitler depended on the consent of associates who would carry out his monstrous plans; he needed hundreds, thousands, perhaps tens of thousands of assistants at all levels, from the most highly-placed, sophisticated and 'well-bred' intimates who participated in the decision making, down to the lowliest apprentice in the arts of homicide – the sadistic killer or the mindless robot.

The deviation from the traditional, the hallowed, the almost instinctive norm enshrined in the injunction 'Thou shalt not kill' – nor take life without proper trial, nor kill the defenceless, nor harm the innocent – was in this case so violent and unprecedented that it is difficult to grasp how even an insane or half-sane fanatic could find it in himself not only to conceive such a plan, but to decree that 'Thou shalt kill' millions, an entire nation, without evoking the immediate horrified reaction, 'Why, you must be out of your mind'.

How, we wonder, did he obtain the consent and cooperation of his closest associates, the compliance of the mass of executioners and the resigned acceptance of the very many who did not care or who were unwilling to get into trouble but who all knew, fully, partially or dimly, what was going on, and chose not to ask questions, but to look away?

Even an Oriental despot in bygone days would have shrunk from committing – indeed would not have been able to contemplate – certain actions which would constitute an attack on established beliefs, violate certain taboos, strike a blow to deep-seated feelings or ancient traditions. In every period in history there have been things that people 'simply will not accept', come what may; things that are so unbearable that it is better to die than be a party to them.

Fear alone cannot explain everything, even the most arbitrary act of an unbridled tyrant is in some measure a function of the general climate, the spirit of the times, the social structure, the standard of values. For instance, the interference of the military with the political process by overthrowing the government or imposing its will by force on the nation, is utterly inconceivable in England and the United States, while it is a daily occurrence in Latin America and the Third World. In this sense one can perhaps speak of a consensus by silence, of acquiescence through indifference. Between the ruthless tyrant and the silent majority there is a quantitative difference that gradually expands into a qualitative one; this development, however, does not invalidate the basic premise, the common point of departure.

Release from awe and respect, the disappearance of inhibitions against deviant acts does not take place overnight; it is a protracted, gradual process of dialectical development. However, the transition from absence of inhibition to the actual commission of acts without precedent is not a result of structure only, but also of opportunity, of a state of emergency giving rise to storms of emotion, of a situation in which all restraint is jettisoned, of a period of danger and peril which gives a certain legitimacy to acts and methods required by desperate circumstances where all other methods have failed. The sense of exceptional emergency unleashes instincts of violence and sweeps away inhibitions imposed by institutional framework, by sentiment, and by the labyrinthine workings of the subconscious mind. There is great importance in the tools and the techniques which allow such acts to be carried out with speed, efficiency and a minimum of publicity, for it is essential to confront everybody as quickly as possible with the fact that they have all become, in Goebbels' words, accomplices in a crime for which they can expect no excuse and no pardon.

We shall try to penetrate the 'geological', historical, social, ideological and psychological layers from which this terrible act of *hubris*, the decision on the Holocaust, sprouted forth. The question that must be asked is, whether the point of departure, the core of the entire development was anti-Semitism, hatred of the Jews, and nothing else. Such a limited answer does not seem adequate to me. Even if we agree that antagonism to the Jews is an unchanging element, a primary factor, continuous and identical from Hellenistic times until today, and not merely a cluster of superstitions that erupt from time to time in waves of hostile agitation, in persecution and riots – even then we shall be obliged to recognize a multiplicity of formulations, expressions, methods of implementation, modes of incitement, types of accusation, all dependent on place, time, political and socio-economic conditions, moral and spiritual values and psychological factors. In short, anti-Semitism may be an autonomous, or more exactly, a primary phenomenon, but in one way or another it is a function of external factors. Anti-Semitism is part of a wider context.

The whole pattern of relations between Christians and Jews has from the beginning been saturated with neurotic elements, on both sides, and it could not have been otherwise. Neurosis consists in the compulsive tendency to react disproportionately to stimuli as the result of a shattering experience at the dawn of youth. The birth of Christianity, its central *mysterium* and all its most decisive events tie it inextricably to Judaism.

Judaism is Christianity's parent, but Jews are at the same time deicides, the murderers of the Messiah, of the Redeemer. Christians are mankind redeemed by Jesus, but they are also the new Israel, the heirs of the election taken away from the old Israel because it rejected God's Messiah and thus God himself.

Murder within the family, the murder of a father or brother according to Freud, and murder as a consequence of incest in the view of various anthropologists, is the cornerstone of every culture, every order of values, every ethical system and code of behaviour (*vide* Cain and Abel, Oedipus, Romulus and Remus). Instincts of aggression boil up to the point of murder; the participants in the act are deeply shaken and their feeling of guilt gives birth to conscience; mourning unites the family or the tribe in the cult of the deceased relative; anxiety to prevent the recurrence of a similar crime gives birth to a system of laws, ethics and taboos; the memory of the experience inspires storytellers, poets, and artists.

How much more true is all this of the murder of God. The believers of the murdered God are full of hatred and craving for vengeance against the murderers, but they can never forget that Jesus, his mother, the apostles and the apostolic community sprang from the nation of the murderers. They cannot forget that the Old Testament and everything in it, the idea of election and the prophecy of the saviour who shall come at the end of the days, is the pre-history, the *preparation* of Christianity, its seedbed, a preparatory stage of the true faith that could not be skipped. Gratitude acts as a brake upon hatred, but gratitude is stifled by hostility.

We shall ignore the background of Hellenistic anti-Semitism, the hatred of a strange, alien people, avoiding contact with all other peoples and exalting itself in the belief of its uniqueness and election, a nation of 'mankind haters'. We shall also ignore the influence of these sentiments on the final rupture between Christians and Jews, on the formation of Christian anti-Semitism and on its adoption of philosophical, ethical, social and other anti-Jewish arguments. The peculiar neurosis referred to above is wholly due to the original dichotomy contained in the affinity of Christianity to Judaism. It becomes visible not only in homicidal hostility and in the urge to persecute, but also in manifestations of a strikingly sympathetic attitude, for example, towards Zionism in its early days, in the first years after the Holocaust and in the period of the establishment of the State of Israel. This attitude stems from feelings of remorse, duty, and shame. In other words, the feelings of gentiles towards Jews are marked by an absence of balance, impartiality and ease. They gravitate between opposite poles. Amos Ox succeeded beautifully in describing the Christian's reaction to the Jew as the expression of the worst and the best in him.

The encounter between the Jews and the Germanic and Slavic

tribes in the centuries following the demise of the Roman Empire added complications to this neurosis. The new masters, ignorant uncivilized barbarians, were confronted by a people of ancient culture, incomparably higher than theirs, a people with a strange faith, mentality and customs, a race shrouded in mystery and a people descended from those who killed God.

At first sight, these people were weak and helpless, but at the same time astonishingly resourceful, vital and tenacious. In the eyes of the Church, they were a permanent reproach and challenge because of their refusal to acknowledge the Saviour and the fact that they were no longer the chosen people. Despised and outcast, they were, however, neither pagan nor infidels. One could and should persecute them, but it was forbidden to kill them, because with the sign of Cain on their foreheads they were living proof of the Church's victory and Israel's forfeiture of election, and therefore of the truth of Christianity. Outcasts, they do not belong anywhere; 'they cannot enter the congregation of the Lord'; the warrior class is closed to them; they are not permitted to join the guilds of artisans and merchants; they are not found among peasants or serfs; their business dealings are not considered legitimate by the God-fearing masses; and they are despised by the well-born and the well-bred. They thrive on the misfortunes of others, and the very sight of them evokes the image of Judas Iscariot and Shylock.

Then comes the 19th century, the century in which the walls of separation come tumbling down and the Jews suddenly leap on to the stage of history. And lo and behold, yesterday's outcast is achieving phenomenal success. He climbs higher and higher, his touch is felt everywhere. Energy pent up for centuries spurts out in a torrent, sweeping away the old and changing things that had seemed as immutable as the laws of nature. He is the pariah risen to sudden pre-eminence, the slave become king.

The images of Judas and Shylock, of the crafty and deceitful Jew, of the heretic harbouring eternal hatred for the faithful – these images are so deeply ingrained that it is impossible for gentiles to believe that Jewish achievements have been attained honestly and are the proper rewards of talent, industry and hard work. The liberals are disturbed and annoyed by the obvious discrepancy between the abstract principles of the equality of man and equal opportunity on which they pride themselves and their instinctive aversion to having live Jews in their midst. The frustrated losers from the vast revolutionary changes of the 19th century, as well as those whose expectations of imminent redemption by revolution have been disappointed, are bewildered when they look around and see that the Jews who previously had no place at all in society are the chief beneficiaries of modernization. Jews fatten on other people's losses and misfortunes and, they hasten to conclude, it is they who are responsible for them.

We must now trace the form, the stages, the circumstances and the time of the fateful transformation of the image of the Jew in the eyes of Europe, from God's accursed and evil breed, a harmful force, and an embarrassing problem, to the concept of the Jew as the root and incarceration of all evil in the Manichean sense, as the source of all the evils that come together to form the one pervasive and all-encompassing evil. This transformation, in its turn, was to help change the mechanism of alleged defence against the spread of the baneful Jewish influence into the idea of the necessity and the legitimacy of a plan for a Final Solution that would put an end, once and for all, to the irrepressible absolute and eternal evil. These concepts, images and plans were to help erode, weaken and finally sweep away the inhibition before a violation of 'thou shalt not kill' as soon as circumstances combined to produce a climate of emergency and of supreme danger.

Developments in European civilization and society at large contributed their share. These developments were not caused or occasioned by the Jews, but their edge was turned against them, directly or indirectly, for more or less objective reasons or because the gentiles, affected as they were with an anti-Jewish neurosis, were bound to link them with the Jews. For the obsessive Jew-haters, of course, animosity to the Jews came first for they were always on the lookout for a pretext to magnify the evil and the danger of the Jews.

One must not put racist Manichean anti-Semitism on the same level as manifestations of hatred of the Jews throughout the generations, however great the cumulative influence of the latter in preparing minds for accepting the theory of race. Oppressive medieval edicts limiting the rights of Jews as blasphemers of the living God, enemies of Jesus and the Christian nations, exploiters and even murderers of Christian children, poisoners of wells, carriers of the poison of heresy even after their baptism, as in

Spain after the expulsion; the refusal, at the beginning of the Emancipation, to grant Jews equal rights because they were a nation within the nation, an alien element; the charges levelled, after equal rights had been granted, against the cosmopolitan Jews for their debilitating and perverting influence on the nation, its religion, tradition and national spirit; the propaganda of the Christian Social Party in Germany and Austria against the threat of Jewish infiltration into key positions in public life, and the disproportionate Jewish share of the national capital; the agitation about Jews controlling the stock exchange and corrupting officials and politicians during the great financial-parliamentary scandals in France, for instance, the Panama scandal – all these manifestations can still be regarded as gentile 'defence' reflexes.

It may be argued that this latter-day notion of the Jews as the embodiment of evil in the Manichean sense was only a new version of an ancient motif, belief in the Devil or in witchcraft. In both cases there appears the fear of an omnipotent and omnipresent power, a master of cunning impossible to locate but whose hand is felt in everything. I, however, am inclined to place emphasis on the explicitly modern character of these Manichean ideas, which led to the Jews being stamped as a hopeless evil that must be exterminated and caused the revulsion against killing to dissolve.

As a result of the vast structural and spiritual changes in European society after the French Revolution, the Jews became the target and the victims of a sort of neo-Manicheism from both flanks, the Right and the Left. Despite the individualism, the pluralism, and mobility that characterize modern society, it has become, both in theory and in practice, a single, cohesive, interconnected entity containing many elements. Its blood circulates throughout the body without skipping a single part. Not as in the old society, poor in means of communication, where individuals and groups, social classes and entire regions were able to maintain a largely independent and separate existence, with the king as the principal symbol and embodiment of national unity.

It is not by chance that counter-revolutionary romantic ideology, especially in Germany, echoed the famous slogan, '*La République, une et indivisible*', with the philosophy of an organic state or society, which despite the ancient label of *Standestaat* (corporate state) was wholly dissimilar to the class society of the Middle Ages.

With the increasing consolidation and unification of society the idea took hold that there is a factor of one kind that secures society's health, vigour, prosperity, harmony and justice, while some other single factor works as a poison to distort, corrupt and dissolve the bonds of society. There were those who, frightened by the vertiginous changes, and outraged by what they regarded as the putrescent consuming society, kept their eyes fixed on some idealized image of the past. Others brought up in an ardent faith in progress and in humanity's destined achievement of a free, harmonious and just society, were gripped by an impatient and exasperated hatred of that power which stood in the way and impeded the leap from the kingdom of darkness to the kingdom of light, from bondage to freedom.

The 18th century philosophers, such as Voltaire and Diderot, had placed the responsibility for this on intolerance, superstition and the priests; the Jacobins warned against aristocrats and their fellow-travellers; socialists denounced the bourgeoisie and capitalism; but for the champions of the idealized past, it was the French Jacobin Revolution which spawned the heresies of atheism, materialism, rebellion and anarchy eating away at society and corrupting it.

What characterizes such patterns of thought is the concept of abstract powers, ideas, desires, interests and processes being embodied in entire groups of people, and the condemnation of these groups as guilty, sinful and conspiratorial merely because they exist. In other words, there are entire classes of people whose very existence is objectively a crime and who must therefore be cut out of society's body like a diseased limb. The question of individual guilt or responsibility, of the subjective good character of the individual is irrelevant – it is neither here nor there.

An extreme manifestation of this type of thinking was the indiscriminate 'absolute terror' of the anarchists of the late 19th century, who not only shed the blood of kings, presidents and ministers and their families, but spread death in theatres, concert halls and other places of entertainment and out in the crowded streets. Their contention was that the whole of society was guilty and rotten; that all were accomplices in the evil and responsible for the reign of overweening pride meriting punishment by death or by suffering pain at the deaths of their children, their brothers and their relatives, because none of them showed mercy for the suffering of the innocent who had been struck down by fate or damned by God.

Throughout the 19th century we hear ominous sounds such as these heralding trouble for the Jews. They are heard both from the Left and from the Right. The Fourierist socialist Toussenel writes a complete book entitled *Juifs, rois de l'epoque* (Jews, the Kings of Our Time). Karl Marx produces in two separate pamphlets, his far better known – and far more shocking – definition of the Jews, variously, as the embodiment of the rule of Mammon; the bearers of the 'cash nexus'; the bedrock of the entire capitalist system; and finally, the fount of the poison that consumes money-mad bourgeois society, which has regard only for price and cares nothing for value. The liberation of mankind is liberation from the Jews. Similarly, the German guardians of the traditional German virtues – resourcefulness, fidelity and honesty – identify the egoistic and rapacious *laissez faire* doctrines of the Manchester School with the Jews.

Germany's solid national distinctiveness disintegrates increasingly under the impact of Jewish ideas, imported from France – cosmopolitan ideas about the unity of mankind, an eternal natural law, the rights of the individual, the equality of all men and popular sovereignty. This is what the German Romantics were arguing at the beginning of the 19th century. At its end the French anti-Semite Charles Maurras will be exclaiming bitterly that the viruses of Protestantism and Kantian philosophy were imported to France from Germany by the Jews in their attempt to break down the instinctive and traditional resistance of Catholic France to the infiltration of the alien Jewish element. Houston Stewart Chamberlain, the racist prophet and Hitler's mentor, was to call the 19th century 'the century of the Jews'. I have had occasion to quote the breathtaking prediction of Friedrich Nietzsche whose own attitude to the Jews was highly ambivalent, but whose hatred for anti-Semitic vulgarity is beyond doubt. This prediction was not motivated by anti-Jewish intention. The Jews of Europe had reached their Rubicon, and the 20th century will decide their fate, for 'either they will become masters of Europe or they will lose it', proclaims Nietzsche.

'I have never yet met a German who was favourably inclined to the Jews,' wrote Nietzsche elsewhere, 'and however decided the repudiation of actual anti-Semitism may be on the part of all prudent and political men, this prudence and policy is not perhaps directed against the nature of the sentiment itself, but only against its dangerous excess, and especially against the distasteful and infamous expression of this excess of sentiment — on this point we must not deceive ourselves. That Germany has amply sufficient Jews, that the German stomach, the German blood, has difficulty (and will long have difficulty) in disposing only of this quantity of 'Jew' — as the Italian, the Frenchman, and the Englishman have done by means of a stronger digestion — that is the unmistakable declaration and language of a general instinct, to which one must listen and according to which one must act. Let no more Jews come in! And shut the door (especially towards the East and towards Austria): thus commands the instinct of a people whose nature is still feeble and uncertain, so that it could be easily wiped out, easily extinguished, by a stronger race.

'The Jews, however, are beyond all doubt the strongest, toughest, and purest race at present living in Europe; they know how to succeed even under the worst conditions (in fact better than under unfavourable ones), by means of virtues of some sort, which one would like nowadays to label as vices — owing above all to a resolute faith which does not need to be ashamed before 'modern ideas' . . . It is certain that the Jews, if they desired — or if they were driven to it, as anti-Semites seem to wish — could now have the ascendency, nay, literally the supremacy, over Europe.'

In the light of what the future held in store, it is a shock to read Nietzsche's expressed desire for a fusion of the Jews with the Prussian nobility to create a new ruling caste for Europe.

'That they are not working and planning for that end is equally certain,' he admitted. 'Meanwhile, they rather wish and desire, even somewhat importunely, to be insorbed and absorbed by Europe; they long to be finally settled, authorized, and respected somewhere, and wish to put an end to the nomadic life, to the "wandering Jew"; and one should certainly take account of this impulse and tendency, and make advances to it (it possibly betokens mitigation of the Jewish instincts); for which purpose it would perhaps be useful and fair to banish the anti-Semitic bawlers out of the country.

'One should make advances with all prudence, and with selection, pretty much as the English nobility do. It stands to reason that the more powerful and strongly marked types of new Germanism could enter into relation with the Jews with the least hesitation, for instance, the nobleman officer from the Prussian border: it would be interesting in many ways to see whether the genius for money and patience (and especially some intellect and intellectuality — sadly lacking in the place referred to) could not in addition be annexed and trained to the hereditary art of commanding and obeying — for both of which the country in question has now a classic reputation. But here it is expedient to break off my festal discourse and my sprightly Teutonomania: for I have already reached my *serious topic*, the "European problem" as I understand it, the rearing of a new ruling caste for Europe.'

Writing in a vicious tone reeking of hatred and patrician disdain, Nietzsche's older friend and colleague, the Swiss historian, Jacob Burckhardt, had even earlier uttered dark threats against the Jews. The nations of Europe, he declared, would no longer tolerate Jewish interference in all their affairs and one night there would arise a storm which would rob the Jews of all their conquests: their control of the press, their domination of the judicial system, and so on.

At about the same time, the Frenchman, Drumont, preached a solution of France's social problem at the expense of the Jews by the confiscation of the wealth which he alleged to be derived from exploitation, robbery and usurpation that had given rise to the social problem in the first place. This retribution would not only provide compensation for past injustice; it would also make Jewish property available for distribution among the French victims of Jewish exploitation and for financing national investments, public works and a system of social reform.

It could of course be argued that all this talk – along with the blood-thirsty sermons of German Jew-haters of the time such as Marr, who coined the word 'anti-Semitism' and Dühring, the influential pseudo-socialist philosopher who provoked Engels to write his famous 'Anti-Dühring' – was still nothing but empty rhetoric and propaganda, however vicious and vitriolic. It is one thing to say that the Jews were fated to play a despicable, harmful, even disastrous role in society. It is quite another thing to advocate a doctrine of racial determinism which seeks to settle the fate and destiny of nations from the beginning to the end of time, and legitimizes bloodshed and the taking of life.

Some of this was, however, advocated by – of all people – the populist socialists, Proudhon and Bakunin. In their teachings they went beyond the basic premises of rationality which deny any collective biological determinism and acknowledge the supremacy of reason, and the power of education and social engineering. They proceeded to a glorification of the existential situation, primary instincts, historical roots and the like, though not, in terms, the purity of blood.

Proudhon jotted down some notes on the subject:

> 'The Jews: Write an article against this race which poisons everything by butting in everywhere without linking up with any nation; demand their expulsion from France, except for Jews married to Frenchwomen; liquidate the synagogues; deny them any kind of employment, work for the abolition of their religious practices. Not for nothing did the Christians call them God-killers. The Jew is the enemy of mankind, this race must be sent back to Asia or else be exterminated... whether by fire or by assimilation or by expulsion, the Jew must disappear... the older ones who cannot bear any more children may still be tolerated. There is a task before me... What the Middle Ages loathed by instinct, I loathe upon reflection and irrevocably.'

Darwinism brought down one of the strongest barriers protecting 'thou shalt not kill'. For this reason alone, its great diffusion and enormous influence make it a turning point in the history of mankind. Darwinism deprived man of his uniqueness in the order of creation. Man was no longer created by God; he did not emerge from the womb of nature *ex nihilo*, a final and completed product with a soul that elevates him above other creatures, all creation his footstool. Man no longer enjoyed a direct and special relation with his all-merciful heavenly Father, who spreads the canopy of His peace over man and accompanies him in all his ways, provides him with sustenance, sees into his heart, rewards him for keeping His Commandments, punishes the sinners or visits the iniquities of the fathers upon the children.

Not any longer. Nature, it turns out, is not benevolent; it does not take care of everyone, and most important, it does not take care of the crown of creation, man himself. There is no Providence to look after man; nor can one speak of Nature as having been planned by a Creator or by some cosmic intelligence. The universe was not wrought by God, nor is it the handiwork of abstract reason. There is no order in the universe, no plan, no harmony, that could prove the concern of a Creator. Rather, it is characterized by confusion and contradiction, by waste and antagonism and by the struggle of all against all.

Such ordered harmony as does strike the eye and provoke wonder and gratitude – because it seems to indicate the possibility of progress and harmony – is in fact only the product of a struggle for existence, paid for in blood, pain, and suffering. There is no end to this desperate struggle in which the strong, the fit and the talented rule the roost, while the weak, the botched, the unfit and the inefficient bow themselves out or else become the tools of those with greater vitality, and the instruments of their will. The notion of the sanctity of life therefore has no meaning. The whole earth, man's battleground, is strewn with the corpses of creatures that have been obliterated because they could not adapt to or resist their betters.

Now, if mankind is not distinctive, it becomes difficult to speak of the unity of mankind. If there is no soul, then there is no reason either, for reason is the only quality that distinguishes man from the rest of the animal kingdom. Reason is but one of the tools evolved in the course of the struggle for existence, a particular expression of animal vitality.

It also becomes impossible to acknowledge objective morality, for the only purpose of morality is to safeguard existence by cementing the unity of the race in its struggle against rivals and enemies. In a Nature 'red in tooth and claw', the sanctity of life is a contradiction in terms. Not only are the weak doomed to die, but the progress of the universe virtually demands their extinction or extermination, so that the fittest shall survive to employ the power that Nature has given them for the conquest of Nature.

We know full well the moral boost Darwinism gave the 'robber barons' in the United States during the early 'storm and stress' period of rampaging American capitalism – a time when 'jungle' was the only word for relations between workers and employers. And we know the rationalization Darwinism provided for imperialism – nay, more, it was a hymn of praise – in its heyday at the end of the last century, especially for the Anglo-American variety. Although one cannot equate Darwinism with racist theory, it would be impossible to imagine racism without Darwin. And I am speaking here not of an indirect affinity but of a direct connection.

In the *Descent of Man* Darwin writes:

> 'With savages, the weak in body or mind are soon eliminated; and those that survive exhibit a vigorous state of health. We civilized men, on the other hand, do our utmost to check the process of elimination; we build asylums for the imbecile, the maimed, and the sick; we institute poor-laws; and our medical men exert their utmost skill to save the life of everyone to the last moment. There is reason to believe that vaccination

has preserved thousands, who from a weak constitution would formerly have succumbed to smallpox. Thus the weak members of civilized societies propagate their kind.

'No one who has attended to the breeding of animals will doubt that this must be highly injurious to the race of man... Care, or care wrongly directed, leads to the degeneration of a domestic race; but excepting in the case of man himself, hardly anyone is so ignorant as to allow his worst animals to breed.'

Darwin states this more explicitly in a letter of 3 July 1881, where he writes: 'Looking at the world at no very distant date, what an endless number of the lower races will have been eliminated by the higher civilized races throughout the world.'

The idea of natural selection brought Darwin to an elitist and authoritarian view of society and the state. Thus, in his *Origin of Species* he writes: 'I regard pure democracy as visionary as a country peopled by one invariable species. This with me is no question of what is good or bad, but of what must ever be, and I do hold that a government must always eventually get into the hands of an individual, or a family, or a class, or there is no truth in natural selection.'

The doctrine of racism, especially its German version, represents a fusion of German Romanticism and the science of biology, mainly in its Darwinist form. Neither Herder, who coined the virtually untranslatable expression *Eigentümlichkeit*, nor the other German thinkers who spread the idea of *Volkgeist*, had at first any intention of going beyond the realms of language, literature, religion, aesthetics, folklore or historical research. However, even during the Napoleonic period, the cult of exclusive German identity, personified in the ancient German hero Arminius, who rebelled against cosmopolitan Rome, spilled over into the domain of political ideas and the relations between nations.

Before long, there sprang up a whole school of thought – led by the jurist Savigny – which repudiated the idea of a natural law based on universal human reason and moral perception. In its place, this 'historical' school posited the laws of nations against a background of natural and geographical factors, national character, specific traditions, *Volkgeist*, local customs and ancient myths. In short, a complete *Weltanschauung* was formulated on the basis of the rejection of the unity of mankind in so far as such unity is founded on universal reason, morality and law.

The racist doctrine constituted a spurious scientific systemization of these theories, and they paved the way for Auschwitz. Blood, the biological prerequisite of our existence, became a substance which determines every aspect and manifestation of personality, from the structure of the skull to the minutest results of scientific research and the finest nuances of artistic expression, to say nothing of emotional predilections, character traits and patterns of behaviour.

This implies that society – the community, the race or the tribe – possesses an immeasurably higher degree of reality than the individual, who has no existence apart from – nor any prospect of escaping – this all-determining, all-embracing reality. Thus scientism reaches back into the dark recesses of the most distant past and, in the case of Richard Wagner, is invested with the hypnotic halo of spellbinding religious symbolism.

Ancient legends, myths, and symbols are like hieroglyphs, whose decipherment lays bare the primordial life of the soul, mode of existence and pattern of conduct. Monumental in their pristine simplicity, they assert themselves continuously anew, in one variation or another.

These primeval patterns, which spell the integrity of the soul and the immediacy, the intensity of original experience, must be protected against the pernicious intrusion of bad alien blood, against the analytical intellectualism that disrupts, debilitates, distorts and destroys original, intuitive and instinctive truth.

This primordial purity, integrity, rootedness and uniqueness fed on the apocalyptic fears that were widespread at the end of the 19th century, and found its own expression in the obsessive interest in the mystery of the decline of civilizations, the downfall of empires such as ancient Rome, the eclipse of great powers and the death of nations.

The mystery seemed to have been resolved, however. It was the result of the admixture of alien blood which helped to weaken the authentic instinct of survival and undermine the sense of pre-intellectual assurance.

And who is the alien but the Jew, who lies in wait for the nations of Europe, at once an outsider and an insider, foreign and familiar, preaching a system of universal values – the primacy of abstract reason, of a pure, universal morality and of the unity of mankind – and scorning the voice of the blood and of primordial instincts.

He himself, meanwhile, manifests an impregnable racial distinctiveness. A rationalist cosmopolitan, he clings to his exclusive heritage and preserves the purity of his own race. Though he may marry off his daughter to princes and counts so as to corrupt their blood, he remains for ever a nation apart, although he is dispersed among the nations.

All history, to be exact, is but a series of incessant conflicts between the races, the chronicle of the rise and fall of racial entities imbued with their own authentic ideas and principles of survival. It is not the mode of production, but rather changes in the composition of human blood, that provide the motive force of history. And wars are waged not over universal truth, equal justice or abstract ideas, but for self-assertion through the accumulation of power, the demonstration of power, the exercise of power, the deployment of power.

Was this cult of power and vitality a revolutionary innovation? In some measure, it is true, this has been the way of the world from time immemorial. The way of the world, perhaps, but not its conviction – the kind of conviction one would be prepared to express in public, or even to oneself, without feeling uncomfortable, without any pricks of conscience. For beside – or, rather, against – the primordial urge, had stood the system of Judeo-Christian ethics, preaching humility, meekness, reciprocity, love of man, regard for others, abstinence, asceticism, the need for truth, the claims of justice and the virtue of equality.

Then came Nietzsche, the mad apostle of naked and unvarnished truth, and proceeded to rip off all the veils of schizophrenia, hypocrisy, deceit and self-hatred that beset the dichotomy between the pagan heritage on the one side and Jewish ethics on the other, and to expose the unbridgeable gulf which separates Rome and Jerusalem.

Nietzsche hailed the *Will to Power* as the primary, authentic and noble urge, and condemned the ethic of asceticism as an invention of weaklings, a conspiracy of misfits and a bit of priestly chicanery designed to emasculate the strong, foster their feelings of guilt, arrest their native powers and defeat them by guile and trickery.

The Jews, according to Nietzsche, are that nation of priests that sired slave morality. All that has been done against the 'aristocrats', the 'tyrants', the 'Masters', the 'mighty' is nothing in comparison to what the Jews did to them. The Jews avenged themselves on their victorious enemies by radically inverting all their values, a most spiritual act of vengeance.

> 'Yet the method was only appropriate to a nation of priests, to a nation of the most jealously nursed priestly vengefulness. It was the Jews who in opposition to the aristocratic equation (good-aristocratic-beautiful-happy-loved by the gods), dared with frightening consistency to suggest the contrary equation, and indeed to maintain with the furious hatred of the underprivileged (the hatred of impotence) this contrary equation, namely that the wretched alone are the good; the suffering, the needy, the sick, the ugly are the only ones who are pious, the only ones who are blessed, for them alone is salvation.
> 'But you, on the other hand, you aristocrats, you men of power, you are to all eternity the evil, the horrible, the covetous, the insatiate, the godless; eternally also shall you be the unblessed, the cursed, the damned! We know who has fallen heir to this Jewish inversion of values. In the context of the monstrous and inordinately fateful initiative which the Jews have exhibited in connection with this most fundamental of all declarations of war, I remember the passage which came to my pen on another occasion – that it was, in fact, with the Jews that the revolt of the slaves begins in the sphere of morals; that revolt which has behind it a history of two millennia, and which we have lost sight of today simply because it has triumphed so completely.'

The heirs to and followers of the Jewish legacy are the Christians, the French revolutionaries, the liberals, the democrats, the socialists – indeed, every movement of social rebellion and liberation throughout history. The war between Rome and Jerusalem has been going on for 2,000 years, but now at last, says Nietzsche, the war is reaching a stage of ultimate confrontation.

> 'Which of them has been temporarily victorious, Rome or Judea? There is no shadow of doubt. Just consider to whom in Rome itself you nowadays bow down, as though before the quintessence of all the highest values. And not only in Rome, but over almost half the world, everywhere where man has been tamed or is about to be tamed – to three Jews, as we know, and one Jewess (to Jesus of Nazareth, to Peter the fisherman, to Paul the tentmaker, and to the mother of the aforesaid Jesus, named Mary). This is very remarkable: Rome is undoubtedly defeated. At any rate there took place in the Renaissance a brilliantly sinister revival of the classical ideal, of the aristocratic valuation of all things. Rome herself, like a man waking up from a trance, stirred beneath the burden of the

new Judaized Rome that had been built over her, which presented the appearance of an ecumenical synagogue and was called the church!

'But immediately Judea triumphed again, thanks to that fundamentally popular (German and English) movement of revenge, which is called the Reformation, and taking into account its inevitable corollary, the restoration of the Church – the restoration also of the ancient graveyard peace of classical Rome. Judea proved yet once more victorious over the classical idea in the French Revolution, and in a sense which was even more crucial and even more profound. The last political aristocracy that existed in Europe, that of the French 17th and 18th centuries, broke into pieces beneath the instincts of a resentful populace – never had the world heard a greater jubilation, a more uproarious enthusiasm.

'Indeed, there took place in the midst of it the most monstrous and unexpected phenomenon; the ancient ideal itself swept before the eyes and conscience of humanity with all its life and with unheard-of splendour. And in opposition to resentment's lying war-cry of the prerogative of the most, in opposition to the will to lowliness, abasement, and equalization, the will to a retrogression and twilight of humanity, there rang out once again, stronger, simpler, more penetrating than ever, the terrible and enchanting counter-war-cry of the prerogative of the few! Like a final signpost to other ways there appeared Napoleon, the most unique and violent anachronism that ever existed, and in him the incarnate problem of the aristocratic ideal itself – consider well what a problem it is: Napoleon, that synthesis of Monster and Superman.'

The issue could not have been more clearly stated. On one side, there is the idea that all men are created equal, and that they are endowed with equal rights and proper universal reason. On the other side, and as a direct consequence of the denial of these same truths, there is the doctrine which claims that life in this world is worthless and meaningless except in so far as it consists in the self-realization of the elite of the strong and the powerful – a workshop for superior specimens who employ the common people as mere slavish instruments of their own will.

All religions and movements originating in Judaism have drawn their inspiration from the Messianic vision – a vision of ultimate universal reconciliation when all shall become one true community, when nation shall not lift up sword against nation and when justice shall rule the world.

Nietzsche, however, rejects this vision with angry contempt; to his mind, it is nothing but a consolation for the meek and the cowardly – the virus of infirmity and helplessness. Instead, he conjures up the vision of an eternal war that fortifies the strong, assures natural selection, and advances the select few. Racist theoreticians hastened to avail themselves of this gift of this convention-demolishing philosopher; champions of elitist inequality found in it ample support for the cult of personality.

'The universal degeneracy of mankind,' writes Nietzsche, to the level of the "man of the future" – as idealized by the socialistic fools and shallow-pates – this degeneracy and dwarfing of man to an absolutely gregarious animal (or as they call it, to a man of "free society"), this brutalizing of man into a pigmy with equal rights and claims, is undoubtedly possible! He who has thought out this possibility to its ultimate conclusion knows another loathing unknown to the rest of mankind – and perhaps also a new mission!' In other words, a war of annihilation against socialist egalitarianism.

All these trends of thought combined to remove the remaining barriers around the commandment, 'thou shalt not kill'. The racist doctrine forbade contact with any Jews as the carriers of a deadly poison – going as far as Houston Stewart Chamberlain's ban on the reading of any literature written by Jews. It closed for Jews all avenues of escape from collective determinism, and assigned a cosmic dimension and a crucial metaphysical and historical significance to the confrontation – nay, the unbridgeable Manichean antagonism – between Jewry and the world, i.e. the Aryan race.

If one assumes that the distinctiveness and the cohesion of a race provide the vital impulse of its culture, then it follows that the anti-race characteristics of the Jews, as well as their cunning and their materialism, must devitalize the primal instinct of race by means of an abstract intellectualism that sows doubts, saps self-assurance and desecrates hallowed symbols. This it does with the help of an egotistic individualism that disrupts social unity, with the help of a pacifism that puts the warriors' vigilance to sleep, and through the manipulation of capitalism and socialism – both of them cosmopolitan forces that split the nation up into embattled factions.

Anti-Semitism was elevated to the rank of a substitute for or, more exactly, an antidote to, scientific socialism. Jewish financial capitalism became the exploiting class; blood replaced the modes of production as the key to history; the struggle over the seizure of power by the Jews took the place of class warfare; and liberation from the Jewish yoke was presented as the victory of a classless, nationalist society – a convenant of brothers.

When one of his disciples objected that anti-Semitism did not amount to a political programme, Charles Maurras replied:

> 'One of these days it will be shown that, on the contrary, it is as a function of the anti-Semitic programme that all the rest of nationalist and monarchist programmes will be able to pass from conception to execution.'

Similarly Hitler was to declare:

> 'We are confronted with a (Jewish) question, without the solution of which all the efforts to awaken Germany and bring it back to life shall be in vain ... This is a vital question for entire mankind since the fate of all non-Jewish peoples depends on its solution.'

The great role played by Jewish Marxists in the reinterpretation of the socialist canon – by tying up the success of revolutionary socialism with the looming confrontation between world imperialism and the world proletariat, especially in the nationally oppressed and socially exploited colonial countries – was seized upon by Hitler, following the Bolshevik revolution and the establishment of the Comintern, as positive proof of a global, satanic conspiracy to destroy the native national elites and thus to bring about the ruin of all gentile peoples. This, he claimed, had been the traditional Jewish strategy 'from Moses to Lenin', finding its expression both in the ancient prophets of Israel, and in the new Jewish revolutionaries who incited the rabble against the elites, and provoked the inferior races to war against the superior races – all to insure world dominion for the Jews, as is written in the 'Protocols of the Elders of Zion'.

Cosmological lucubrations, nightmarish visions, provocative and inflammatory rhetoric – all these combined to remove ancient inhibitions, to break down existing barriers, to awaken dormant instincts and cravings. They were forged into forces of terrifying efficacy under the impact of mighty historical events: the First World War, the Bolshevik Revolution and the civil wars that followed them.

The bloody frenzy of the years 1914–18 threw humanity into a state of confusion without any precedent. First the war, then the inflation that followed it, and finally the great crisis of 1929 – which was widely regarded as the harbinger of the collapse of

Western civilization – destroyed all sense of cohesion, continuity, certainty and confidence. Age-old moral constraints were swept away in the desperate rage which seized millions of people. Sacrosanct commandments and prohibitions were turned upside down by a false and distorted idealism – the violation of a precept became its fulfilment.

Defeated Germany developed the psychosis of a 'nation under siege' threatened by the whole world, with the Jews as the insidious agents of that world conspiracy inside Germany itself. For by spreading their liberal-cosmopolitan-pacifist propaganda, by working inside the Socialist opposition parties, by preaching defeatism, and by degrading the symbolic national myths, the Jews stuck a knife in the back of the fighting German people. No sooner has the Reich collapsed than they appear – these vultures preying on a corpse – as the new rulers and the chief spokesmen of reconciliation with the West and observance of the Versailles Treaty – in other words, of capitulation and slavery.

Even a humanist such as Thomas Mann, married to a Jewish woman, in his famous speech of reconciliation with the Democratic Republic, exhorted German youth to 'take the wind out of the sails of the clever young Jews' who were pushing to the head of the line. General Hans van Seeckt, virtual dictator of Germany in the old days of the Weimar Republic, a conservative, aristocratic officer of the old school, would say that despite differences in background, mentality and viewpoint he was able to find a common language with Ebert, Scheidemann and Noske; but in no circumstances could he talk to the Jewish journalists of the *Berliner Tageblatt* and the *Vossische Zeitung* such as Theodor Wolff and George Berhard, for he was convinced that they never said what they thought.

Dr Friedrich Thieme, a principal assistant of Karl Legien, leader of the Socialist trade union movement in the Weimar Republic, wrote of the well-known Jewish publicist, Maximilian Harden, in the journal of the movement: 'The German people is honour bound to reject this leper. German people, you cannot sink so low as to have truck with this Judas Iscariot ... German people, do your duty!'

Even deeper was the abhorrence felt in all strata of German society for the Jewish satirical writer, Kurt Tucholsky, who certainly went to extremes in his virulent lampoons on the national mythology, German patriotic slogans, Prussian militarism and the Teutonic mentality.

There is no stronger testimony to the consent by silence and indifference – more than that, the readiness to welcome the 'thou shalt kill' measures when the time comes – than the following extract from an article which appeared in 1921 in *Die Neue Zeit*, the official ideological organ of the German Social Democratic Party, on the penetration of 'Ostjuden' into Germany.

> 'East German Jews are mainly a proletarian population, sunk in squalor and wretched poverty, on the lowest rung of business morality ... they are unable to enter industry ... they are unfit for work on the soil. The great majority of them lack any sense of order or cleanliness; their clothes are full of stains and holes, their houses are unbelievably filthy ... The memory of the Jews of Eastern Europe will remain one of the most nauseating experiences in the minds of our soldiers.'

In the same spirit, a Socialist member of the Reichstag declared during a debate on smuggling offences: 'This gang (of Jewish smugglers) does not deserve to live. These parasites ... must be wiped off the face of the earth.'

And now, to quote Lord Keynes, appears a lunatic who declares that he 'hears voices from on high', which are in fact but the echoes of phrases he has read in the brochures of some vulgar popularizers of racist theories. But this lunatic has no longer any inhibitions whatsoever about drawing the most extreme conclusions from these theories and putting them into practice.

'Even if there had never been a synagogue, or a Jewish school, or the Bible, the Jewish spirit would still exist and exert its influence. It has been there from the beginning and there is no Jew, not a single one, who does not personify it.' Thus declares Hitler in the famous dialogue with his mentor, Dietrich Eckart. There is therefore no alternative to the physical annihilation of this 'flesh and blood' substance.

Hitler's angry, violent, fanaticism sweeps along the mass of the impoverished and rudderless middle-class. Put to shame by the well-to-do and the well-bred, fearful of being assimilated into the proletariat, the middle-class is left with only one single – but most cherished – asset: its German blood. The members of this class yearn for a strong hand to lead them, and at the same time they long for the power and the glory of treading on other nations.

Meanwhile, the German intelligentsia, their minds deformed by theories of mighty primordial forces gushing forth from the depths of the collective soul, are deeply stirred and prostrate themselves before this expression of elemental forces – this colossal natural phenomenon, this veritable volcano, the epitome of their hopes and aspirations, the quintessence of the Nordic spirit. As such, he is above the law, and above all moral codes; a man such as he cannot be held to account for the violation of legal rules and regulations.

And thus it came about, as Ernst Nolte has observed, that Hitler was greeted in 1933 with shouts of joy by Germany's leading philosopher, best playwright, greatest jurist and foremost composer. But long before Hitler, the Jew had become for most Germans an enemy and an outcast, and an embarrassment even for liberals and socialists.

It would be impossible to exaggerate the contribution of the Bolshevik Revolution to the collapse of moral barriers and to the process of man's brutalization throughout the world. The Russian civil war, the G.P.U. terror, the physical liquidation of entire social classes during collectivization and industrialization, the hideous show trials, the mass purges, the slave-labour camps, the bloody, lawless dictatorship – all these provided an example, a challenge and a licence.

After the first terrorist attempts on the lives of Lenin and the two Jews, Uritski and Volodarski – incidentally, at the hands of Jews – Zinoviev, also a Jew, and then at the peak of his career as secretary-general of the Comintern, declared: 'We shall liquidate not only individuals, but entire classes.'

It was Zinoviev who, in a four-hour speech at an historic congress of the German Communist Party, led the German comrades down a path that was eventually to serve as a springboard for Hitler's leap to power. Zinoviev's humiliating and bitter end came in 1936 when, early one morning, the odious man was dragged, screaming and kicking, to his execution in a G.P.U. cellar.

To the new nation-states of Eastern Europe, reborn after a prolonged period of subjection, the victory of Bolshevism seemed not only a danger to their feudal and capitalist classes; it was an even greater threat to their national distinctiveness and political independence – their sole possession – than their traditional enemy Czarist Russia.

The Jewish leaders of the revolutionary régime in Russia and the Jewish Communists in their own countries were identified in their eyes with the Jewish masses who inhabited their cities and towns. These they had come to regard not as God's creatures, people who had lived among them for more than a thousand years, but as an alien growth, a vicious exploiter, a punishment from heaven. They were searching the whole time for some way of getting rid of the Jews, waiting for someone to save them from this mass of strangers blocking the road to a national and social cohesion, to genuine self-expression.

Poland's National Democrats, for example, insisted that the most dangerous of the four Powers that had divided Poland among them was still around. It was the most dangerous precisely because it was not an army of occupation, like Russia, Germany and Austria, but was settled in Poland and could not be uprooted. Thus the Jews became the Trojan horse of the world conspiracy headed by Poland's age-old enemy, which was now scheming to devour the infant state minutes after its rebirth.

No wonder, then, that the Polish Ambassador to Berlin, Josef Lipski, could applaud Hitler after hearing from him of his Madagascar plan, and declare that for such a noble service – the removal of the Jews from Poland – the Polish people would raise a monument to the Fuehrer in Warsaw. No wonder, either, that at the time of Auschwitz, the Polish underground press was capable of thanking Providence for solving a most difficult problem for the Polish people in a way that nobody could have imagined previously.

But for this Polish attitude – and without the participation of Ukrainian, Lithuanian, Lettish and Bielorussian auxiliaries – the Nazi campaign of extermination could not have been carried through; nor without the systematic dehumanization of the Jews in the minds of millions of Germans.

To them, the Jew had become, as Hitler wrote to Eckart: 'a parasitic growth over the whole earth, sometimes creeping, sometimes leaping ... sucking ... at first the bursting abundance, finally the dried-up sap. No people in the world, not even Attila's race of murderers, would allow him (the Jew) to remain alive if it could suddenly see him for what he is, what he desires; screaming with horror, it would strangle him the very next instant.'

However, there were two other necessary preconditions without which the Final Solution would never have been ordered or executed. One was the war with the Soviet Union; the other, modern technology. Only in the frenzy of an Armageddon for the rich lands of the Ukraine, coveted by the rapidly expanding master race – in the mood of a crusade for the extermination of the Communist monster, personified by the Jews and other inferior races – was it possible for the ancient cry of the First Crusade to be sounded again across a gulf of eight centuries. Since one must travel thousands of miles to kill the infidel, one should start by discharging this sacred duty at home.

After the war, neo-Nazis of all types put forward the claim that the gas chambers had been merely the 20th-century version of the guillotine – a more effective, speedy and humane instrument for killing people. Although the *Einsatztruppen* (Extermination Squads) carried out mass murders, using machine guns and other weapons of death, it is inconceivable that they would have been able to complete the Final Solution by this method alone. It is extremely doubtful whether they would have been able to stand the psychological strain for any length of time, even though the arch-murderers, Himmler and Globocnik, kept praising the fervent idealism and steadfast loyalty of their subordinates who, wading knee-deep in rivers of blood and climbing over pyramids of corpses, persevered fearlessly with their sacred mission on behalf of the fatherland, the nation and the race.

The historian who, perhaps unconsciously, seeks to punish himself because he neither perished in Auschwitz, nor endured hunger and torture in the bunkers, nor witnessed the death agonies of his dear ones, nor froze as a partisan in the forests of Bielorussia, nor fell in action during the Warsaw ghetto revolt – such an historian buries himself for years under piles of papers and books which represent his own personal valley of the shadow of death, and asks himself: What is the meaning of history's greatest horror within the scheme of universal history – what is its sense, its purpose, its logic?

Could the Holocaust be the conclusive proof that history moves by no law, offers no lesson, and serves no purpose? That it is merely a succession of irrational accidents, insipid banalities and gratuitous horrors. Their mere inclination to accept this point of view suggests a surrender to the mentality of the perpetrators of the Holocaust. After all, they ended up where they did partly as a result of their desperate denial of a final station of redemption in history.

This heresy of theirs gave birth to the cult of power and vitality for their own sake, as a substitute for the search for truth and justice. Because they ceased to believe in eternal verities, they were ensnared by a perverted, murderous idealism which gave them absolute belief in their own superiority and in everyone else's inferiority. This is the kind of idealism that unleashes the beast in man, and turns high-flown ideas into a mere rationalization of the urge to murder.

In parenthesis, let us not disregard the modern technocratic philosophy which finds satisfaction in a job well done, and hails the challenge of solving a scientific or technical problem, regardless of the nature of the eventual uses to which they might be put.

As Aristotle wrote in his 'Treatise on Government':

> 'In this particular man differs from other animals, that he alone has a perception of good and evil, of just and unjust, and it is a participation of these common sentiments which forms a family and a city ... for as by the completion of it man is the most excellent of all living beings, so without law and justice he would be the worst of all, for nothing is so difficult to subdue as injustice in arms: but these arms man is born with, namely, prudence and valour, which he may apply to the most opposite purposes, for he who abuses them will be the most wicked, the most cruel, the most lustful, and most gluttonous being imaginable.'

The Holocaust put an end to over a thousand years of Jewish history in Central and Eastern Europe. It solved the entire Jewish problem – a product of special historical conditions – in that region. Are we then to conclude that every diaspora is similarly doomed? I find it difficult to accept this thesis when I think of the downfall of great powers, and of the disasters that have befallen so many nations, states and cultures in the course of history.

I recall, for example, the Tartar invasion early in the 13th century, which enslaved Russia and cut it off from all contact with Europe for more than 300 years; the extinction of the entire Czech social and intellectual elite for several generations following the battle of the White Mountain in 1620; the years of the Polish 'flood' in the middle of the 17th century – Chmielnicki's uprising and the Swedish invasion, which put an end to Poland's urban culture – not to mention the period of partitions which wiped Poland off the map of Europe; the horrors of the Thirty Years War, which turned a large part of Germany into wasteland and sent entire regions back to cannibalism; the bloody histories of the Armenians and the Irish, and the destruction of the Byzantine Empire, Bulgaria, Serbia and the other Balkan states, by the Ottoman conquerors.

True, none of these catastrophes ended in the total physical annihilation of a whole people; but it is entirely possible that this is the end that still awaits many races and nations – maybe all of them. And the Jews will then prove to have been not the last, but the first victim of this new experiment.

Some people profess to see the Holocaust as an ineluctable stage in Jewish history – the labour pains of national rebirth, so to speak, or the price of redemption. One hears this kind of interpretation from extreme nationalists as well as from certain extremely religious Jews.

This I shall never be able to understand. I shall never be able to believe in a Guardian of Israel who claims the lives of a million children as the price of national revival. One must not confuse a metaphysical and theological question with historical and empirical statements about the role of Jewish despair after Auschwitz, the guilt feelings of the Christian world, and the fluid situation at the end of the war aiding the restoration of Jewish statehood in modern Israel. There is, of course, unparalleled grandeur in the explosion of Jewish energies and the display of an inconquerable will to live on the morrow of the most horrible blood-letting and deepest degradation and wretchedness that any people has ever experienced – in the struggle for independent Jewish nationhood.

Did those million die a martyr's death for the Sanctification of the Name? A great many of them were killed without ever having had this feeling. Did they, then, die in vain, more of the innumerable victims of man's bestiality throughout history?

Was the Holocaust nothing but an act of degradation which can only arouse searing pain and endless horror? Or was there, perhaps, beyond the unbelievable indignity, some terrible majesty and magnificence to the Holocaust? By this I do not mean only the manifestations of heroism and courage in the Warsaw ghetto revolt and the struggle of the Jewish partisans.

Rather do I mean that in the vast perspective of history, the

Holocaust assumes the grandiose dimensions of a confrontation between the two diametrically opposed world views about which Nietzsche spoke: between morality and paganism; between the sanctity of life and the cult of warfare; between the equality of all men and the supremacy of the select few; between the search for truth and the display of vitality; between the quest for justice and the discharge of instinctive impulses; between the vision of a genuine society of equals and the prospect of a society of masters lording it over slaves.

In these times of population explosion and racial struggles, when we have at our disposal all the means necessary to ensure either a Golden Age for all or destruction of all, the future of mankind seems to depend on a choice between two alternatives: either the establishment of a genuine world community, or the outbreak of Armageddon over world domination and the rule of the strong over the weak. In other words, the awesome question is, has Auschwitz become an eternal warning, or merely the first station on the road to the extermination of all races and the suicide of humanity?

It would perhaps be appropriate to conclude with Nietzsche himself. In 'The Genealogy of Morals' he says:

> 'Let us come to a conclusion. The two opposing values, "good and bad", "good and evil" have fought a dreadful, thousand-year fight in the world, and though indubitably the second value has been for a long time in the preponderance, there are not wanting places where the fortune of the fight is still indecisive. It can almost be said that in the meanwhile the fight reaches a higher and higher level, and that in the meanwhile it has become more and more intense, and always more and more psychological; so that nowadays there is perhaps no more decisive mark of the higher nature, of the more psychological nature, than to be in that sense self-contradictory, and to be actually still a battleground for those two opposites.
>
> 'The symbol of this fight, written in a writing which has remained worthy of perusal throughout the course of history up to the present time, is called "Rome against Judea, Judea against Rome". Hitherto there has been no greater event than that fight, the putting of that question, that deadly antagonism. Rome found in the Jew the incarnation of the unnatural, as though it were its diametrically opposed monstrosity, and in Rome the Jew was held to be convicted of hatred of the whole human race, and rightly so in so far as it is right to link the wellbeing and the future of the human race to the unconditional mastery of the aristocratic values, of the Roman values.'

Nietzsche goes on to describe the long-drawn-out struggle between Judea and Rome, with its climax in the French Revolution. Hinting that the battle between the aristocratic ideal of Rome and the democratic-socialist egalitarian vision of Judea is still going on, he adds:

> 'Was it therewith over? Was that greatest of all antithesis of ideals thereby relegated *ad acta* for all time? Or only postponed, postponed for a long time? May there not take place at some time or other a much more awful, much more carefully prepared flaring up of the old conflagration? Further! Should not one wish that consummation with all one's strength? – Will it one's self? Demand it one's self? He who at this juncture begins, like my readers, to reflect, to think further, will have difficulty in coming quickly to a conclusion.'

As to himself – Nietzsche continues in his oracular style – he has 'ground enough to come to a conclusion, taking it for granted that for some time past what I mean has been sufficiently clear, what I exactly mean by the dangerous motto which is inscribed on the body of my last book, *Beyond Good and Evil (Vorspiel einer Philosphie der Zukunft)* – at any rate that is not the same as "Beyond Good and Bad".' Nietzsche would certainly have been shocked to learn that one day he would be officially celebrated as the prophet of the Third Reich.

On the eve of his squalid suicide in the Berlin bunker Hitler still had enough spirit (or madness) in him to claim the world's 'eternal gratitude' for National Socialism: 'For having eliminated the Jews from Germany and Central Europe... who wanted war and engineered it.'

Terrible and bloody are the ironies of History.

1973

The Disputation

HYAM MACCOBY

The following are extracts from a play, The Disputation, *based on the famous Christian-Jewish disputation at Barcelona in 1263 C.E. In this debate, the Jewish speaker was the renowned Moses Nahmanides (Ramban), who has left us his own account, written with style and wit. The Christian disputant was Pablo Christiani, a Jewish convert to Christianity. A Christian account of the Disputation also exists (see Y. Baer,* Tarbiz II, *pp. 185–87). A new translation of Nahmanides' account (the Viqquah) has been made by Mr Maccoby, and will be published in his forthcoming* Jewish-Christian Medieval Disputations *('Littman Library of Jewish Civilisation').*

The first Act deals with the personal and political manoeuvring preceding the debate. Our first extract comprises the first scene of the second Act, where the Disputation begins. The controller is King James of Aragon, a complex character, whose sporting sense of fair play ensured that, for once, a Disputation took place on almost equal terms. The second extract is from the third Act, where the disputants deliver their final speeches.

ACT 2: SCENE 1

(*The curtain rises to a scene of magnificence – the Throne-room is now arranged for the Disputation, with two long tables at each side of the throne in the centre. A crowd of splendidly-dressed courtiers sit in positions of vantage, chatting in scornful oblivion of the crowd of bourgeois and working people, who are in attendance too. Some Jews sit apart in the crowd, conspicuous by their long beards. The throne and tables are as yet empty; but a hush comes over the crowd as some minor officials enter and occupy the less prominent parts of the tables. Then more important figures enter, exciting more reverence: Raymund de Penjaforte and Pablo Christiani, together with a serene-looking priest, the legate of the Pope. Then entering alone, comes Rabbi Moses, who looks around and goes to a seat near a big lectern on left. Pablo takes a corresponding seat on the right. Now all rise in silence as the King and Queen enter and occupy the two thrones. The King nods to an attendant who strikes a gong. Raymund de Penjaforte comes forward, and bows deeply to the King and Queen.)*

RAYMUND: Your majesties, lords, ladies and citizens of the kingdom of Aragon: by the order of his Christian Majesty King James we begin today a Disputation between Christianity and Judaism. His Majesty's object in holding this Disputation is to draw his Jewish subjects to Christ not by violence but by reasoning and persuasion. And since the Jews everywhere are upheld in their aversion to the Christian religion by love of their book known as the Talmud, his Majesty has graciously approved that the chief part in this Disputation should be played by my colleague Pablo Christiani, who is an expert in the study of the Talmud, having studied it in the greatest detail before he was converted to our religion from Judaism. And on the Jewish side, we have as chief arguer and speaker the Rabbi known as Rabbi Moses ben Nachman, who is well qualified to express the Jewish point of view, and who has promised to consider carefully the arguments which shall be put to him, and to acknowledge them as true if his reason is convinced by them. And this is all that we ask of him, since we are confident that the Christian religion must be acknowledged as true by anyone who approaches it in the light of reason and with an open mind. Rabbi Moses will begin.

(Rabbi Moses rises and comes to his lectern. He begins to speak quietly.)

MOSES: Your majesties, lords, ladies and fellow-citizens, I thank the General of the Dominicans. It would indeed be a great thing if your Majesty's example were followed throughout Christendom, and the differences that exist bewatern Christians and Jews were handled by verbal disputation and not by the method of violence and coercion. (*A stir in the audience.*) I too believe that reason is sufficient to settle these matters. As my first contribution to this discussion, I should like to suggest certain lines on which the discussion should proceed. There are obviously hundreds or even thousands of differences in detail between Chistianity and Judaism, and if we were to discuss them all, our life-time would not be sufficient – certainly not my life-time. Only three or four days have been set aside for this Disputation. I suggest therefore that we should devote ourselves to two questions which, in my view, are the most vital.

JAMES: What are they, Rabbi Moses?

MOSES: The first question is: 'Has the Messiah come, or is he yet to come?' The second question is: 'Is the Messiah prophesied in Scripture a man or a divine being?'

JAMES: What is your opinion about this suggestion, Pablo Christiani? (*Pablo comes forward.*)

PABLO: It seems to me, your majesty, that the questions proposed by Rabbi Moses are certainly very good ones which ought to be discussed before any others, but that our discussion would be narrowed down too much if we undertook to confine ourselves entirely to these two questions. Surely there are also profounder matters at issue between Christianity and Judaism than these?

MOSES: I agree that there are profounder differences which belong to the realm of philosophy. However, though I am myself a student of philosophy, I have observed that philosophical discussions seldom arrive at any conclusion. That is why I proposed that we should confine ourselves to questions on which there is some hope of eventual agreement. On philosophical questions, your majesty, there is no common ground on which all men agree. But there is one area of agreement between Christians and Jews on which we can build a fruitful discussion: we both believe in the truth of the Holy Scripture, which you Christians call the Old Testament, which prophesies the coming of the Messiah. It is the opinion of the Jews that the Messiah has not yet come. It is the opinion of Christians that the Messiah *has* come, and that Jesus was that Messiah. If this matter could be settled one way or the other, there would be no need for philosophical discussion. However, I do not wish to be rigid about my proposal. I observe that Pablo Christiani agrees that the Messiah should be discussed first, and philosophical questions later. This proposal is quite sufficient for my purposes, and I agree to it willingly.

JAMES: I am glad that we have reached agreement on procedure so quickly. The agenda of this Disputation will therefore be as follows: first, the question 'Has the Messiah come or not?'; second, the question 'Is the Messiah prophesied in the Old Testament a divine being or a human being?'; third, philosophical differences between Christianity and Judaism. Is there anything else before we proceed with the discussion?

(Pablo, who has been conferring with Raymund, comes forward.)

PABLO: Your majesty, there is just one point I wish to raise. Rabbi Moses has referred to the Old Testament, but not to the Talmud. That the Messiah has come and that he was Jesus and that the promised Messiah was to be a divine Messiah – all these points can certainly be proved conclusively from the Old Testament. But it is my contention that they can be proved conclusively from the Talmud too, and I wish to lay great emphasis in my argument on this aspect of the matter, since I know that it carries much weight with the Jews.

JAMES: Thank you, Brother Christiani. Perhaps it would not be a bad idea at this point to tell us a little more about the Talmud. I confess that I personally am not as fully informed on the subject as perhaps I ought to be. In fact, not to put too fine a point on it, I know nothing whatever about it.

PABLO: Your majesty, the Talmud was written down about 400 years after the birth of Christ, but it contains traditions which go back to a time long before this. It is the book of the Jewish tradition and explains and amplifies the laws and stories and prophecies of the Old Testament in such a thoroughgoing way that the Jewish faith without the Talmud would be shorn of most of its content. In fact, it is not too much to say that the Talmud rather than the Bible is the Holy Book of the Jews. That is why I consider it so important that it should figure prominently in our discussion.

JAMES: Do you agree with this account of the Talmud, Rabbi Moses?

MOSES: Brother Christiani's account of the Talmud was too brief to be adequate, but I agreed with it as far as it went. He was right in pointing out the great importance of the Talmud to us Jews.

JAMES: Do you agree then that the Talmud should be brought into our discussion?

MOSES: I have no objection. However, I should like to give Brother Christiani a friendly warning which may save him a great deal of time and trouble.

JAMES: And what is that?

MOSES: Simply that we Jews do not always agree with everything we find in the Talmud.

JAMES (*surprised*): I don't quite understand this. You accepted just now that the Talmud is a Holy Book to the Jews?

MOSES: Yes, your majesty.

JAMES: Yet you say now that you don't agree with everything in it?

MOSES: Yes, your majesty. The Talmud is a record of discussions. These discussions took place between Rabbis over the course of about 500 years on every aspect of the Jewish religion. Obviously, when two Rabbis disagree, which happens on every page of the Talmud, both cannot be right. Consequently, many sayings in the Talmud are not accepted by the Jews, though they consider every saying of the Rabbis, whether accepted or not, as worth studying.

JAMES (*still rather puzzled*): I see.

MOSES: Moreover, your majesty, there is another point to be considered.

JAMES: Yes?

MOSES: It is only the legal parts of the Talmud which Jews consider binding. The non-legal parts, being poetical and open to various interpretations, are not considered binding. The topic of the Messiah belongs to this poetical part of the Talmud.

JAMES (*after a thoughtful pause*): Let me get this quite clear, Rabbi Moses. You say the poetical part of the Talmud has no authority?

MOSES: That is correct.

JAMES: And even of the legal part, only a portion has authority?

MOSES: Quite so.

JAMES: This is a very strange Holy Book. There seems to be very little in it to which you give your unqualified assent.

MOSES: That is true, your majesty. The Talmud is a Holy Book, but it is not what Christians mean by a Holy Book. It is not a closed book. It is open and alive. In fact, it is not even finished.

JAMES: What do you mean?

MOSES: It is still being written. Wherever Jewish rabbis come together for discussion, an extension to the Talmud is being written. I have had the great honour of adding a few pages myself. The Jews are called the people of the Book, and that is true, for the Book is the Talmud. But we are not a people who *have* a Book; we are a people who are continually writing a Book.

JAMES: But what about the Bible? Is that not your Book, rather than the Talmud?

MOSES: Yes, that is true. The Bible is the Book, and the Talmud is talk about the Book. That is why it is with reluctance that we write down the Talmud; because then it turns into another book. The Talmud should always be talk.

JAMES: And do you consider everything in the Bible to be binding and authoritative?

MOSES: Yes, we do. But then we are seldom sure what the Bible means. That is what we are continually talking about.

JAMES: But are not the words of the Bible plain and simple? Are they so hard to understand?

MOSES: They are very brief. They require expansion and elucidation if they are to be of use in everyday life. I think your confessor, Brother Raymund, will agree with me in this.

RAYMUND: I do, your majesty. To say that Holy Writ does not require elucidation is a dangerous heresy, and an attack on the authority of the Church.

MOSES: Yes, you have your Talmud too – a stricter one than ours.

JAMES: It seems that you are going to be very hard to pin down in this discussion, Rabbi Moses. For if Brother Christiani appeals to the words of Holy Writ, you will say that it cannot be understood without the commentary of the Rabbis. And if Brother Christiani appeals to the Talmud, you will say that the words of the Rabbis in the Talmud are not necessarily binding on you. I think we must get this point clear before we go any further; otherwise we shall all be wasting our breath. Brother Christiani, I hand the examination over to you now. Can you elicit from Rabbi Moses a clear statement as to what writings or sayings or pronouncements he regards as authoritative?

PABLO: I shall do my best, your majesty. (*To Moses*) Now Rabbi Moses, I think you have been overstating the flexibility of the Jewish religious attitude a little. I was a Jew myself for many years, and your description of Judaism does not quite tally with my recollection of it.

MOSES: Perhaps you have forgotten some things since you became a Christian.

PABLO: I do not think so.

MOSES: Or perhaps there were certain things about Judaism that you never understood.

PABLO: Again, I do not think so. Tell me, Rabbi Moses, is there such a thing as heresy in the Jewish religion?

MOSES: Yes, there is.

PABLO: What is a heretic, then, in Jewish law?

MOSES: One who denies an essential principle of the Jewish faith, while still adhering to Judaism in part.

PABLO: And what are the essential principles of the Jewish faith?

MOSES: That is a matter of dispute.

(*The audience bursts into laughter.*)

PABLO (*after waiting patiently for the laughter to subside*): Surely there are some articles of faith which are beyond dispute?

MOSES: Yes, there are some. The Unity of God is one. The Revelation on Mount Sinai is another. But we have no agreed and definitive set of theological doctrines, as you Christians have. That is why heretics are so rare among us. Theology is for us not a subject on which definite rules and principles can be laid down. Theology belongs to the realm of poetry, not of law. What we Jews are very precise about is the rules of behaviour and action. Here there is no room for poetry. There must be a clear, unambiguous decision, if suffering and injustice are to be avoided.

Even to make no decision is still a decision, and a bad one. You Christians are just the opposite – you do not care much about rules of action, but you have a very strict code of law regulating beliefs. You will burn a man alive because of his views on a matter of poetry, such as the nature of the Trinity, but the fact that your society is organized on a basis of violence and injustice does not seem important to you. (*He pauses.*) But we are getting away from the point.

PABLO: Yes, we *are* getting away from the point. Let us get back to it. Is it a point of belief to you Jews that the Talmud is an authoritative work?

MOSES: Yes.

PABLO: Is a person who denies the authority of the Talmud a heretic?

MOSES: Yes.

PABLO: I am glad you have acknowledged that, because I was about to remind you of the existence of the Karaite sect, who are regarded by orthodox Jews as heretics because they refuse to acknowledge the authority of the Talmud.

MOSES: That is quite true. The Sadducees too were heretics of a similar kind.

PABLO: Well, then, Rabbi Moses, am I to conclude that you, who have just said that the major portion of the Talmud is without authority, are a heretic?

MOSES: No, I am not a heretic, because what I mean by authority and what you mean by authority are two quite different things. We Jews believe that God gave us the Law, and then left us to make what we could of it. It was His will that our attempts to master his Law should be subject to human error. This attempt to master God's law – an attempt full of groping and disagreement and patchy decisions – is the Talmud. All this groping and disagreement is part of God's plan for us. That is why we preserve every dissenting view; we preserve the struggle. All the decisions which were over-ruled by the majority are to be found in the Talmud. They too are part of the truth. And the argument itself, the disagreement which led to a decision, this too is part of the truth. And yet the decision of the majority must be adhered to, or it was not a decision.

PABLO: And what do the Karaites think?

MOSES: The Karaites think that the Talmud is unnecessary

because the meaning of God's word in Holy Writ is plain and obvious, and needs no discussion. You too have heretics like this, who deny the authority of your Church to interpret the words of the Bible.

PABLO: We have a few such heretics. They are not important.

MOSES: One day you will find them very important. They will split your Church in two.

PABLO (*laughing*): Are you a prophet now, Rabbi Moses?

MOSES: No, I am not a prophet. But this is an easy thing to foresee. Your Church is different from our Talmud. You have added the divinity of the Church to the divinity of Scripture. You do not give respect to dissenting views. You burn all dissenters as heretics. Your law is all decisions, and no discussion. The Karaites are heretics to us not because they refuse to worship the Talmud as a second God – as you worship your infallible Church, which you call the body of God – but because they do not recognize the necessity for discussion. The necessity for discussion is authoritative.

ACT 3: SCENE 2

PABLO: Your majesties, lords, ladies and fellow-citizens. So far in this Disputation we have argued about the meaning of texts and phrases, and this was an important task, for those phrases came from Holy writings inspired by God Himself. But now we must probe into the deeper mysteries of life in order to display the truth of our most profound religion . . . Remember the story told by Christ himself about the Pharisee and the tax-gatherer, who stood side by side in prayer. The Pharisee said, as he prayed, 'Thank God I am not as other men are.' But the tax-gatherer smote upon his breast and said, 'God be merciful to me a sinner.' And Christ tells us that the sinner not the Pharisee was justified in the eyes of God. This is the whole difference between Christianity and Judaism. He who looks into his own heart and is appalled by the corruption he finds there must become a Christian. For he knows that without a Saviour, he is lost. And that Saviour is our Lord Jesus Christ, who died for our sins on the Cross, and enabled us to lift ourselves from the abyss. To look into the abyss and be appalled – that is the beginning of wisdom, and the Jews, for all their superficial cleverness, do not have this wisdom. We Christians stand poised between Heaven and Hell, with the pit at our feet and our arms stretched out to our Saviour who draws us from the brink of destruction. Is this a true picture of our life on earth? Or is the complacent, self-satisfied Jewish picture a truer one? I pause now, in the hope that, with God's help, I may have touched the heart of the Jew.

MOSES: (*Rises. He ponders deeply before replying.*) Complacent, self-satisfied, superficial – these are heavy charges. And you Christians, you claim you have looked into the abyss and seen your own unworthiness before the glory of God. To acknowledge one's own sinfulness is certainly a great thing; but shall we go further and call ourselves utterly worthless? Were we not created by God? And is it not an insult to God who created us to call ourselves worthless? . . . To criticize oneself is good, and where in the whole world can you find more examples of self-criticism than in our Jewish writings? What nation except the Jews has put on record in its sacred book every backsliding, every weakness, every sin and disloyalty of which it has been guilty? The sins of the Jews are on record in the Bible, and our enemies are not slow to use this record against us; but blessed is the nation which is not afraid to give such a handle to its enemies. But let us consider; what is the aim and purpose of humility and self-criticism? Is it not to learn by one's errors and do better in the future? But if humility is carried to such a point that one says, 'I am utterly worthless; no action of mine can ever be good,' then the incentive to improvement has been abolished, and excessive humility has become an excuse for lack of effort. This is what you Christians do; you ask God to take you over; you give up the task for which He put you into the world, like a child who refuses to learn to walk. And then a worse result comes about; you fancy that God *has* taken you over; that your Saviour has snatched you from the abyss into a state of sinlessness in which you can do nothing wrong. From a state of abject humility you emerge into a state of incredible arrogance, and proclaim that you are 'saved', and that God is now speaking through your mouth. But we Jews know that no man on this earth is ever without sin, not Moses, not even the Messiah . . . We must grapple with it from the first day of our lives to the last . . . Is this our complacency? Is this self-righteousness? We Jews, you say, are proud, because we reckon ourselves the chosen people of God. But for what were we chosen? To show all the nations an example of a people who are not afraid to walk upright on the earth, to regard no man as God, to look even God in the face and not to be overwhelmed, to stand up for human worth, not human worthlessness. This is what makes us the chosen people of God, for God does not want us human beings to be snivelling wretches and cowards who dare not stand up on our own feet. And this makes us hated by all the nations of the earth, who think that we are endangering their life-lines, their saviours and demi-gods, who look after them and save them from the effort of living like men. We are proud, yes, but we want all men to be proud. We were chosen, yes, but for what? For power? For happiness? For rest and security in our possessions? No; for pain and misery and persecution and wandering over the face of the earth ... But do not say that we have not seen the abyss, we who are on the brink of it every day of our lives; we who began our story crossing the great Desert with only the pillar of fire to guide us. We have seen the abyss, yet we continue our journey, with the guidance of God's Law, which was made for men, not for angels or devils. Moses, who delivered the Law to us, gave us also a saying, when he stood before his death on the border of the Promised Land. Here is the saying of Moses, in which is to be found our message: 'Be strong and of good courage.'

(*The lights fade.*)

Diogo Pires

MEIR WIENER

Meir Wiener (1893–1941), poet, novelist, literary historian and critic, was born in Cracow, Western Galicia. At the outbreak of the First World War his family moved to Vienna, where he completed his education, continuing his studies at the universities of Zurich and Lausanne. In his early twenties he wrote highly complex poetry in German, contributed to Martin Buber's famous journal, Der Jude, *and collaborated in the compilation of the first comprehensive anthology of medieval Hebrew poets. For a time he lived in Berlin and Paris where he began writing in Yiddish. He wrote three novels which were subsequently published in Moscow where he settled in 1926. In the Soviet Union he became associated with the Kiev Institute of Yiddish Studies as a highly respected authority on Yiddish literature of the 19th century.*

In 1941 while fighting with a Red Army unit at the gates of Moscow, Meir Wiener was taken prisoner by the Germans and shot on the spot as were other Jews in this unit in accordance with the German practice of selecting 'Jews and Communists' for execution.

The following extract is from the final section of a long poem in a cycle of three poems, Messiahs.

Born as a Marrano in Portugal around 1500, Diogo Pires was sentenced to death by an edict of Charles V. With his mouth

*gagged he was burned at the stake in Mantua, Anno Domini
1532.*

. . . One night the Spirit visited him once again and spoke thus:
There will come a time when the men in the Western Lands will,
in a sudden awareness, lift up their eyes to the Cross,
and with great astonishment they will ask: Are you one of us?
Are you blood of our blood, you pain-stricken man?
And with whips and knouts in their fists they will come
and call out in horror: You phantom!
And they will say: You ugly-crooked man, what do you want in
   our midst?
An evil spirit adoring the cross for a thousand years,
you terrified us with ghosts, enslaved us with cries of pain,
poured poison into our souls, glistening with humble contrition.
We have recognized you at last: a Jew! A Jew!

Once more they'll take Jesus down from the Cross
on which he was hanging in comfort so long.
His stiffened legs will cause him to fall,
looking mildly amazed at his new tormentors.
But they will only raise their hands to shade their eyes,
and swing their rods and roar:
Enough of the holy gestures!
We've suffered too long your cunning face.
Make haste, Jew!

There will resound a mighty laughter
among the nations of the Western lands.
They will stand there, lining the roads,
to watch him be driven away in shame and disgrace.

Suddenly he will turn round, a quick glance in his eye,
the gesture of one who is hunted –
and by this gesture they will recognize him once more,
                shouting with scorn:
Jew! Jew! Laughter will roar all around him.
Lifting the seams of his cloth he'll start running, torn by pain.

The world's suffering he will bear once again.
But they will laugh and, laughing, swing their knouts,
not bringing them down lest thereby he'd regain his strength.
They will only laugh and swing their knouts.

Wherever he passes, they take his image down from the crosses,
and throw them after him –
and he loads them on his shoulders.
The burden of the empty crosses grows heavy and heavier still.
And once again he breaks down under their weight.
Greater than ever before is the pain he suffers last.

And then there will come the wayfarers, their backs bent low,
their eyes to the ground, with the heavy looks of the hunted.
They will recognize their brother, take mercy on the outcast,
and, removing the load of the useless, discarded crosses,
will throw them with horror into the open abyss.
Then, shaking off a bad dream, Jesus will sigh with relief.

The Rabbi, approaching, will take down the thorny crown from his hair,
and clean the blood from the dried-up wound.
He will wind the black strap around his left arm
and put on his forehead the black diadem –
thus henceforth he will accompany them
on the beggars' rounds through the lands.

The nations of the world, however, who have watched all this,
will no longer laugh,
only shrug their shoulders and turn their backs with contempt,
as is their way.

The poem was written in the autumn of 1916, and first published in Vienna in 1920.

Translated from the German, 1974

Baruch of Amsterdam

CHAIM SLOVES (Paris)

DRAMA IN FOUR ACTS
EXTRACT FROM THE FIRST ACT, SCENE TWO

At the house of Manuella, Baruch's aunt.

BARUCH (*enters, pale and shattered*): Manuella... Rachel... (*with difficulty*) You... you know already?
RACHEL: And you know, too...
BARUCH: I met Henriques, and he told me.
MANUELLA: Sit down, Baruch.
BARUCH (*not hearing*): It's impossible!... It's nonsense!... They have no right!... As often I was called to the Rabbis' Court, I went, and I went there with a clear conscience. And each time I explained: I am innocent! The truth is with me!... What do they think there, in the House of Law – that you can curse away the truth, strangle it by hatred, kill it, kill the truth?...
RACHEL: Baruch, Grandfather says: if you will do what you are told, if you will recant...
BARUCH (*interrupting*): Recant – what have I to recant?... Did I ever publish something in writing... or in print...? Did I preach or engage in public discussion?... And what if I did – is it not my right?
MANUELLA: That's exactly what I am saying: it's madness... Sit down, Baruch... Don't run about the room!... Take my advice – go to the Signores Rabbis and agree to everything they ask you...

BARUCH: Everything they ask?... Everything – nothing less, not a bit less? (*Laughs bitterly.*) And do you know what they ask?... I will tell you: I should say that human reason is all vanity, that one must not question, not seek, not think, not search... And what else? That the heavens are full of angels and seraphim: and that the earth is crawling with devils and spirits, with witches and incarnations!... That God dwells in Heaven, sits on a Golden Throne, has hands, feet, walks, stands up, is jealous, errs, feels regret... Is that all? No, it's not all!... The main thing I nearly forgot – that our people have been chosen from among all peoples – and that the Signores, the Rabbis, are naturally the chosen from among the chosen... Is this, Manuella, what you want me to say – this kind of truth?

MANUELLA: The main thing is not the truth, it's human happiness. All this talk is not worth a single tear shed by Rachel.

BARUCH: There can be no happiness that is based on lies. I will go to the Rabbis' Court and tell them: your zeal for the holiness of each dead letter has transformed true faith into superstition... Our Jodenbort – it is not orthodox, it is ossified... Turned on itself like an oyster in its shell... Superstition chokes each living thought, extinguishes each spark of reason, makes of thinking man a foolish creature, not able to tell truth from falsehood. Jodenbort must wake up! We live in the Netherlands! In a new age!... I have a right to think... and I have a right to say what I think! For this I must not be excommunicated... I shall prove it to the Court...

RACHEL: No, no! You'll only make it worse!

MANUELLA: And all this – what for? Words, words... You're mad, all of you! (*Exits.*)

RACHEL: Baruch, they will banish you!... What will happen to us? To me? I told you I would go with you to the end of the world... I was ready to marry you even against the will of my grandfather, but you refused. You still believed that in the end he would give his consent. And what now? After your excommunication?

BARUCH: Rachel... Don't cry! When I see you cry, I feel so unhappy! What shall I do?... God is my witness – I didn't want it should come to this! I would gladly give up half my life, it should not come to this! For your sake, and also my own. You know it. But what can I do – tell me...

RACHEL (*through tears*): O, what a life, Baruch!... How is one to live in this world of God, which knows no pity?

BARUCH: If I could only find an answer to this question: How to live? What is our life, anyway — is it no more than blood circulating in our veins, our lungs drawing breath, no more than eating, drinking, having children — exactly the same as other living creatures?... But human life — is it not in the main the life of the spirit? If it is — and Rachel, I am sure it is — then no force on earth could make man's mind believe in that which is contrary to what he believes to be true! What reward or punishment could convince me that a body is infinite when I clearly see its limits? By what reward or punishment can it be proved to me that the angles of a triangle do not amount to one hundred and eighty degrees, and that this will be so in all eternity? The spirit of man is invincible!

RACHEL: But nobody forces you to think otherwise. Only you should say...

BARUCH: Rachel — now you, too, ask me to betray myself? I should betray that which is the most precious of all things given to us — our thoughts?

RACHEL: I don't ask anything, Baruch... Do as you think. I can see — you don't love me any more...

BARUCH: But Rachel, I do love you. There isn't a human being who could love you more than I do.

RACHEL: Once you were good to me, and fond of me, as a *fiancé* should be, but lately... You know how hard it is for me to leave the house, grandfather should not know. And then, when I am with you, it is as if you did not even notice me. You keep on telling me about your friends, the gentiles. Only last week you spoke the whole evening with great excitement about the very important arguments they have among themselves, whether Jesus is, or is not, the son of God, and whether Mary was really a virgin when she bore the Holy Spirit, or an ordinary woman... What does it matter to me? I am a Jewess, and don't believe either in Jesus or in the Holy Virgin! I don't want to know about them. And you, too, Baruch, if you are really a Jew, must not think about these things. I begin to be afraid of you!

BARUCH: Rachel! My child! Don't you understand — it's the awakening of the human spirit... There may be different people and different religions, but human reason is one and the same!... Man's thoughts...

RACHEL (*interrupting*): Only thoughts... Only reason... And where is your heart? I begin asking myself: perhaps you have no heart at all, Baruch? Perhaps you consist of reason only, of dry and cold reason? Why don't you have pity on me? Don't you see, how all this bears down on me?

BARUCH: Am I the guilty one? I – and not those who persecute me so unjustly?

RACHEL: What difference does it make, who is guilty? The important thing is, you don't do anything – nothing at all – to prevent the disaster from happening... Forgive me, Baruch, I am so unhappy... Perhaps it's really something good you're after, but what is the good of it if it ends so badly?

BARUCH: So what is it you want, tell me...

RACHEL: I want... I want that we should not destroy our happiness, Baruch, not destroy our lives...

BARUCH (*in despair*): Rachel! What should I do?... If only I could view things quietly, coolly... If only I could come to some final conclusion! My thoughts are like a fishing boat during a storm. Waves beat at it from all sides, the sails are torn, the rudder's broken... and soon the boat will sink into the abyss... Rachel, why should the road to truth lead me away from life and everything that up till now has been my world, all my hopes, my dreams, and my desires?... Must the road to freedom and happiness be the road to loneliness? O, how I fear loneliness! (*He embraces Rachel.*) My soul is with a thousand threads bound to this city and the narrow alleyways of our Jodenbort. The sad songs of mothers leaning over the cradles, the tearful glances in Jewish eyes – it is all part of me! And so is the sing-song of Talmud students, their feverish search in holy books, day and night, to quench the burning doubts, to find the liberating truth. It's all part of me! And you are part of me, too, a part of my soul. My love to you is like a flame that lights up my darkness. Must I cover myself with ashes and bury my own heart in them? Do I know whether there is anywhere else a spring of greater joy, of greater happiness, deep and pure? I dreamt of bringing light and freedom to Jodenbort, to my own people here. This is my place... I must not be cast out from here! (*Pause.*)

RACHEL: You are right, Baruch. There must be no *Cherem*. You'll go, won't you, you'll go to the House of Law and tell them that you recant. You will, won't you?

BARUCH: Recant! (*Not understanding.*) What do you mean, child? Deny the truth? You want me to deny the truth?

RACHEL: Don't ask me anything, anymore. I can see, you have not changed, you are obstinate. You are as hard and pitiless as a rock!

BARUCH: But Rachel ... !

RACHEL: Yes, like a rock! ... Do as you like ... (*She runs off the stage.*)

BARUCH: (*tries to hold her back, but she tears herself away. Exits*): Rachel! Rachel! (*Alone. After a pause.*) If only I could think quietly, if only I could contemplate ...

(*curtain*)

Translated from the Yiddish, 1964

Judaism for the Intellectual

LIONEL KOCHAN

'It is not your duty to complete the work, but neither are you free to desist from it.'
                                                    Rabbi Tarfon

The value of the intellect, the cultivation of the intellect, and respect for the intellectual certainly belong to the heart of Judaism – perhaps, even, they *are* its heart. Speaking in sociological terms, is not one of the 'ideal types' that Judaism has created that of the dedicated scholar? To scholarship is even attributed social value – 'the students of the wise multiply peace in the world'.

Yet in our own day and indeed for the last few centuries, Judaism has not been a religion for intellectuals. Many of the foremost intellectuals of Jewish origin have taken up an attitude of indifference or even hostility to Judaism. There is a rabbinic saying – 'an ignorant man cannot be pious'. In terms of the present perspective it would be more appropriate to turn this the other way round and to say that a man of intellect cannot be pious. Furthermore, there is a great deal of evidence to suggest that this trend of the past is maintaining itself in the present day.

A few years ago, the U.S. monthly journal *Commentary* submitted to a wide span of American-Jewish intellectuals – though perhaps not a representative span – a number of questions concerning the nature of their response to Jewish tradition. Did they feel any sense of obligation to it, for example? Did this sense of obligation, assuming it were there, include a desire to become involved in Jewish community life, or a desire to transmit to their children a knowledge of Judaism, or a desire to acknowledge any merit in the claim that the Jewish people had created or preserved certain special values? There were also other questions so that it is by no means easy to generalize from the diversity of answers. Even so, making full allowance for this distorting factor, it would be true to conclude that a common denominator to all the answers was some appreciation of Jewish values in a humanitarian sense, a distaste for any communal affiliation and some consciousness of Jewish identity. But this was all very tenuous and vague; above all, there was very little recognition of the traditional Jewish obligation to become familiar with Judaism as a preparation for the transmission of its teachings to the next generation.

This dispiriting but not surprising picture is not of course limited to the United States. It is equally evident among the Anglo-Jewish intelligentsia. It is noticeable, for example, that only a tiny minority of the Jewish members of university teaching staffs is at all interested in Judaism. I am quite convinced that if they were confronted with the same set of questions as their United States counterparts then the same picture would present itself.

A book entitled *Walls are Crumbling*, edited by a Catholic convert from Judaism, was published in 1954. The 'Walls' of the title are the divisions between Judaism and Catholicism and the book itself discusses the sympathy for Catholicism, extending in most, but not all cases, to the actual conversion of a number of Jewish philosophers. The latter included such influential modern thinkers as Bergson, Husserl and Scheler – an indication of the true dimensions of the estrangement of the intellectual Jew from Judaism. The tradition of Spinoza in the 17th century is being maintained in the 20th.

If it is incontrovertible that Judaism is losing the adherence of Jewish intellectuals – then this, in the case of a religion that has always set such store by the cultivation of the intellect, cannot but be the forerunner of further disintegration.

Why has this situation come about? And how may it be remedied? To these twin questions I now propose to address myself.

I would like to suggest, first of all, that a chief obstacle to the intellectual acceptance of Judaism has been and continues to be the latter's hostility to speculative thought. Here there is a marked contrast with Christianity. Although much is made of the intellectual assent and intellectual sacrifice demanded of Christian thinkers, intellectual speculation does not seem thereby to have been greatly impaired. There is a notable contrast with Judaism in this respect.

Whereas Christianity can take pride in a most distinguished line of thinkers who have devoted their lives to the understanding of their religion, from one or the other point of view, Judaism in the modern period has little of such tradition to display. One might say that a number of the Jewish historians of the nineteenth century have sought to widen the boundaries of Jewish existence. And there do continue to be isolated Jewish thinkers. But this is very little by comparison with the long and unbroken line of Christian thinkers. It is also little by comparison with those Jewish thinkers who have made their contribution outside and sometimes in opposition to Judaism.

This tradition of hostility to speculative thought is indeed highly pervasive. By the early rabbis it is expressed in the form of an answer to the question why the world was created with the letter *beth*: 'Just as the letter *beth* is enclosed on three sides and only open towards the front, so you are not permitted to be concerned with what is below or above the earth, nor with what happened before this world came to be. Rather, you should be concerned with what happened since the creation of the world, with what lies before you on earth.' Of similar tenor is the warning, 'Whoever reflects on four things it were better he had never come into the world – i.e. what is above, what is beneath, what is before and what is after.' Again, the Talmud approvingly quotes Ben Sira: 'Seek not the things that are too hard for thee, and into the things that are hidden from thee, do not enquire. In what is permitted to thee, instruct thyself; thou hath no business with secret things.' Even so bold a thinker as Maimonides declares at length that 'if ... you do not aspire to apprehend that which you are unable to apprehend you will have attained perfection and attained the rank of Rabbi Akiba ... when engaged in the theoretical study of these metaphysical matters.' Maimonides also interprets a verse from *Proverbs* to state that the nature of intellectual apprehension, if not made to stop at its proper limit and not conducted with circumspection may be converted into a defect ...

No one will deny of course that the injunction to concern oneself with what lies before one on earth has produced a corpus of law of incomparable richness. But part of the price exacted has been the impediment presented to the development of speculation, and this contradicts the *raison d'être* of the intellect.

An additional impediment to this development of speculation has been the rôle of tradition in Judaism. In essence, the claim that the Oral Law enjoys revelatory status with the written law has produced the closely related view that the latter was in some way part of revelation itself; and, furthermore, the view that the expository work of each generation of scholars has also been in some sense part of the original revelation. In other words, that the scholarship of each generation is prefigured in the original revelation, that the latter took place in an all-encompassing present without distinction of past and future. That is why we find such dicta as the following: that in the forty days that Moses spent on Mount Sinai he learned the Torah with all its implications; that, according to a third-century rabbi, Torah, Mishna, Talmud, and Aggadah – and even the comments that some bright student will one day make to his teacher – were already given to Moses on Mount Sinai – and even the questions that such a bright student will some day *ask* his teacher. You may also recall the dictum: 'The Holy One, blessed be He, speaks Torah out of the mouths of our rabbis.'

These remarks indicate a concept of tradition in which, although knowledge is revealed progressively, everything has in effect already been made known. The task of succeeding generations is therefore not to discover new truths – because the full truth has already been made known – but to elaborate a continuity or rebuild a continuity of truth that may have been broken. It is for this reason that commentary plays such a dominating part in Jewish scholarship.

Now, however reassuring such a view will undoubtedly be, it is equally clear that it cannot but inhibit deviation from tradition. Of course, the rabbis, expositors and commentators do not repeat each other; and of course Jewish law does have a history and not merely a tradition; also, the wealth of Torah commentary does include very differing views. It is equally worthy of note that there are one or two passages, I believe, where the Talmud itself makes fun of some of its own more far-fetched interpretations. Even so, taking all these factors into consideration, there seems to me no doubt that the rabbinic conception of the nature of truth has seriously thwarted systematic thought, as distinct from commentary.

To advance several centuries is to be able to discern some of the effects that the emphasis on a revealed tradition and the anti-speculative component in the Judaism rabbinic outlook have had on the development of Jewish thought. It is evident, for example, that Maimonides, in his *Guide for the Perplexed*, finds himself in need of a legal justification for the philosophy he is about to propound. It is evident also in the way in which Spinoza in his *Theologico-Political Treatise* declares that the Jews 'despise' philosophy. In the following century, in 1765, we find Moses Mendelssohn under the necessity of apologizing when he recommends the study of logic and of arguing that the prohibition of the reading of profane literature does not apply to works on logic. At another level again, it is worth taking a glance at the autobiography of the philosopher Solomon Maimon. He was born in Polish Lithuania in 1754 and afterwards became one of the first European thinkers to appreciate the new Kantian philosophy. Maimon also exercised an important influence on the evolution of German idealist thought in the 19th century. In his autobiography he relates how his father had forbidden him to study any book but the Talmud. Now Maimon was very precocious – not only intellectually, I may say. He was married at the age of 12 and became a father at the age of 14.

In his bachelor years, the young Maimon took advantage of his father's preoccupation with household affairs to make a raid on some other books in the household and there he found works which compared most favourably with the Talmud in so far as 'natural events are related in an instructional and agreeable manner, and with a knowledge of the world's structure, by which the outlook into nature is widened, and the vast whole is brought into a well-ordered system'.

In the last century and a half or so another dimension has been added to the challenge that Judaism has already encountered through its hostility to speculative thought – and here I have in mind all those techniques that can be used to investigate the past. It is neither paradoxical nor fortuitous that the development of historical studies should have introduced another threat to traditional Judaism.

We might see the tremendous significance of history to Judaism somewhat as follows: not only does a large part of its constituent documents take the form of a narrative of events, i.e. a history, but one of the most outstanding characteristics of later documents is their repeated reference to events in the Jewish past. At every step the divine and the historical are interwoven. This includes attributing the fulfilment of the divine promises to observance of the divine commandments. If the Hebrews perform certain acts and conduct themselves in certain specified ways, then their history will be affected accordingly. This preoccupation with the national past, as a demonstration of divine purpose and power, is a reiterated feature of the Scriptures. All in all, Judaism, as no other religion perhaps, has rooted itself in a certain attitude to its past, i.e. to its history and to the requirements imposed by a specific understanding of that history. Judaism and its past have become inseparable and the traditional nature of the former has similarly become characteristic of the latter. If, therefore, it can be said that Judaism has no history, in the sense that the events at Sinai and the Oral Law constitute a *final* revelation to which only commentary is possible, then the past is likewise solidified into an unalterable edifice.

Suppose however, it can be shown that that edifice is not in fact unalterable, that it does have a history of its own, that there is not only a divine dimension to the formation of the past, but also a human one – then much of our certainty must necessarily disappear. One of the most eloquent statements of the change wrought by the new historical approach was made by Lord Acton in his inaugural lecture as Regius Professor of Modern History at Cambridge in 1894.

> 'The jurists taught us that law of continuous growth which has transformed history from a chronicle of casual occurrences into the likeness of something organic. Toward 1820 divines began to recast their doctrines on the lines of development... Even the Economists, who were practical men, dissolved their science into liquid history, affirming that it is not an auxiliary, but the actual subject-matter of their inquiry. Philosophers claim that, as early as 1804, they began to bow the metaphysical neck beneath the historical yoke. They taught that philosophy is only the amended sum of all philosophies, that systems pass with the

age whose impress they bear, that the problem is to focus the rays of wandering but extant truth, and that history is the source of philosophy, if not quite a substitute for it. Comte begins a volume with the words that the preponderance of history over philosophy was the characteristic of the time he lived in. Since Cuvier first recognized the conjunction between the course of inductive discovery and the course of civilization ... the depressing names historicism and historical-mindedness have been devised.'

What does this mean in the context of Judaism? How has the past, as understood by traditional Judaism, been modified, if at all, by that influence which Acton calls 'historicism and historical-mindedness'?

At its most extreme it would mean that Judaism ceased to exist as a fixed and self-sufficient entity but became a part of history, that is to say, that it existed as something in a perpetual state of becoming, lacking all finality. However, that position has not yet been reached. But sufficient historical treatment has been given to Judaism to illuminate the threat. In one sense this process can already be seen at work in Maimonides, for example, who in certain respects is prepared to understand certain of the basic concepts of the Pentateuch in a historical context, as historically conditioned – that is to say, to interpret them within the context of their time. I have in mind the regulations concerning what are known as the Sacrifices. Maimonides interprets these with regard to the circumstances of the time – i.e. as a concession to those Hebrews to whom the Pentateuch was originally addressed: 'Man, according to his nature is not capable of abandoning all to which he was accustomed ... and as at that time the way of life generally accepted and customary in the whole world and the universal service upon which we were brought up consisted of offering various species of living beings in the temples in which images were set up, in worshipping the latter and burning incense before them ... Therefore He suffered the above-mentioned kinds of worship to remain, but transferred them from created or imaginary and unreal things to His own name ... Thus He commanded us to build a temple for them, to have an altar for His name, to have the sacrifice offered up to Him, to bow down in worship before Him and to burn incense before Him. And He forbade the performance of any of these actions with a view to someone else ... Through this divine ruse it came about that the memory of idolatry was effaced and that the grandest and true foundation of our belief, namely, the existence and oneness of the deity – was firmly established while at the same time the souls had no feeling of repugnance and were not repelled because of the abolition of modes of worship to which they were accustomed, and no other mode of worship was known at that time.'

How valid this is as an explanation of the Sacrifices I do not know. What concerns me at the moment is that it anticipates in a small way the application to the Pentateuch of the principle of historical understanding and analysis; that is to say, it presupposes that a text can be understood – perhaps, *must* be understood, as in some measure a product of its time, as in some way related to its time; and therefore that in the particular instance of the Sacrifices, their observance is only of limited validity.

But of course it is only within the last century and a half, say, that historical-mindedness of this type can be said to have developed seriously as a medium of scholarly investigation. Other techniques for the intellectual understanding of the past, such as anthropology, social psychology, textual criticism have also come to the aid of historical-mindedness (insofar as they were not already dependent on the latter for their very existence).

Even during this comparatively short period of a century and a half a great deal has been accomplished to show that Judaism does in fact have a history, that is to say, to take one example, that it is doubtful, to say the least, whether it can still be maintained that the Pentateuch can be held to have emanated from a revelation made to Moses; or that the Oral Law has itself not known development, even though it may only be by way of interpretation; or that Hegelian or sociological theories of Jewish history cannot plausibly be maintained.

On the specific question, for example, of the law governing the relationship between Jew and Gentile I have recently been reading a study which shows not only that the Talmud itself took up a less restrictionist attitude in this matter in the course of its compilation but also that the restrictions were gradually relaxed during the whole of the post-Talmudic period. The reason for this was the disappearance of the Talmudic situation when legislation was conceived in terms of a compact self-supporting body, whereas in the post-Talmudic period the Jewish situation was one of small dispersed bodies economically dependent to a varying and sometimes quite considerable extent on their Gentile neighbours.

So far as Jewish history is concerned, as distinct from the practice and understanding of religion, it is also noteworthy that the traditional pattern, centred on a divine disposition and relationship, such as I have tried to outline above, has been complemented by other interpretations. For many centuries of Jewish existence in Europe I think it would be true to say that Jewish historical consciousness was barely developed. Certainly, Jews were only too well aware that their fate was most intimately bound up with events in the areas where they lived. But this was very different from being emotionally involved in the past of the particular area. When, however, this degree of involvement did grow – say, at about the end of the eighteenth and beginning of the nineteenth century, then it was not long before the Jewish past also began to be comprehended in a setting rather different from that which had hitherto prevailed. We no longer have the God-centred narrative of the Pentateuch and the Prophets but interpretations on Hegelian lines (as in the work of Hirsch) or, a little later, interpretations on sociological lines as in the work of Dubnov. In all these there is manifest a spirit of comprehension very divergent from that of tradition.

So far as traditional Judaism is concerned this means that truth itself has a history. And this view I take to be of fundamental importance for it is wholly incompatible with the view that the Torah can stand as an unshaken edifice in the commonly accepted sense. A certain fluidity is introduced into the conception of the Jewish past. The end result of this process, as I have suggested earlier, can only be to turn Judaism itself into a historical manifestation, to consider all its claim to embody the truth as but the evolution of a claim to see Judaism purely as history. If this were to happen then it would be very difficult indeed, if not impossible, to assert of Judaism that it contained any prescriptions that deserved to be commended and observed by reason of their truth-value. It seems to me that this is the challenge that Judaism must be prepared to face. The history on which traditional Judaism has taken its stand has now turned into the enemy of that Judaism.

The proposition that Judaism possesses truth value can no longer be asserted by reference to the past – because the past has itself been undermined by historical investigation. The proposition will have to be proved by other means.

The journal to which I have already referred, *Commentary*, does not only quiz intellectuals; it also quizzes rabbis. And in a recent issue it asked Rabbi Jakobovits, amongst others, such questions as these: In what sense do you believe the Torah to be divine revelation? In what sense do you believe that the Jews are a chosen people? What aspects of modern thought do you think pose the most serious challenge to Jewish belief? In the course of his answer Rabbi Jakobovits referred to the need for

> 'a reappraisal of Jewish teachings in the light of modern thought, just as Judaism reacted to similar challenges in the past. The confrontation with the ritualistic paganism of antiquity witnessed the rise of prophecy, which stressed the then neglected ethical elements of the Torah. The impact of the Graeco-Roman age was met by the Talmud, the presentation of Judaism in pre-eminently legal terms. This encounter with Arabic philosophy during the Spanish period produced the classics of Jewish philosophy, or the formulation of Judaism in philosophical terms. Conditions in 18th century Poland led to the rise of Hasidism, while the rational humanism of 19th century Germany found its Jewish reaction in the Orthodoxy of Samson Raphael Hirsch and other thinkers. All these developments and movements were equally authentic expressions of Judaism, beginning and ending — as the prophetic books do (Joshua 1:7 and Malachi 3:22) — with an unqualified endorsement of "the Torah of Moses, My servant", though particularly stressing or evolving different facets of it in response to the challenges of the times.'

Jakobovits ended his reply with Hillel's dictum: 'Now, go and study'. The question is where? *Where* does one go to study and *what* does one study? To a *Yeshivah*, for example? We must all take pride in the history of the *Yeshivah* and in the succession of great scholars whom it has produced. An institution which has shown such vitality is not one that any historian would wish to deprecate. It precedes the earliest university in the western world and its undiminished strength is attested to in the establishment of so many *Yeshivot* in this country in our own generation.

At the same time we must, however, also ask ourselves whether the traditional curriculum of a *Yeshiva* is the best adapted to the particular contemporary problems we have to confront. Jakobovits, in the extract I quoted, referred to the Talmud as 'the presentation of Judaism in pre-eminently legal terms' in response to the Graeco-Roman age. But does it follow from this that a response to the position of one age can be similarly valid and effective to the position in another age?

The very fact that the response of Judaism has in fact, over the centuries, been couched in varying terms strongly suggests that this is not the case. Whereas the *Yeshiva* has fully retained its capacity as a medium of instruction it has lost its capacity to formulate the necessary response to the contemporary challenge.

But can learning alone provide us with the answers to questions that belong to a later age? It is precisely those questions which will reveal whether Judaism is still intellectually alive, whether Judaism can still provide satisfying answers couched in a contemporary idiom. In order to answer those new questions that are already being posed and will assuredly be posed in the future something additional will be required. Apart from what is indestructibly true in the work of thinkers of an earlier period, it would also be clear that they themselves had formulated their ideas in response to the challenge of their age – and this, by definition, could not be the challenge of our age. Their example is one that should be a stimulus to emulation and not a reason for contentment. Besides, it would be a confession of something akin to intellectual bankruptcy were we to assume that nothing more can be added to what our predecessors have said. Surely we have something of our own to add.

And that is what brings me to the question of a Jewish philosophy and the role that it is called upon to undertake. I think we may visualize this in two categories. The first is what we might call an internal Jewish category. It would work within the framework of an already existing Judaism and seek to make explicit the Jewish theory of some specific theme or perhaps the evolution of Jewish theory; the idea of prophecy, the content of Messianism, the theories of the Jewish mystics, the schools and methods of Biblical interpretation. This 'internal' category does not, of course, mean excluding non-Jewish comparisons and affiliations. On the contrary, they would be essential for the purpose of illuminating what Judaism has to say on these subjects. However, it would still remain true that such a philosophy took its starting point and its *raison d'être* in the exposition and formulation of the particular Jewish doctrine in question. Such a philosophy would find its natural climax in an attempt to determine the divine attributes and thus renew the thought of the medieval Jewish philosophers. It is a remarkable fact, and one testifying to the large-scale abandonment of Judaism by Jewish intellectuals, that the wealth of medieval speculation on this theme is followed in later centuries by barely two thinkers – Moses Mendelssohn and Hermann Cohen. Moreover, the task will be all the more difficult in that it will no longer be possible to take for granted a conception of God that has prevailed for many centuries. It will no longer be able to carry conviction by referring to a commandment but will have to validate that commandment in terms of the divine attributes.

There is another category of Jewish philosophical thought and this is much more closely related to the non-Jewish cultural and intellectual world. It involves the use of contemporary techniques to explore this or that aspect of Judaism; for example, we have recently had a socio-anthropological work dealing in a comparative manner with such crucial concepts of Judaism as cleanness and uncleanness. But I envisage this second category rather in the form of a dialogue that will be concerned with the problem of formulating an answer to Epicurus, to adapt the classic phrase. I had hoped to avoid the use of the term 'dialogue' altogether but it has at last crept in. Generally speaking when a dialogue is held so much noise is generated that the speakers cannot be heard. However, this must not obscure the need for a Jewish response to the contemporary world. The point is this – as Judaism moves through the ages it is confronted by an ever-changing intellectual environment of all degrees of friendship and hostility and endless combinations of these two. The movement of the human mind is very rarely halted for long and if Judaism is to retain its intellectual respectability then it must be prepared to relate itself to this ever-changing environment. This is what Christianity has succeeded in doing and its continued intellectual vitality is due to this responsiveness. But this is by no means true to the same extent in the case of Judaism.

We might take as one type of example of what I have in mind the hostile portrait of Judaism presented by Toynbee. A principal indictment that he makes against Judaism is what he calls the latter's 'Futurism', i.e. the supposed attempt to hasten the advent of the Messianic age. This is in concert with Toynbee's sympathy for the Christian transfiguration of the world. Associated with this 'Futurism' in Toynbee's hostile portrait is the Jewish notion of election. These two notions are of course crucial to Judaism and I would hope that they might be re-examined and re-considered.

Such a re-examination would not only have value as a historical exposition but also serve as an organ of the renewal of Judaism. Toynbee's challenge is couched in contemporary terms and undoubtedly draws strength from attempts to enforce a utopia and to invest a particular national and popular grouping with transcendental values. To this extent, it could not have been made before the nineteenth or twentieth century. That is why it must receive an answer that is made in contemporary terms and not in terms of a second-century quotation. For if Judaism is to be continually renewed in its contact with time, then the world of that time, the world outside traditional Judaism, must be grasped in its fullness – and that in addition to acquiring familiarity with the body of Jewish knowledge. I do not under-estimate the magnitude of this task. But by way of consolation I would recall a dictum of Rabbi Tarfon: '*It is not your duty to complete the work, but neither are you free to desist from it.*'

1967

Lionel Kochan is Bearstead Reader in Jewish History at the University of Warwick. His published works include *Russia in Revolution 1890–1918*; *Russia and the Weimar Republic*; *Struggle for Germany 1914–1945*; *Acton on History*; *The Making of Modern Russia*.

ON BEING ENGLISH AND JEWISH

An Inquiry

In 1963 The Jewish Quarterly *published a series of interviews with a number of Anglo-Jewish writers on 'Being English and Jewish'. The writers were Alexander Baron, Brian Glanville, Frederic Raphael, Gerda Charles, Dannie Abse, Wolf Mankowitz, and Michael Hamburger. The same set of questions, with slight variations, was put to each of them. In the pages that follow are answers to two of the questions:*
1. *Basically are you a Jewish writer or an English writer?*
2. *What has been the impact on your work by the war-time destruction of the Jews in Europe?*

   Although the two questions were linked with others and, consequently, the answers were similarly linked, we confine ourselves here to the direct answers to the two direct questions, in exactly the same form as they were given then.

ALEXANDER BARON:

'Jewish Preoccupations...'

'Jewish preoccupations... have more and more taken possession of me...'

Q. *Basically are you a Jewish writer or an English writer?*

I am still trying to find out. The Question is so big, and so much at the centre of my life, that I feel as helpless as you might if you were suddenly asked to answer the question, 'What are you on earth for?' We have had a lot of symposiums about this, of course, and for the last year or two I have refused to speak at any more of them. All the argument on Anglo-Jewish writing seems to me to be of the cat-chasing-tail kind, and a waste of time. The only way a writer can even grope towards a solution is through his work. What he writes will tell him what he is.

It seems strange to me that after sixteen years I have to answer so evasively. Certainly, at the beginning of my writing career I had no doubts. I was an English writer. I would have gone on to add, as perhaps some of the younger writers may assert, that there is no contradiction between this and my Jewishness. After all, the work that established me was a trilogy about British soldiers. These three books have become, in a sense, classics. I don't over-estimate myself, or wish to make claims. But after many years they still sell in enormous numbers, they are used in whole or part as school books in this and other countries, and as their author I have come to be regarded as a kind of spokesman of the voiceless British soldier of World War Two. My later London novels, I think, are as deeply rooted in the people they describe. I am English in the third generation on one side, the second on the other, but I have the most profound emotional attachment to this country. The novelist's business is with the state of man, but he usually sees mankind through his own neighbours and I feel the same obsessive fascination in the English character, the English mystery if you like, and the same pride in it as – without comparing myself to these great masters – Faulkner did in his neighbours of Yoknapatwpha County, as Silone does in the peasants of Fontamara. People often ask me why, since I have freedom of movement, I don't live abroad. I can't for any long period. I can't even stay away from London for long. As a writer I am under the spell of the English, and particularly of those multitudes who were once known as 'the lower classes', of their extraordinary virtues, their patience, moderation, courtesy, deep humour, all the qualities that are embodied in the humane and temperate progress of English society, and also by their vices, their ugliness, pettiness, the great national streak of Saxon stupidity, the Puritan poison in the spirit (there are also Puritan virtues) and the vicious prejudices of race and class which sometimes seem to me a purulence caused by the Puritan wounding of the spirit. I am a worshipper of the incomparable literature of England. I believe I spend more time reading than writing, and for most of it I am shut up in the treasure-house that lies between Chaucer and Thomas Hardy. I barely keep in touch with present-day novels, and don't at all mind not being in the swim. I am appalled when I meet younger writers, people of reputation and genuine talent, who tell me happily that they haven't read, or have hardly read, the classical English novelists. In fact they regard such reading as old hat, fuddy-duddy. The work of a writer, like that of a painter, doesn't only derive from life, but from that of earlier writers. Art is a process of handing down. Writers who derive from no one earlier or greater than D. H. Lawrence are going to be awfully small people. I also feel an immense responsibility towards the English language. I don't speak Hebrew or Yiddish. I think and dream in English. It is my greatest possession. Too many cried-up modern novels degrade the language. I believe that every writer, whatever his style and however limited his talent, must try with all his power to do honour to the language. So? Surely I'm English?

All the same, as time goes on, Jewish preoccupations, obsessions, and symbols have more and more taken possession of me and consequently entered into my work. I have to admit that there is a conflict here, perhaps an insoluble one. Perhaps this conflict is what makes me write. I have always believed in the theory put forward by Edmund Wilson in *The Wound and the Bow* that inside every writer, making him write, is the irritation of a wound that can't be healed.

Two thousand years of history have made the Jew, however assimilated he may be, into a nationality, into an incurable outsider. Or perhaps I should say that part of him is an outsider – the outsider living inside the insider.

I don't want to be sentimental about the Jew. Those two thousand years have made him into a strange animal. Scoop up a handful of Jews and you will find some of the ugliest human characteristics in the most exaggerated form. But you will also find certain virtues in heightened form. For instance, the lack of statehood, of chauvinism, and the continuous experience of suffering, the dispersion of the Jewish people and of thousands of individual Jewish families have made it easier for a Jew to have a more universal outlook than his fellow-countrymen, even if he is no less patriotic. Bitter experience has taught him the need for tolerance. He is less easily taken in by propaganda (Mr Khruschev is said to have complained that a Jew always asks 'Why?') because he has heard it all before. In fact I'd sum it up, rather than continue this catalogue of qualities, by suggesting that whereas people generally have no sense of the past and their minds live in small parishes, Jews are dominated by a long past and by its lessons, and they are forced to encompass the whole world in their view. All this makes the Jew a born critic. In short, an outsider. It may be said in reply that every writer, even the most 'inside' and integrated of men or women, has to be at the same time an outsider in the nature of things. The mere taking up of a position from which to observe other people, the act of lending form to a work, implies judgment, criticism. Well, yes, but then we have to add to this that a Jew has grown up as a member of an insulted – even in this country – minority, as the heir to an appalling history of persecution, as the witness (and surely spiritual fellow-victim) of the gas chambers, as the bearer of the knowledge that, even after the gas chambers, the human species, even some of the nations that fought Hitler, can still persecute Jews. And if he is religious, he has been brought up in a faith that, unlike any other I know, imposes on each human being, without the get-outs of after-lives or pardon easily bought by prayers, the responsibility of acting rightly during this lifetime. Is it too much to say that in a Jewish writer you may well find the moral sense and the sensitivity not only to all human suffering but to all human weakness unbearably intensified?

In my own work – who knows? I don't believe that a novel should contain overt preachment, but my intention is always didactic. It's not my place to say now what that intention is. In the first place, books should speak for themselves. In the second place a writer often doesn't know what he has really said. This he may learn, perhaps with surprise, from other people. After all, when he writes he doesn't set down thoughts that are already clear in his head. He is beset by a vague conflict of perceptions, moods, ideas, and his work is a combined struggle to make something clear to himself and communicate something to other people.

Certainly I find myself again and again using a Jewish character as a critical spokesman, a chorus to the drama. This is the role of Trifon in my historical novel, *The Golden Princess*. In my television play, *The Harsh World*, the little Jewish furrier speaks what is in effect a moral epilogue. In my new novel, *The Lowlife*, the central character, Harryboy Boas, plays a complex part which no other than a Jew could have fulfilled. He himself has to have sufficient vision, sufficient inherited wisdom – even poetry, in a sense – to comment with sufficient clarity on the action of the story. He embodies in his own person a number of universal problems, above all, that of guilt – and the supreme symbol of guilt in our times, as seen in the book, is the mass murder of Jewish children by the Nazis. He is, though he is scarcely aware of it, a religious Jew, which reinforces his critical position. And in his relation to the English family, the Deaners, he is able to view from the outside the whole complex of character and *mores* that they represent.

Q. *What has been the impact on your work by the war-time destruction of the Jews in Europe?*

Perhaps it would be more useful for me to discuss this question with the psycho-analyst than with an interviewer. For many years after the war the whole business of the *Churban* (The Destruction) had no profound effect on me. I knew about it, I thought it was a terrible thing, I drew conclusions from it, and so on, but *it had done nothing to change me*.

About ten years ago a personal incident – I am not concerned to describe it now – broke through whatever membrane of resistance had formed in my mind, and I was completely invaded by the knowledge of what had happened, by horror at it, and also by horror at my own previous superficial reaction to it all. Since then it has been the master obsession of my life. It is a literal truth that at the present time not a single day passes without some thought or picture of the *Churban* assailing me. It is usually a picture. Sometimes I go off into a train of generalized thought about it, but mostly one small sharp film or photograph appears in my mind – for instance, I see again and again the children of the Warsaw Jewish Orphanage marching through the streets on their way to the death train; or I see myself in a room with my own family waiting for the S.S. to come, and trying to imagine (to hear, rather) what I am saying to my parents and my wife. It penetrates and darkens every moment of pleasure, a wedding dinner, say, or an afternoon on a Mediterranean beach. At such moments of course there is a complex reaction. I feel that the moment of anguish is itself a hypocrisy, for it passes and I go on enjoying myself, I go on living. One accuses one's self at such times of using even pain as a form of self-indulgence, of easy absolution.

At one level it seems to me that the effect on my work is negative. I can see no way of coping with it in literary form. I try to find a way of doing so, often, if only in the hope of freeing myself a little from the obsession. No, what happens to me is that I can't write about it, but it stops me writing about anything at all for quite long periods. There are times when I can do nothing but walk about in the streets brooding about it and looking at the films inside my head.

It does keep on invading my work. You know, when mentally

disturbed people are invited to write or draw, they introduce into whatever they do symbols – words or pictures, always the same – deriving from their own state. In the same way, whatever I write, on any subject, I find myself in the first draft introducing some reference-back to the Nazi holocaust. When I revise, I recognize that it is quite out of place in this particular piece of work, and delete it.

Only in my novel, *The Lowlife*, have I found a way of creating a link between present-day experience and this obsession. Even then, one perceptive critic told me that this element was an intrusion into the book; and while I do not agree, I wonder myself if I have introduced the theme in a too small, oblique and unworthy manner.

Yet this tendency of mine, this neurotic tendency if you like, has a seed of rightness in it. The *Churban* was not a private Jewish experience. It was not one of many comparable and terrible historical episodes. It is different in kind from anything else we have seen. It calls into question most of our previous assumptions about civilization, about how far man has got in the twentieth century, about the very nature of man. And what is the fundamental job of writers? Whatever area of reality we explore, in whatever genre or mood we write, we are all (if we are of serious intention) research workers adding our small findings, our personal illuminations, to the great self-exploration of man, the attempt to learn what the real nature and destiny of the species is. And this being the case, how can we, who have lived in the time of the *Churban*, side-step it? How can we fail to take it into account when we are making *any* statement about the human kind? Even if we don't write a word about it, we must give some evidence that it is present in our consciousness.

So that, after all, I come to wonder why *all* writers aren't obsessed as I am. Perhaps it's a good thing that they're not. However I look for it, and I think I have a right to look for it, in other people's work, and especially in the work of those talented young Jewish writers who were only children or even babies when all this happened. I don't expect them necessarily to deal with it. I do hope for some clue, however obscure and indirect, to *awareness*, not only because they are Jews but because they are writers – spokesmen.

In this connection it is again interesting to look at the work of

Gentile writers. A Pole told me that in his country the great obsession of the younger writers is with the Jew, the Jewish suffering. 'The years go by,' he said, 'but they can't break out of it. They can't get away from it.' I understand that the same is true of Czech and Yugoslav writers and film-makers, although in all three countries the writers are criticized and even attacked by the authorities for their 'obsession with the past'. Of course they are – because it isn't the past, it's still the present. The questions posed by the *Churban* are still not answered. The behaviour of man in that time may be a clue to how he will behave in the future, with H-bombs in his hands. A Pole cannot work out an attitude to his own countrymen without thinking about the Jews. How can he create characters without wondering if they were indifferent, if they were among the heroic few who helped, or if they were like those Poles who jeered from the pavements at the marching column of Jewish infants (I'm thinking again of that terrible day when they took the children from the orphanage) and shouted to them that they were going to the ovens? This thing has become a kind of chemical test for human character.

1963

BRIAN GLANVILLE:
'At a Deeper Level one is and remains Jewish.'

Q. *Basically are you a Jewish writer or an English writer?*

Both. My father was born in Dublin, my mother in London, but their parents all came from Eastern Europe, and in many ways our family was a pretty typical London-Jewish one. (Though my father was a dentist, not a businessman, and the Irish Jews differ a good deal from the London Jews.) At the age of nine, I was sent away to boarding school and was subjected for the next eight and a half years to a typical, upper-middle-class English educational processing. Both at prep. school and in my house at public school, I was the only Jew. In each case, this brought about an exceedingly painful period of adaptation, after which (but somewhat late to avoid emotional scars) came acceptance. School for me – and for most of us – was a mere, pale shadow-world by comparison with home, but its effect was nevertheless considerable.

English is my language – this in itself is a most potent conditioner of the personality – and compulsory chapel attendance probably means I have (most reluctantly) attended more Anglican services than Jewish. At the deeper level, one is and remains Jewish, partly because the roots are so much more profound, partly because one's temperamental inheritance and early, determining experience are Jewish, partly because it was made so clear to one in a Gentile society that one *was* Jewish. I love England and I love the English; I tried to live in Italy, and found I had to come back. Now, I could not envisage living anywhere but London. This love isn't unqualified, or sentimental. English inhibitions, English xenophobia, English class consciousness; I'm aware of all these. But I feel tremendously at home with the English; even soothed. I love their humour and their tolerance and their decency. English literature says far more to me than any other; its ethos is immeasurably more graceful than the French, more sympathetic to me than the Italian, less strange and alien than the Russian. I feel that the tragedy of the First World War was my tragedy, just as the Warsaw Ghetto and Auschwitz and Buchenwald were my tragedies.

Although I have published two 'Jewish' novels, I have written largely about English – and Italian – subjects; English dialogue rhythms fascinate me, and I was the first to write serious fiction about the world of football; a quintessentially British world. And yet of course I am, in a sense, a Jewish writer. I say, in a sense, because I believe Isaac Bashevis Singer was right and logical when he said that the majority of so-called American-Jewish writers were not Jewish writers at all; they had little or no Yiddish or

Hebrew background, they were merely Americans of Jewish ancestry, writing on Jewish themes. One must not carry the comparison too far; there *is* a certain national (if not racial) mainstream here, whereas America is a racial synthesis, a somewhat uneasy blending of ethnic groups. But I do not derive from Jewish writers, can neither read nor write Hebrew or Yiddish; in what useful sense, then, can I call myself a Jewish writer? Yet the fact remains that I consider myself a Jew, am poignantly aware of the Jewish experience, and find that experience central to my apprehension of life. I am, then, both a Jewish writer and an English writer . . . I remember Isaiah Berlin once writing that the Jew could never be a great creative artist because he was always faced with the problem of adjustment; what the great creators took for granted, he had to work out for himself. Thus, his usual role was that of explainer and interpreter of nations to themselves. I think there is much truth in this, though Heine, Kafka, Babel and Proust stand as contradictions. Yet at this particular moment in English history, when vigour and purpose are impaired and the middle class, from which most literature has sprung for the past century, has lost so much blood and vigour, I believe the Jewish writer's dilemma is an advantage, a source of passion and vitality. If he has been brought up among the English, their mentality will not be foreign to him; it will be accessible, and he will have two strings to his bow. The process of finding out who he is, which must involve any writer, will for him be peculiarly painful and immediate; but this again, may benefit him, as an artist.

Q. *What has been the impact on your work by the war-time destruction of the Jews in Europe?*

It seems to me that my life, all life, is in some sense no more than a coda to that destruction. It obsesses and horrifies me; I find it unbearably painful. The reports which still come through from trials, the memoirs of murder, torture and persecution, stun the mind with outrageous and incredible cruelties. In theory, of course, one easily explains the phenomenon of anti-Semitism; paranoia, minority groups, projection of guilt, abreaction of repressed violence. But of course one cannot come to terms with it, with the brutal gratuitousness of it all, the vile murder of little children, the sadism and above all the Germanic *coldness*; sadism not just spontaneous but organized, rationalized, put into effect like any other daily project. That violence will always exist, of course; just as the psychic economy makes it inevitable that minorities will always be vulnerable as scapegoats. Yet I do not believe that any other nation but the Germans, with their persecution mania and what Freud, fifty-five years ago, called their 'morbid craving for authority', could have systematized and codified evil in this way. I am also horrified by how little difference it has made. Even the English, who tolerate Jews, even if they do not like them very much, are quite unaffected in their cheerful anti-Semitism. Only a humane minority, here or anywhere else, *sympathized* with the Jews; the rest seemed, and seem, merely indifferent. Again and again, one tried to come to terms with the persisting horror of it all; to try in some way to excuse the murders and the sadists and the butchers; excuse them in political terms, in psychopathological terms – but one can't. And if all this affects my work, it must be indirectly. The subject – for me – cannot be treated in terms of fiction, because by the side of such gigantic suffering and such monumental cruelty, artefact is cheap.

FREDERIC RAPHAEL:

'Something to be Serious About . . .'

Q. *Basically are you a Jewish writer or an English writer?*

Without quibbling about the word 'basically' (after all, the question has to be phrased somehow), I would be inclined to say that I am basically myself and do not have any general characteristics which would designate me Jewish or English, though of course English is the language in which I work. In this sense I am basically English but this sense is not very much more than tautologous. I am not basically a Jewish writer at all if by Jewish one means working within the Jewish community or finding my characters among the figures of traditional Jewish writing. My Jewishness is extremely personal, not in the sense that I claim any special philosophical insights or theological revelations, not in the sense that it is better or more valuable than anyone else's, but in the sense that the way in which I find Jewishness a creative concept for me is so closely related to my whole private grammar and has so curious a place in it that any pretence that it meshes with the Jewishness of the community, of the Jewish religion, of the State of Israel or of ghetto writing would be delusive. I do not think, quite frankly, that I am a Jewish writer at all and I sometimes feel that it is more common politeness than our common heritage which makes Jewish circles welcome me and which makes me prone to accept their welcome. I have no interest in saving the phenomenon of Jewishness, but I find it senseless to proclaim my divorce from a group in which my family quite recently took an active part and whose fate has so deeply impressed itself on me that I shall never forget it.

No public experience can ever affect me as the discovery of what happened to European Jewry did, no experience, I mean, of which I am not the witness, in which I am not a participant. By a pun, by being called the same thing as those who died, I am linked with them. Yet I am, in de Gaulle's sense, very Anglo-Saxon! I am as influenced by American as by British writing. The Americans excite me because they seem less cosy, less strutted with the institutions Henry James thought so vital to monumental fiction, the English because the English novel has employed so much more effectively and purposefully the humorous surface which I feel to be a vital part of the novel: the English novel understands verbal impasto better than the American. I also admire much French writing, because of its lack of coyness in dealing with politics and psychology. I do not admire the new French novel, however, with its conspicuous aesthetic vacuity. I do not have faith in anything. Hence my work is lonely.

My Jewishness is the Jewishness of the disillusioned diaspora

Jew, the Jewishness of loneliness. When I was at school I believed myself to be the only Jew in the school. I realize now that there were plentiful and obvious proofs that this was not so. Yet I continued to believe it. And when other Jews forced themselves on my attention I found neither comfort nor comradeship in their presence. I have always believed myself to be alone and I daresay I always shall. To me Jewishness is the symbol of inexorable loneliness. My attempts to associate myself with the community are either polite or hypocritical, depending on how you look at it. I do not believe in salvation, either through community or religion. Thus I am not English either, for I feel myself wholly excluded from the community of Britons. I function within it, but I am not absorbed or satisfied by it. I feel myself alien from everyone. This is my kind of Jewishness. This sounds very sad! As if I were asking for sympathy. This has to be watched, but of course the 'my' here is the my of my language, not of my person (I hope). The heroic Jew (like Lindmann) is to me a figure who accepts responsibility without hope. He need not, in this way, be a circumcised, paid-up Jew.

Q. *Why do the Jewish obsessions conflict with the English obsessions and how do they enter your work?*

The essence of the matter to me is that the Jewish obsessions reveal the limitations of the English obsessions, whatever they are, and insist on the language changing. At the present, too much English writing exudes a glum, brutal resentment and very little else; a wilful contraction of the language, a wilful diminishing of what the unsentimental writer will accept as 'honest', is leaving us less and less able to express anything except the grunts and groans of primitive vulgarians. The other typically English pose is that of those who still ape the Mandarin attitudes of Forster and others. They still think of sensitivity and love as master forces and with them God is, if not in his heaven, out there somewhere, ripening the corn. He may doze now and again, but on the whole he keeps an eye on the British. More than Jewish obsessions or English obsessions, one is the victim, the interpreter, the prisoner and the guardian, of one's own obsessions: sexuality, pain, love and death, missed opportunity, lost friendship, failure, success and so on. How do they all conflict? Dramatically. One hopes.

Q. *What has been the impact of the war-time destruction of the Jews in Europe on your work?*

Unfathomable. I have dealt with this already in a way. It has prevented me from being optimistic, from being complacent, from being pious. How to cope with it without seeming to appropriate it has concerned me very much recently. *We* didn't suffer (*I* didn't suffer), yet I cannot avoid this feeling of – what? – associate membership in – what? – *something*. Wisdom said: 'Say it if you like, but be careful.' I am careful of what I say because of the fate of European Jewry. It needs to be honoured. Nothing can be said which suggests that it did not happen, not without loss of honour.

1963

GERDA CHARLES:

'I Believe . . .'

Q. *Basically are you a Jewish writer or an English writer?*

'Basically' I really don't know what this means. Questions which presuppose a dichotomy between one's English self and one's Jewish self always leave me slightly bewildered. These 'conflicts' one hears so much about . . . what are they? I suspect that they occur (apart from experiences of brute anti-semitism which come into a different category) at those moments in our lives when we notice with pain that we are alien to the society around us and, looking around for something or someone to blame, just like everybody else, the first scapegoat which comes to mind is the Jew in us.

Jewishness is our Jew; to be blamed for our failures in society, accused, held responsible, drummed out, disowned, at best endured with irritated liberalism, at worst vilified and if possible destroyed.

In a life not otherwise noted for good fortune, I count myself lucky at least in this; that I do not feel like that at all about my own Jewishness... for several reasons. Perhaps the most important is that for a long time now I have accepted (though certainly not to a fanatical degree) a great many of the disciplines of orthodox Judaism. This has greatly simplified my life in some ways which is something I am very grateful for since all this conflict and so on I feel to be a terrible, needless cluttering up of the imagination. I have not so much mental or spiritual energy that I can afford to waste it on eternal dialogues with myself on my Jewishness. I *am* Jewish. I relax within this accepted condition. I accept the moral laws given on Sinai. I accept the teachings (so marvellous in their delicacy and understanding of the human heart) of our great sages. I accept the lessons of history, I accept the mystical belief in the Jew's special purpose... in other words, *I believe*. I believe not with blind faith but because I see that, however outraged or distorted in the practice, orthodox Judaism *works*. If it didn't we wouldn't be here to deny it... If the Jew is born to the disability of his Jewishness he must, as they say these days, learn to live with it. If it causes him suffering he must learn how to use his suffering. That is what it is for. In my last novel, *A Slanting Light*, I tried to show this acceptance-of-difference attitude in action. One of the many ways in which the Jewish hero of that book differs from myself however is that he did not undertake the day to day practice of orthodoxy. I do. I do so not because I find blind acceptance so easy nor because I think it so terrible to eat bacon or smoke a cigarette on the Sabbath but because I think it terrible not to be able to submit oneself to disciplines in the region where disciplines matter; that is, in everyday life. Anyone can key themselves to the large, splendid and (if possible) public gesture. But we do not live by such gestures. We live by the thousand, small decisions of our every day lives. These decisions make our morality. The intended function of small, daily, religious observances is to keep both our self-discipline and our sense of marvel constantly exercised and supple and responsive; they *remind*. There are, generally speaking, good, sound reasons for most of the prohibitions and injunctions of Judaic law. But even if there weren't I am grateful to be reminded by them of the necessity of law in society. How can it matter if we eat a ham sandwich? What matters is not the ham but the rule, the discipline. I sometimes wonder that the sheer, radiant common sense of Judaic law is not more obvious. *Of course* the rules are sometimes interpreted idiotically, applied tyrannically, made to seem stupid, empty, narrowing; but good law should not be confused with idiot practitioners.

I believe that some of our Jewish writers and intellectuals reject orthodoxy not so much with their hearts or even with their heads (however much they may try to rationalize) but with their engagement books, since it is, in contemporary society, *socially* a drag and a burden. I have found it so myself on occasion, have found myself obliged to miss an experience or a friendship which might have been interesting or valuable because of it. I do not and hope I never shall resent the deprivations I have to endure every now and then ... nor even the sometimes open hostility provoked. It is curious that while I make generally no criticism of non-orthodoxy in others (regarding it as none of my business) I have myself to withstand a good deal of what appears to be deeply uneasy nagging and sniping. But about the deprivations ... I believe that undertaken, if not willingly at least with a cheerful grumble, they hold no sting. If they entail a feeling of loneliness – and since I know of practically no other creative Jewish artist of any standing in any media in this country who is even remotely orthodox, I do feel very much alone – then I must endure being alone. There are worse conditions.

Q. *For instance anti-semitism. Does anti-semitism frighten or obsess you?*

Neither. At least, in the abstract I may feel a little frightened. But in an odd sort of way (and I realize that this sounds very odd indeed) I don't associate anti-semitism particularly with Nazi Germany (though I find I do a little with Czarist Russia). I believe this feeling has been shaped by the fact that from my earliest years I have seen low natures, meanness, cruelty, despicable acts committed against men's dignity and self-respect everywhere. I detested that part of my own society which bullied and despised the weak and defenceless amongst them so much that I spent most of my early life trying to avoid it by a sort of willed sleep of my own sensibility. This was a difficult thing to wake myself out of and accounts for my very late development as a writer. I didn't have to know about Germany to have a pretty clear idea of what, given a small twist of the wheel, people can do to each other. I *know* what so-called ordinary people can do. It is human nature in general which I distrust and believe barely containable within civilized boundaries. The Nazis were devils; but I have seen (and still see) hysteria, malevolent lying, terrible injustices, rampant, mad egotisms, every ploy of Victorian melodrama still being played out before my eyes. I couldn't live at all without the concept of Divine Justice; the thought that *somewhere*, somehow, the balance is being redressed.

1963

WOLF MANKOWITZ:

'I Have a very Strong Sense of Origin.'

Q. *Basically are you a Jewish writer or an English writer?*

I am a Jewish writer, writing in the English language. My work is a synthesis of English and Jewish cultural elements.

Q. *Why do the Jewish obsessions conflict with the English obsessions and how do they enter your work?*

I am continuously interested in certain basic Judaic and Yiddish themes – by the teachings of Hillel on the one hand and by the medievalist fantasy on the other. They occasionally enter my work in an archetypal way, but I tend to reformulate them in situations and characters of local reference. I think that the Yiddish forces are strongly present in the unconscious background of a good deal of what I write. But English language and the society that has produced it is much in the foreground. I consider myself to be essentially an ironist and fanatasist, so that both the unconscious and the conscious images have great force for me.

Q. *What has been the impact on your work of the war-time destruction of the Jews in Europe?*

Very profound. The destruction of the Yiddish-speaking communities of Eastern Europe and the present threat to the remaining three million living in the Soviet Union by the antagonism of Government and Communist Party officials, is to me a very personal threat. This may be sentimental to some extent. However, I have a very strong sense of origin and feel deep loyalty and gratitude to it. For me, one's feeling towards the people from whom one has originated is close to the sense of honour which the Decalogue insists we should maintain towards our parents. It is one Commandment which I respect profoundly.

Q. *You have mentioned the Jewish religion. Is your Jewishness as a writer based merely on the awareness of Jewish experience or on Judaism?*

On Jewish experience. The general clutter of no-longer meaningful ritual of any religion seems to me to be out of place except for the least religious of individuals. For those who have no profound religion in them, systematized and inexplicable routines may well have a value. For my own part, I find them a meaningless hindrance to a true appreciation of basic philosophical truths. My 'Jewishness' as a writer is an important element in the complex that is 'me' – whether I am writing or not. Such as it is, it is a compound of awareness – of historical experience, of traditional wisdom, of an ethical system and of ways of feeling.

Some people maintain that one is not Jewish unless one is a Jew in the strict and orthodox religious sense. But the Jews are bound to each other not only because of their religion and religious past; they are also bound together because of their immediate, secular history, their common heroes, their common enemies, their common contemporary predicament, their common myths and needs, their common concern for the State of Israel, by the common positive as well as negative aspects of 'otherness', and even because of their present liking for certain foods, trivial as that may seem. I believe if one reaches 'God', one does it through the enlargement of life and the pleasure of the senses: through the amazement of looking, and hearing, and tasting, and touching, and smelling; or through certain pleasureful activities – like making love when one is in love, or like singing and congenial working. And writing poetry, by the way, is a kind of singing and a kind of beautiful work that names things. And the naming of things, itself, ultimately – a country or a star, a flower or a baby – is a kind of worship.

1963

DANNIE ABSE:

'Jews are bound to each other...'

Q. *Basically are you a Jewish poet or an English poet?*

Generally, I don't feel myself to be a poet at all. I finish some five or six poems a year. Only then, after a poem has been completed satisfactorily, for a few hours only do I feel myself to be a poet. Between times, for months, I am uncertain whether I shall ever write a poem again. I think Dylan Thomas once said something like, 'Art is an accident of craft.' But the craft doesn't exist separately from the 'art' of the poem. The whole activity, craft included, seems to me like an accident; so that afterwards I am not quite sure how it happened. Since the poem seems partly 'given' I am never sure whether another 'gift' will be offered again. Indeed, I look back at certain poems I've written with continued surprise. Often I find this or that poem to be much cleverer than I am; more lyrical than I could ever be; more sharp than the sharpness I think I contain; more tender than the tenderness I know; and these poems, when they work, use words with a skill that I can hardly believe myself to own. I am not suggesting that the making of poems is purely a visceral activity, or that the poet is a dummy for the ventriloquist Muse, White Goddess, or some pristine Jungian divinity. Simply, poetry is written in the brain but the brain is bathed in blood.

Sometimes, I discover the poem, when I look at it later as an analytical observer, contains a Jewish note – this has happened more frequently in recent years; there are more 'Jewish' poems in my most recent volume, *Poems, Golders Green*, than in previous volumes. Still I don't think of myself, when I think of myself as a poet at all, as a Jewish poet or as an English poet, or for that matter as a Welsh poet, or a five foot eight and a half poet, or a younger, growing-older poet, or whatever.

Q. *But Jewish notes, as you put it, do enter your work?*

Sometimes, yes; and often in an obscure or arcane way. Without conscious design on my part, I find myself working, for example, on a poem about the remnant of a tree that has been previously struck by lightning. In short, a misfit of a tree rather than say, a tall, straight, beautiful elm. Or I take as subject matter a shunter – you know those slow, slave-like engines you see on railway tracks – rather than an express train. That I choose one object rather than another, even if not consciously, seems to me to have something to do with the fact that I am a Jew living in the 20th century; and therefore someone who must be aware of the situational predicament of the Jew in a special, close way. Not that I'm using the misfit tree or the shunter by way of allegory or symbol. I'm not: I intend to write only about a tree as tree, and shunter as shunter.

In any case, apart from poems of this kind, I have published poems which own a Jewish theme more explicitly. It doesn't often happen; though I've written more poems of this kind than I've ever published. Generally, they don't work as poems – and finally, I'm committed not to any one single theme, but to poetry. So it is, sometimes, that one tells a lie in a poem for the sake of the poem, or advocates a viewpoint that one doesn't wholly accept. Oddly, you see, poetry is fiction.

Q. *What has been the impact on your work of the war-time destruction of the Jews in Europe?*

I think my work would be even less Jewish than it is if that bestial event hadn't occurred. I mean Hitler has made me more of a Jew than Moses. Indeed, as the years have passed, as I take in more fully the unbearable reality of what has happened in Europe, as I read biographies of Hitler, Himmler, Goebbels, Goering, as I read the testimony of survivors, as I see films, as I come to know the documents of history, then gradually I feel myself to be more of a Jew than ever. It takes a long time to become aware that here, in England, one is a survivor also. The realization of the destruction of the Jews, of one single event only – that two million Jews have been exterminated in Auschwitz alone, that thousands of children, there, were thrown on the pyre alive and not even gassed – changes, poisons subtly, one's attitude to other people. I am aware that ordinary, decent people one has met, with ordinary passive prejudices, could be, under other circumstances, the murderers or one's own children, or the executioners of adults whom one loves and reveres. This is not a paranoic delusion, alas. As a doctor, I know that listening to say, Mr Robinson sitting opposite me, complaining of this or that minor symptom and ventilating strange anxieties, that I am hearing the muted voice of some potential Gestapo official. I have heard in the course of one week the heart beat of Eichmann, palpated the liver of Goering, seen the x-rays of Himmler, read the electroencephalogram of Hitler. Almost every Jewish father and mother, however much they disaffiliate themselves from Judaism or Jewry have, perhaps once a year, because of a remark uttered inadvertently, or because of a headline, looked across the table at their young children and wondered for half a second whether one day their beloved offspring might be forced to enter the gas chambers of another decade. Even the most optimistic Jew must admit the possibility to be there. This is something that many non-Jews can hardly credit.

Of course, it is difficult to sustain suspicious attitudes towards other people, now, here, in tolerant, liberal, mild, decent, democratic England. No doubt it would be sick to do so. It also might be sick not to do so. As a Jew, I was brought up to believe that man was essentially good. Didn't I, as a boy, say in my morning prayer: *My God, the soul which thou has given me is pure . . . ?* Karl Marx explained the evil in society in environmental terms. He wasn't a Jew, and an optimist, for nothing. But Sigmund Freud, another Jew, has given us back Original Sin not as a genetic or theological proposition, but clandestinely and more realistically in terms of our early and inevitable Oedipus complex. How can we be anything but (neurotically?) afraid of anti-semitism seeing what has happened in Europe? Why is it that every Jew overreacts, however much he feels himself to be delivered from a ghetto mentality, when a Jewish figure like Peter Rachman, features villainously in some contemporary scandal? The fact is, I don't believe any Jew in the Diaspora, however much he proclaims the contrary, is other than a Ghetto Jew, in the deepest sense – and this is, above all, because of the war-time destruction of the Jew in Europe. As for writing – well, a writer brings into his work more of himself than he realizes. I don't know in concrete terms what the impact on my work is of the Jewish catastrophe. I am certain, though, that in devious ways it is there.

1963

MICHAEL HAMBURGER:

'How my Jewishness was brought home to me'

Q. *How does your German-Jewish background effect your work as an English writer, if at all?*

In a hundred different ways, which I can't deal with fully here. To begin with, the need to translate German poetry has a lot to do with my displacement at the age of nine. I see it now as an obscure urge to be 'transplanted', rather than an uprooted writer, though the original urge has been modified by the sheer pleasure of the thing, or 'the fascination of what's difficult'. As for the effects of the displacement on my own work, I can't presume to judge them even now; for all I know, my poetry may never have been anything but 'naturalized' English poetry. For a long time I resisted this possibility, and one reviewer of an early collection of mine said that I was 'ghosting for the ghost of Yeats'. Now I am perfectly happy to be myself, whatever that may be. What I do know is that I have retained an intense concern with everything pertaining to my first environment and to Germany in general.

Q. *While in your earlier poetry there seemed little awareness of Jewishness, there are indications of some awareness of it in your more recent poems, for instance the poems about Eichmann. Is this so?*

Here I must explain that, although I remember hearing one of my grandmothers mention a visit to what she called the

'Temple', my upbringing, from the start, was such as to leave me in total ignorance of Judaism. The only religious instruction I received was Christian. Awareness of Jewishness, therefore, was not an obvious or a simple matter for me; but my personal experiences of Nazism most definitely brought home to me one sense in which I was and am Jewish. It is true that my early poems contain no direct references to Jewish matters; but I think that indirectly they must reflect the peculiar way in which my Jewishness was brought home to me. It may be, too, that these early experiences of mine amounted to what the psychologists call a trauma. That would explain why it took me a long time to be able to deal with them directly; and even then a good deal of delving and exploring was required.

One instance of an indirectly Jewish preoccupation that occurs to me is the sequence *From the Notebook of a European Tramp* in my first book, written while I was a soldier in Italy and Austria. The myth of Ahasuerus – a Christian myth, admittedly – has always held a special significance for me, and this invisible presence, never actually named anywhere in my poems, links the early poems to the later. Again, it is only in recent years that I have recognized this presence, and positively welcomed it. The poem on Eichmann is one of several poems in my last book in which this change or break-through is recorded. Some of the people who objected to this poem complained of its 'softness'. I had hoped that it was hard enough to cut through complacencies which seem soft to me, because they take the easy way out. Mercy, to me, seems harder, not softer, than justice; it takes a risk, creates something new and purifies the air. Retribution only buries the stench. The poem was translated into Hebrew and published in Israel. It did no good, of course, and since it was intended to do good, rather than to be good, it may prove an embarrassment to me when I come to re-read it.

Q. *In your work as a translator and interpreter of German literature, do you see your role as a mediator between German and English culture?*

My work as a translator and critic of German literature has come as naturally in my peculiar circumstances as the writing of my own poems. It has grown out of my personal preoccupations, not out of the wish to carry out any particular function.

Q. *Do you see any special merit in an attempt to preserve the works of German-Jewish poets and novelists of the past in English translation, as a monument to past glories and achievements?*

Good literature is its own monument. And I think I have already answered this question in my reply earlier on. The glories and achievements of German-Jewish writers are inextricably bound up with those of the non-Jewish writers. One can isolate certain theological, social and moral concerns in the works of the Jewish writers, but not without running the danger of doing the same kind of violence to them in order to glorify them as the Nazis did in order to expunge them from German literature. The reason, quite simply, is that one's criteria would be reduced to racial ones in the absence of the cultural tradition to which I have referred; and if racialism is wrong, as I believe, it is wrong for everyone.

1964

EMANUEL LITVINOFF:

A Jewish Writer in England

The following statement was presented at the First Anglo-Jewish Israeli Symposium, held in Tel Aviv in the summer of 1966. The Symposium was initiated by The Jewish Quarterly *and co-sponsored by the Hebrew Writers' Associa-*

tion. Mr Litvinoff was one of the five Anglo-Jewish writers who participated in the Symposium, the others being Dannie Abse, Chaim Bermant, Karen Gershon, Jon Silkin and Jacob Sonntag.

Before me as I write is a school photograph: I am the fourth boy on the right. Forty-six of the other boys in the photograph are also Jews – Kantorovich, Zelinikoff, Cohen, Dubovsky, Shrebnik, Abramovich, Segal, and others whose names I cannot now recall. The one *goy* stands forlornly in the back row, and across the fading years I still remember how lonesome he was, the unreflective cruelty of our indifference.

Outside the school yard where we self-consciously pose are the backstreets of Whitechapel and Bethnal Green, a hard-working district of sinewy cabinet-makers, round-shouldered tailors, itinerant street-vendors hoarsely praising the goods on their barrows, furriers, button-hole makers, housewives battling the daily grime that seeps in from the littered pavements. Backrooms vibrate to the noise of machines. There are shops heaped with rags, cracked gramophone records, chipped crockery, old iron, ancient magazines. Whatever it is, someone can make a living out of it. The district stinks of too many people occupying too little space, of drains ill-equipped to flush away the waste of so many bodies, and this effluvia of poverty is spiced with the smell of sour pickles, herring, garlic and meat rotting in the open windows of kosher butcher shops. People stand on pavements speaking Yiddish, but they avoid the corners occupied by pubs, which are numerous, and they seldom stand for more than a few moments near the marble crucifix implanted on the grass-bearded forecourt of the Catholic church. East London 1929 . . .

I lived near the school in a street of small two-storied cottages, some with cellars under the pavements in which whole families spent their days in artificial light. My home was in the tallest building of the street, a tenement of sooty brick whose squalor in retrospect seems unbelievable. But conditions were much the same all around us, acreages of slums boiling with humanity, and we were not at all conscious of special hardship. Most of the people in our street were East European immigrants and even if they could afford the luxury of privacy I doubt if they would have thought it worth buying.

Life varied according to light and season. In summer, when it was hot, we were both more languid and more violent, occupying our doorsteps like the sands of a Mediterranean beach; in winter, we hurried indoors to jostle peevishly for a warm place near the fire. Twilight transformed people's faces and voices, enveloping them in a kind of loneliness. The sluggish movement of life at the day's end made even us children reflective and philosophical, like old men on park benches; but when street-lamps lit up the night people came out to enjoy themselves, with a feeling that they'd earned it. The fat started to sizzle in fish-and-chips shops, thumping pianos sounded from pubs, brilliantined young fellows in sharp suits stared with insolent lust at the plump buttocks of high-stepping girls, and crowds skirmished around the picture-palaces trailing peanut shells wherever they went.

I have a habit of thinking about that past in collective terms, partly because my memories have become generalized but chiefly because in my childhood we were still members of a tribal community, our neighbourhood a village remote in spirit from the adjacent cosmopolitanism of the great city of London. The way of life was still much like that of the small Jewish towns scattered across the lands of Eastern Europe from Poland in the north to the southern Black Sea town of Odessa, where my own parents had been born. We shared the same Sabbaths and festivals, ate the same food, sang traditional songs in the same minor key, laughed at the same Jewish jokes. We were a foreign colony, like the Italians of Saffron Hill or the Chinese of Pennyfields, but unlike them I do not think that as children we felt at all un-English, or regarded the *goyim* in the next street as more native than ourselves. If anything, we thought ourselves to be a superior kind of English, because we were also Jewish and, therefore, cleverer, cleaner, more industrious and sober, less a different race than another class, and any hostility we encountered was put down to envy of our superior qualities.

My first serious experience of anti-semitism was in my fourteenth year when I won a trade scholarship. Successful candidates were allowed to nominate, in order of preference, the trades they wished to learn. I chose, first, a school of lithography, then one for catering and, finally, a study course in electrical engineering.

The school of lithography rejected me without explanation

after an interview, in which I had politely and correctly answered a number of simple general knowledge questions, submitted a short written essay and produced a decently carpentered towel-rack as an example of my handiwork. The one question I did not apparently answer to the interviewer's satisfaction was that relating to my religion. The other schools granted me no interview at all. Instead the London County Council offered a place at a Cordwainers' technical college, which turned out to be an institute for shoe-making near an offal yard in Smithfield market. I was the only Jewish pupil. From the very first roll-call the headmaster improvised variations on my name. It became Litintoott, Levypotsky, Levinskinoff, Litmuspaperoff and – on one hilarious public occasion – Lavatoryoffsky. For the rest of the term I endured ridicule and humiliation at the hands of both teaching staff and boys, the headmaster proving the most inventive of all. But I did not generalize from this experience. The barbarities of Cordwainers' technical college seemed localized, like the stench of decaying offal which permeated its classrooms.

As far as I can recall, therefore, the problem of identity did not begin to raise until the onset of adolescence with all its emotional and intellectual uncertainties. In my case, it coincided with the beginning of the thirties, as it must have done for many young Jews in Germany. I was then a young communist with a rather apocalyptic notion of political salvation, and one day I was walking with another young communist, a big-nosed lad named Izzy Birnbaum, in the alien territory of Hoxton, where Jews were unwelcome. It was not politics that brought us there, but girls. Jewish adolescents had an idea that Gentile girls were complaisant and we skirmished the neighbourhood in the hope of finding it true. Rather unwisely, Izzy had made himself conspicuous in a jazzy pullover and my hair was glistening with a dressing of margarine. Instead of attracting female attention, we ran into a gang of youths who spread themselves across the pavement and told us to get back to Palestine. It wasn't the first time in my life I'd been given that advice. The usual rejoinder was 'go to Palestine your f—g self', or 'this is my bloody country', or 'I'm as good a f—g Englishman as you'. But it was somehow no longer possible to say such things with conviction, and the Hoxton boys looked as if they wouldn't stop at trading insults. We got shoved around a bit and retreated from Hoxton bruised in body and self-esteem. Uneasiness had begun.

The day of Mosley and his fascists had arrived and a frightening change came over the East End. Snotty-nosed kids with whom one had exchanged fairly harmless abuse suddenly appeared buckled and booted in black uniforms, looking anything but juvenile as they tramped through the district shouting: *'We gotta get rid of the Yids, the Yids! We gotta get rid of the Yids!'* And it was even difficult to laugh at the bespoke-tailored fascists who came from the suburbs to officer these eager troops. Black was not the only para-military colour. A green-shirted organization which had practised woodcraft with religious fanatacism abruptly expelled its Jewish members and turned to anti-semitism. Also green-shirted, the Social Credit movement took up back-street drilling with wooden rifles in preparation for armed insurrection against the international Jewish financiers of Whitechapel Road. Young communists marched to meetings in red; Zionist youths went around in blue; Jewish ex-servicemen paraded in their war-medals. Sir Oswald's bodyguarded visits to his stronghold in Roman Road, Bethnal Green, were ludicrous and, at the same time, sinister. He looked to us as we skirted the crowds with a prickly sense of peril like a comic 'toff' playing at Mussolini; and his hot-eyed, rigid expression suggested that he derived from the slum streets and shabby onlookers an onanistic illusion of conquest. As he stood on a platform orating in a prissy upper-class English voice he aroused more derision among us than fear. We could not hate him in the way we did his followers, because we could never take altogether seriously a man with an accent like that. What came across unmistakably was a kind of hysterical evil. It penetrated to the marrow of my Jewish bones. There was something inevitable about it all; it was as if all my life I had been waiting for it to happen.

Every child of East European Jews has grown up with a working knowledge of persecution. When his elders exchanged reminiscences at the family table, there was usually a curse or two for the Tsarist police, government officials and Christian clergy. Anti-semitism was a sort of unwanted inheritance: you were lumbered with it. Now it was on the doorstep again and if you were shocked, as I was, it was because it didn't seem possible that it could happen in England, the country of freedom, justice and tolerance.

When I was about 16 or 17, I was abnormally sensitive about my appearance, having the notion that my nose was too long, my lips too thick and my walk flat-footed and ungainly. I tried to remember not to talk with my hands, but the moment I got excited they jumped out of my pockets and made un-British gestures. When I shoved them out of sight my tongue stumbled on the simplest of phrases. At the same time, I had a secret conviction that people were justified in despising me.

This self-contempt made me intolerant of the imperfections of other Jews that I had begun to recognize with sickening frequency. Every time a woman with a foreign accent made a scene on a bus, or two men argued loudly in Yiddish over a business deal, or a music-hall comedian got a few laughs by jamming a bowler-hat over his ears and retracting his neck into his shoulders, I was miserably ashamed. I started to look at my surroundings in a different way, although all my life had been spent in the same neighbourhood. Now the foreign names on shop fronts seemed grotesque and provocative; the Kosher signs and Yiddish lettering were embarrassing advertisements of alienation; there was too much huckstering in street-markets; and flies crawling over exposed meat and groceries were proof of ingrained backwardness and squalor. I was equally affronted by the sight of a Hassid walking through the street in outlandish garb, impervious to the effect of his own strangeness, and of the herring-women down the Lane, plunging their chapped and swollen fingers into the open barrels of pickled fish.

Much had changed since those innocent days when I had taken it for granted that Englishmen were simply people born in England. Until the age of ten I had not seen a country lane, a field, or the sea. England's green and pleasant land was a green and pleasant conceit in a school poem. Reality was the ghetto of East London, the only England I knew, the only place in the whole wide world to which I was truly native. And if I ever thought of it at all, what else was I but English, and what else was I but Jewish, and why should the one be inconsistent with the other? True, a hostile English tribe lived on our perimeter incomprehensibly ordering us to go back to this or that place – anywhere but here. So we were intermittently troubled: but in our teeming streets we dwelt unchallenged and secure except for the ills of poverty. I have been asked, generally by other Jews who grew up as a separate people among the nations of Eastern Europe, if it did not occur to me to wonder how my forefathers fitted into the kind of history we were taught at school. I can only reply that it did not. We got little beyond those narratives in which Canute ordered the tide to halt and Alfred burned the cakes, and what, in any case, had history to do with a boy's dreams and disappointments?

But in my early years a line was drawn through your life at 14 and everything changed. One day you were a schoolboy in short trousers, the next a putative adult dressed like a man of 40, and shoved out to earn a living. You came abruptly into contact, and sometimes collision, with the complicated society in which people competed for work, advancement and opportunity at a time when these were not easily come by. It was then that I began to learn that some were more English than others. In the first place the lesson had a class character. The kind of occupations open to a working-class boy of little education were restricted. It goes without saying that in the thirties it was still unthinkable for anyone from Bethnal Green to aspire to become a bank manager (or cashier), a newspaper reporter, a sanitary inspector or a commissioned military officer, even with a carefully adjusted accent.

Soon I discovered an additional handicap. Being reasonably intelligent and writing a fair hand, I hoped to break out of the tailoring, cabinet-making, fur-manufacturing, hairdressing circuit in which Jewish boys of my background sought a livelihood. Painstaking letters of application went out advising insurance companies, shipping lines, city commercial houses and similar respectable establishments that I had all the qualities required for the post of office boy. No one ever replied. I rushed to be first in the queue for direct interviews. Some people were frank enough to tell me that it was their policy not to employ people of the Jewish faith, others preferred ambiguity.

The 'Situations Vacant' columns of newspapers exploited the prevailing insecurity. We unemployed youths pushed and jostled around copies of the *Daily Telegraph* in public libraries, daydreaming of wonderful opportunities for salesmen, of learning to make £6 a week in our spare time, of having a healthy and interesting career with free travel all over the world in the armed forces, of becoming masters of our fate by a short course in

Pelmanism. One advertisement invited the reader to obtain lucrative employment in His Majesty's Civil Service as a Grade Three Officer or something through a correspondence school that guaranteed success in entrance examinations on a money-back basis. Not having more than a shilling or two at any time, I applied directly to the authorities for the conditions of entry in the hope that it would be possible to read for the examinations in the free library. This was how I made the dismal discovery that I was not quite British enough even to empty the waste-paper baskets in the civil service. Without British-born parents, I learned, they would have nothing to do with you as a postman, a policeman, a naval rating, a customs and excise officer, a government cipher clerk or a weights and measures inspector. In fact, you weren't particularly wanted, and it seemed quite obvious to you why.

So far, my experiences had been singularly parochial, not at all lessened by a growing sense of alienation. The people I best understood were those amongst whom I'd always lived, the East End Jews, and I knew little about others with whom I was linked by fate. But more and more of them were appearing in London, uprooted men, women and children, some with scuffed cardboard or wooden suitcases, some still showing signs of recent affluence, all subdued, apologetic, unwanted.

Many hundreds of other refugees were shuffling through the wintry streets of Paris. They queued in cellars for bowls of soup, huddled for warmth in cheap bistros, hoarded their misery. In Germany thousands of others bartered vainly for passports, scurried from frontier to frontier, crawled through thickets of clawing wire towards the rifle-muzzles of vigilant border-guards. One could not then know that after the migrant search for a chance to live would come the enforced migration of millions to certain death. In Paris it seems to me then that the symbol of rootlessness could be taken no further. A few months earlier, I had been down, if not out, eating in soup-kitchens and sleeping in doss-houses. But the umbilical cord of group and family belonging had not been severed: there was always the knowledge that friendship, or a new job, would put everything right. If Fascism conquered Britain, in what wintry city would I, too, seek transient companionship, bread, sex, forgetfulness?

A proletarian life could not prepare me for the society of the refugee artists, writers, musicians and scholars with whom I now occasionally came into contact and my East European antecedents made it even more difficult to understand them. In the Whitechapel ghetto we were never in any doubt about being Jews, but many of these new acquaintances had travelled far from their Jewish origins. Some were entirely deracinated, baptized Jews, Germanized Czechs, Marxist intellectuals, elite representatives of German culture, only the crude generalizations of Nazi racial philosophers could herd them into a common category. They were to prove far more adaptable than that earlier generation of Jewish immigrants from Poland, Russia and Lithuania who, by and large, left it to their children to assimilate. These newcomers swam in the mainstream of European culture: they had style, facility, sometimes erudition. All they required was a period of acclimatization. Within a decade, their accents perfected, there was little to distinguish them from born Englishmen, Frenchmen or Americans.

During the war I was commissioned into an alien company of the Pioneer Corps composed of these Jewish refugees. There cannot be a single civilized language for which we did not have an expert. We could easily have mustered the academic qualifications to staff a small university, assemble a decent orchestra, script, direct and shoot a movie, or launch a newspaper. One day an order came from the War Office authorizing alien personnel to change their nominal identities in case they were ever captured by the enemy. For some strange reason Scottish clan-names were most favoured and few, if any, ever reverted to their former titles.

The war, when it came, had unexpected benevolences. I travelled north to an army depot in Glasgow with a draft of conscripts from all parts of East London, young Cockneys leaving the smoke with reluctance. When the train left Euston a few of the Jews grouped themselves together, exchanging glances of recognition and commiseration. There were other regional groupings, for local patriotism used to be strong in the poor districts of London. Bermondsey boys eyed natives of Shoreditch with misgiving, Hoxton stared through Homerton as if X-raying his backbone. Upper-class conscripts avoided conversation for fear of giving their class away by their accents. Once battle-dress was on and square-bashing began we were as alike as if hatched together from the same gigantic womb. For my own part, this anonymity was convalescent. The army offered little hardship. For the first time I was eating three square meals a day and still feeling hungry. I got the first warm overcoat of my life, free boot repairs and laundry, a primitive sense of well-being. Without being a good soldier, I was skilful at tempering the rigours of military discipline and kept out of serious trouble. My Jewish neuroses vanished as I learned to turn the occasional anti-semitic remark against its perpetrator with nonchalant good humour. Friendships took no account of religion or race, anyway. There was an unbelligerent war going on somewhere; if there were also rumours of cruelties, practised upon civil populations in German-occupied territory, little of it got into the newspapers, or we didn't think too much about it. In the gentle, soft-hued Ulster countryside troops played war-games and grumbled at the rain. In barrack room, canteen and village hall I stared at nothing, writing poems of frustration.

'We are the soldiers whom no gun awakes. / Whose living fades in dumb monotony of thought, / Whom pain gropes in the urgent thighs, / And in the breast lies numb. / Death is an angel who has passed us by / To grasp another hand sailing an ocean / Or a boy mocking the quiet stars / While we grieve and desire.'

My name appeared in anthologies with titles like *Poems From the Forces*, *Poets in Khaki*, and so on. This gave me modest status at Belfast (we had moved to Ireland) literary gatherings and may have had something to do with my subsequent selection for a commission: it did not change anything much at the time. The poems spoke of sexual deprivation and a melancholy longing for violence. It was a somnambulistic episode in many people's lives. Then came Dunkirk and one awakened to fear.

The horrible prospect that the Nazis might win the war brought home once again that I was involved in the Jewish fate. My friends, in the event of a German occupation, would have the choice of resisting or submitting to conquest. We Jews have no choice: we would die. We had not yet heard the term 'final solution' and the Germans were still conducting experiments to perfect the techniques of mass-murder. But the starvation and sadistic cruelties practised in Dachau, Buchenwald and other places were known even in 'peace-time'. It needed little imagination for a Jew to visualize what awaited him at the hands of the Nazis now that killing was licensed, hallowed by the requirements of war and patriotism.

I began to be haunted by the sufferings of Jews in Europe because these unknown victims took on the features of my own family, of my mother, my young sister and my brothers, three of them soldiers like myself, four still schoolchildren and, therefore, most vulnerable of all. It is curious and, I think, significant, that I was less worried by the immediate danger they were experiencing in the London blitz than by the fear of their helplessness in the events of a Nazi invasion. Bombs falling from the sky made no discrimination between victims: everyone had an equal chance of doom or survival. What horrified me was the cold-blooded selections practised by the Nazis in the name of a warped ideology. I was no longer a soldier like any other soldier; I was a Jew in uniform.

About this time, a small group of Jewish fugitives – men, women and children – succeeded in escaping to the Dalmatian coast and were smuggled aboard an old cargo boat, the *Struma*. It must have seemed a miracle of deliverance. Again, miraculously, they survived a hazardous Mediterranean crossing and reached Turkey, from whence they hoped to travel overland to Palestine. But there was a legal obstacle. The British authorities refused entry certificates for Palestine on the grounds that the quota allocated to Jewish immigrants was exhausted. The fugitives then applied to the Turks for permission to stay in the country. This also was refused. They pleaded that the children, at least, should be permitted to stay, but again the answer was no, and the *Struma* was ordered to leave port. Where were the wretched people to go? Back to the Nazis, who would kill them? The British and Turkish authorities were sorry, but there were rules and regulations. *Struma* sailed. Some distance out at sea, there was an explosion and it foundered. Only one survived. No one knows what caused the explosion. Some say the boat struck a floating mine, others that the fugitives chose to die at sea rather than face torture and death at the hands of the Germans.

The sinking of the *Struma* was desolating news. It blurred the frontiers of evil. Those stony-hearted British and Turkish officials who could send people to their death because their papers were not in order were Hitler's accomplices. They were doing the devil's work, refusing children the right to live because it would upset their book-keeping. No doubt they had consulted with superiors. Coded messages had gone from Ankara to Whitehall. Senior bureaucrats must have found it tiresome to be bothered in the middle of a war by a group of refugees who inconveniently turned up demanding to be let into Palestine. Before they escaped from the Nazis they should have found out if there was room on the quota for them. Didn't they know there was a war on?

After more than twenty years the memory is still painful. This is how I recorded it at the time in an incoherent poem of grief and bitterness.

'For everything the poets have a word. / To everything the soldier brings his sword, / And I who am soldier and poet only bring, / A crushed heart and my tribal suffering. / Too heavy are my eyes for tears, I am dumb of grief. / They mouth the usual promises but I am deaf... / Today I invoke Christ in his heavenly mansion / To come down from the mountain and the sun / And walk into my lowly dwelling place, / My house of mourning, to seek out and bless / Me for my dead, my dead for peace. / I am Matthew, I am Luke, I am twelve Jews / Against many whom my Master knows. / Arrogance of Caesars and Hitlers, lies / Streaming dark through many centuries, / Have stormed and taken many forts of strength, / But mine shall hold until my ally cometh... / Today my khaki is a badge of shame, / It's duty meaningless; my name / Is Moses and I summon plague to Pharoah. / Today my mantle is Sorrow and O / My crown is Thorn. I sit darkly with the years / And centuries of years, bowed by my heritage of tears.'

If it were possible to point to one single episode as a decisive turning point in one's life, the tragic sinking of the *Struma* would be that for me. Never again would I be able to think of myself as an Englishman, or face uncertainty about my identity. In the middle of this century any Jew in Europe was condemned as surely as if he was born with an incurable disease. Only the accident of geography, or astronomically lucky odds, determined his survival. And when the war was won, for me it was also lost six million times over. This exclusive sense of injury lacks generosity, even imagination. It was some time before I was able to recognize that there was no less depravity in the indiscriminate slaughter by mass bomber raids than in the selective killings practised by the Nazis, that both techniques derived from an increasing tendency on the part of people to regard other people as abstractions. But that is not my theme. I am concerned here with my education as a Jew, and it was the *churban*, the destruction, which largely completed it.

Yet England made me. When the State of Israel was established in 1948 it confronted me with a clear-cut choice and I found I would not willingly emigrate from the English language, spoken in English ways by mild, tolerant English people. In reality I have encountered little anti-semitism, most of it inconsequential, some of it the chemical reaction of over-sensitivity. I live in an urbanized English village and am not conscious of segregation from my neighbours, whose reputation for insularity has been exaggerated. I belong to them a little and they belong to me, yet they would probably be faintly astonished to learn that I feel in some ways an outsider having more in common with certain people in New York, Tel Aviv or Moscow than with themselves. They might not understand why I am sometimes overtaken by desolation watching my small daughter playing in the sunshine, why a child's discarded shoe can germinate terrible images in my dreams. But if they ever guessed these things, I would be confident of their compassion. Most of them, anyway.

1966

ASPECTS OF LITERATURE

Some Aspects of Anglo-American Jewish Fiction

DAVID DAICHES

There are three distinguishable elements in fiction with a recognizable Jewish content written by Jews of our time in America and Britain. The first of these is the least obvious: it surfaces occasionally or is echoed intermittently. This is the background of Yiddish literature of the *shtetl* as represented by the work of such writers as Sholom Aleichem, Mendele Mocher Sforim and Isaac Leib Peretz. Not all modern Jewish writers in English have a direct acquaintance with this literature, but many have absorbed something of its flavour through sporadic reading of translations (a fine collection of such translations, edited by Irving Howe and Eliezer Greenberg, was published in 1955) or through an oral tradition which has transmitted something of the tensions and paradoxes of Jewish life and thought and feeling as presented by the Yiddish writers – the counterpointing of pride and humiliation, of irony and sentimentality, of dignity and self-mockery, of humour and agony, of commitment to history and the desire to escape from history. We find conscious or unconscious echoes of this in a variety of writers on both sides of the Atlantic, from Saul Bellow in America to Chaim Bermant in England.

The second element is the documentation of Jewish immigrant life, of which the classic example is Zangwill's *Children of the Ghetto*. These documentaries themselves draw on the humours and ironies of the Yiddish tradition, especially as they are manifested in the dialogue of the characters presented, but their main concern is to illuminate a historical moment of transition between the life of Jewish immigrants still emotionally oriented towards *der heim* and the life of their English- or American-born children. To call such works documentaries is not in any way to belittle them: we know from the history of the film, and particularly from John Grierson's work there (and Grierson invented the term 'documentary'), that the documentation of an area of human activity can be a high art form, involving not mere passive photographic reproduction but an artfully organized and patterned series of vividly rendered scenes. Zangwill evokes the mixed flavour of life as it was among immigrant East End Jews in the early part of the present century, and in doing so has left a record of permanent value to social historians as well as to novel-readers. It is significant that the American Jewish documentary novel emerged most strongly during the Depression of the 1930s, when the objective was to record and so bring home to readers the actualities of poverty and struggle among Jewish immigrants who had originally come to the United States in the hope of finding its streets paved with gold. Mike Gold's *Jews without Money* (1935) presents this world with bitter vividness. Gold (whose real name was Irving Granich) was not himself an immigrant, but was born of immigrant parents on New York's Lower East Side, and he based his novel on his own first-hand knowledge of the bitterness of the lives of poor immigrant Jews and their children. There was a propagandist element here as well as a documentary one. The writers of the Depression who documented Jewish poverty were without exception of the political Left, and, unlike Zangwill in an earlier generation, were at least as much moved by the desire to expose and reform as by the desire to exhibit with love and irony the humours and paradoxes of the immigrant Jewish scene. Indignation was more prominent in their work than empathy. At the same time there were writers of this period who, together with their social and political commitment, had an affection for their subject and an almost Breugelesque feeling for the details of the social scene they described. There is an element of this in Gold, and we see it clearly in Meyer Levin's *The Old Bunch* (1937), presenting the lives of the children of Jewish immigrants in Chicago (where Levin himself was born in 1905).

The most remarkable development of what might be called the documentary tradition is not to be found in novels or short stories but in Alfred Kazin's moving autobiographical account of his childhood and youth in Brownsville, New York, where he was born in 1915 of immigrant parents. This book, *A Walker in the City*, published in 1951, is about the poor immigrant Jews of Brownsville and their families who led there their warm, shabby, picturesque, humble and devoted lives; about the sights, sounds, smells and general atmosphere of Brownsville homes and streets; about the impact on a sensitive Jewish child growing up there of the claims of the big city beyond and of America as a whole beyond that. We see too the Jewish child's eager response to Western culture, his determination to master it and make it his own, which is such a notable characteristic of second-generation Jewish immigrants everywhere and, in America in particular, has led to a brilliant generation of Jewish writers and critics and cultural historians, sons of immigrants to a man. At the same time – and here Kazin's story is typical of that of so many American Jews – the book is also the unconscious record of the failure of an education. For what he was taught formally, either at school or by the *melamed* who taught him the minimum amount of Hebrew to enable him to get by on his Bar Mitzvah, was astonishingly little. His Hebrew teacher was apparently contemptuous of the possibility of giving any real understanding of Jewish history and religion to an American-born child. The result is a curious emptiness where we might have looked for something dominating and central. There is garbled American-Yiddish chatter and 'folkways' but no Hebrew culture at all and no contact whatever with a living religious tradition. Kazin had to discover the Hebrew Bible and the Jewish prayer book later in life for himself. To this extent the sons of Jewish immigrants into America were worse off than the sons of those who came to Britain. Zangwill's characters have a real Jewish culture, and so, though in perhaps a more attenuated way, do the Jewish characters of a later generation who inhabit Louis Golding's Doomington (which is Manchester). The mis-spelt Yiddish, the inaccurately remembered and mistranscribed fragments of Hebrew that spatter American Jewish fiction are a testimony to the gap between the immigrants and their children, to the degree to which America weaned them early from their parents' culture or even to which their parents themselves willingly surrendered them to the claims of the great new country to which they had come in such hope. It is the re-discovery by these sons of immigrants of the symbolic significance – the significance for the literary imagination – of their Jewishness that brings the third element into American Jewish fiction, and from America it spread to Britain.

That element is the symbolic. James Joyce had already presented, in the character of Leopold Bloom in *Ulysses*, the Jew as symbolic of the predicament of alienated man in modern society. Bloom is both Jew and Irishman, he both belongs to Dublin and does not belong to it, he is both accepted and rejected by his fellow Dubliners. When he is shown drinking with fellow citizens in a Dublin pub – and drinking together is one of the archetypal symbols of human communion, preserved as such in the rituals of both Judaism and Christianity – he is at the same time shown as isolated and different from his companions. In his inner consciousness he is always harking back to some eastern magnet at the same time as he longs for total acceptance by his fellow citizens on a basis of generalized feelings of brotherhood and humanity. With the crisis of civilization in the Western world sensitive people felt more and more alienated from society, felt more and more that their needs as individuals were at odds with the social realities of their situation, felt more and more that the common values of their civilization were no longer able to provide a basis for genuine communion between people and that the isolated individual, seeking in vain to cross the barrier of his uniqueness by signalling frantically to his neighbour, was bound to have his signals misread and his individuality misunderstood. In such a situation the Jew was the obviously symbolic character, the true embodiment for the imaginative writer of modern alienated man. A non-Jew discovered this first (but the Jew Kafka had already made his hero-victims of *The Castle* and *The Trial*, though not overtly Jewish, symbolic characters of this very kind); and then the Jewish writers and critics discovered, to their great excitement, that they could use their own Jewish background to make a unique contribution to the literature of alienation. It was as though they said to the literary world at large: 'You want to explore alienation? We Jews, who have been minorities in innumerable societies for two thousand years, are experts both in presenting alienation in our own works of literature and in diagnosing its existence in the work of others.' So the Jewish writer moves away from the documentation of Jewish society to show his imaginative skills in exploring and interpreting alienation.

Before going on to discuss some of the major writers in this third category, we might mention a remarkable American Jewish novel which bridges, as it were, the documentary and the symbolic. This is Henry Roth's *Call it Sleep*, published in 1934, a picture of immigrant Jewish life in New York seen through the eyes of a boy but with the boy's mother as the real heroine. The symbolic element derives from the brilliant use of language: when the boy's mother is talking in her native Yiddish or thinking to herself, her words are rendered in a sensitive and fluent English, mirroring the sensitivity and fluency of her use of her native tongue: but when she communicates with her non-Jewish environment and has to use English, her language is broken, crude and inadequate. The gulf between her real self and the self that communicates with the gentile world around her is thus symbolized by the way language is used in the novel, and this gives a moving new dimension to the work. There are other symbolic elements in the novel's plot, and a rich documentary groundwork that anchors it in social reality.

If the modern Jewish writer has realized that the Jew in a gentile society is an effective symbol of sensitive man in the modern world, then a curious equation results. If all sensitive men are Jews, a man can be a Jew simply by being a sensitive man: and that is the central theme of Bernard Malamud's admirable novel *The Assistant* (1957). Malamud, who is in many ways the most consciously Jewish of living American Jewish novelists and short-story writers, brings echoes of the older Yiddish tragi-comic mode of writing into his novels and stories, and is a master of wry self-mockery as a form simultaneously of self-exploration and moral criticism. This can be seen again and again in the short stories collected in the volume *The Magic Barrel* (1958) and, in a different way, in his novel *A New Life* (1961). The latter does not emphasize the Jewishness of its hero by any insistence on overt Jewish traits; the hero, a teacher of English in a California college, is a sensitive intellectual fated to get involved in personal situations that are at once preposterous and romantic; he is a willing scapegoat, but a sophisticated scapegoat who plays the part with style; a wry self-mocker who is romantically involved in what he mocks. He gets involved, through the best of motives and with the most admirable of feelings, in a situation quite absurd in its human difficulty yet at the same time quite alarming in its moral overtones. Professor Ihab Hassan once categorized one kind of hero of the modern American novel as the self-mocker, where irony, hovering between comedy and tragedy, may border on romance. This is exactly what we find in *The Assistant*.

The Jew is more vulnerable than others, more sensitive, more troubled by the relation between his true self and the society in which he lives, more anxious to find out the truth about the problems which enmesh him. Such a Jew figures in so many American Jewish novels, and especially in those of Saul Bellow. *The Victim* (1947) tells how the moderately prosperous New York Jewish businessman Asa Leventhal is visited and dominated by the anti-semitic gentile Kirby Albee, who insists, against all obvious reason, that Leventhal is responsible for all the misfortunes that have befallen him (Albee). In coming to terms with this extravagant demand on his responsibility, Leventhal is led to continuous and repeated reflection on the nature of man's relationship with his fellows, and this reflection takes place under the constant pressure of the wearing physical realities of life in New York City. The result is both a documentary and a symbolic exploration of alienation. Bellow's heroes are seekers, searchers, generally agonizing intellectuals who respond to the dilemmas posed by experience by testing their reading and thinking against the reality they encounter and, in doing so, constantly modifying the messages they derive from their reading and thinking. In *The Adventures of Augie March* (1953) the hero, born in Chicago of immigrant parents one of whom, the father, has long disappeared, moves through the kaleidoscopic Chicago social scene always, in spite of temporary commitments, shaking off permanent demands made on him, always testing, seeking, re-defining, exploring and exploiting human contacts to the point where they reveal nothing more than that he must seek true relationships elsewhere. Augie March's Jewishness, like the Jewishness of most of the families with whom he comes into contact (the Einhorns, for example), is not solidly grounded in Jewish custom and culture, for there is little enough of these in the novel and only the most casual intermittent references to Jewish religion or tradition: his Jewishness is embodied in his 'adventures', in his questing, his restlessness, and – this is something we find so often in Bellow – his shoring himself with massive cultural supplies from European literature and history to try to provide a world of knowledge and feeling to which he can finally belong. Bellow's heroes are well-read (even when, like Augie, they are without formal education) and continuously reflective, so that his are novels of ideas as well as symbolic novels of alienation. This is particularly noticeable in *Herzog* (1964), where the hero, a university teacher of literature, is a disturbed and victimized intellectual who reacts to his personal misfortunes by writing never-posted letters to living and dead celebrities and formulating and re-formulating generalizations about all aspects of life and its meaning. Before *Herzog*, Bellow published *Henderson the Rain King* (1959), where the hero is not a Jew at all but a millionaire Protestant. Yet, though there are no Jewish characters in this novel, it is in a sense the most Jewish of Bellow's works. Henderson, who finds his life in America unsatisfactory and goes on a quest to Africa to try to discover what it is he really wants, is symbolically a Jew: in his alienation, his questing, his wry self-mockery, his capacity for engaging with other cultures and applying their wisdom to himself, he is acting out a Jewish role. The Africa he visits is a symbolic Africa, an Africa which never existed, and the African characters he meets – notably the wise and doomed King Dahfu of the Wariri – are legendary figures from a kind of secular African *haggadah*.

In the novel immediately preceding *Henderson*, the short *Seize the Day* (1957), Bellow presents Tommy Wilhelm, overwhelmed with financial and personal disaster, wrestling to discover the meaning of it all and achieving some kind of *katharsis* of grief in identifying himself with (and mourning for) an unknown dead Jew. This is a sort of rediscovery of Jewish identity at a symbolic level, paralleled by the hero of Philip Roth's short story *Eli the Fanatic*, the assimilated gentile-oriented Jew who suddenly develops a sense of guilt at having tried to get rid of an embarrassing old-world Jew who is upsetting the wealthy assimilated Jews of the area by running a yeshivah and dressing in traditional Jewish black hat and kaftan; he appeases this sense of guilt by himself adopting this old-world Jewish dress, and as a result is considered literally insane by his friends and treated accordingly. But Roth's story hovers uneasily between documentary and parable: Bellow's novels and stories have a richer intellectual content and a consistent texture of concern and reflectiveness. In *Mr Sammler's Planet* (1970) he brings an elderly survivor of the holocaust to modern New York to let him observe and reflect on the meaning of life in the world he now confronts, and his alienation is ironically emphasized by bringing him into friendly and intellectually rewarding contact with an Indian scientist, who comes from a wholly alien background and thinks in different categories. As so often with Bellow's heroes, Mr Sammler's Jewishness is marginal – he was never orthodox, was already orientated to western culture when a young man in Poland, and he had lived in London and been a friend of H. G. Wells before the war. Yet his Jewishness is also central, for both his fate and his response to it are Jewish.

The combination of the documentary and the symbolic which gives such richness to Bellow's novels can also be found in other novels on both sides of the Atlantic. Mordecai Richler (a Canadian living in England, like Bellow son of Jewish immigrants to Canada) has produced in *St Urbain's Horseman* a savage yet richly comic novel, both acutely observed socially and powerfully disturbing in its symbolic implications. The Jewish background that bubbles through – in Yiddish expressions and jokes, in a knowing Jewish lewdness which represents the detritus of Yiddish culture without its moral and religious content – aerates the book with a kind of black humour. The book is about the complex fate of being a Jew in an aggressive modern free-enterprise society, and the problems of identity and of relationships that result: again, it is a paradigm of sensitive man in the modern world.

The British tradition in the Jewish novel tends on the whole to be documentary rather than symbolic, which is not surprising when we consider that the greatest of all the Jewish writers in the documentary tradition – indeed its founder in the English speaking world – was the English Jew Zangwill. Gerda Charles is a good writer of what might be called Anglo-Jewish documentaries, and when she tries to move into the symbolic dimension (as in that part of *The Destiny Waltz* dealing with the tragic and short-lived East End Jewish poet) her work is less persuasive. (The other aspects of this novel are very impressive: like Chaim Bermant's *Roses are Blooming in Picardy*, they deal with the life and predicament of a Jewish band-leader, though with more sympathy and less comic irony than Bermant shows. But when Bermant in turn moves into a symbolic dimension, as in his recent *The Last Supper*, his themes begin to tangle with each other and the design of the work is less sure.) Frederick Raphael's *Lindeman* is one of the few Anglo-Jewish novels squarely in the symbolic tradition: it is a kind of anti-story to *The Assistant*, where the symbolic Jew is revealed in the end as literally a non-Jew. Another Anglo-Jewish novel in the symbolic tradition – and it perhaps shows that this tradition is now becoming established in England – is Bernice Rubens's *The Elected Member* (1969), a harrowing novel about Jewish psychological suffering in a modern English context. In Canada again, Adele Wiseman's *The Sacrifice* (1956) handled a similar theme in an equally symbolic yet socially and psychologically very different way.

Where the Jewish novel in America and Britain will go now is difficult to see. There is still a lot of mileage in the symbolic tradition and there are many aspects of Jewish life in both countries that await exploration and transfiguration in a symbolic dimension. At the same time, the subject is beginning to lose interest (witness Philip Roth's more recent frenzied attempts to whip up interest in Jewish-American themes, compared to the more restrained and effective stories in his *Goodbye Columbus*). What perhaps Jewish writers in English will now turn to is what might be called the Israeli dimension. For the impact of the existence of Israel, and of the Israel-Arab conflict, raises profound questions of identity and morality that seem to call out for treatment by the literary imagination.

1973

Writing About Jews

RENEE WINEGARTEN

Writing about Jews is still a tricky and perplexing affair. A certain chic cultural philo-Semitism has rapidly bloomed and faded. The phenomenal rise of the American-Jewish novel since the War – perhaps the only modern collective literary enterprise to make a powerful impact outside the United States, and to achieve solid critical and academic recognition – has already inspired a 'backlash', of the kind discussed by Norman Podhoretz in his indispensable, candid memoir, *Making It* (1967). Indeed, as early as 1964, out in California, Christopher Isherwood's university lecturer, George (in *A Single Man*), not only complained about the aggression of an organized minority, but also suggested that it was impossible to discuss Jews objectively and would be so for at least another twenty years. What he seems to have had in mind was a form of Jewish moral blackmail.

A landmark in this contrary movement was undoubtedly Philip Roth's controversial novel, *Portnoy's Complaint* (1969). The American critic of masscult and midcult, Dwight Macdonald, in a revealing parenthesis, said of *Portnoy's Complaint* that it was 'the Jewish novel to end all Jewish novels (which unfortunately it hasn't)'. So much for Saul Bellow, Bernard Malamud, and the rest. In a lively satirical novel, *Bech: A Book* (1970), John Updike had some mild fun with the American Jewish literary establishment and with a peripatetic, blocked American Jewish writer named Harry Bech, whose childhood resembled that of Alex Portnoy, and who possessed a 'strangely anti-Semitic Semitic sensibility'. At a literary party in London, a 'Lady of evident importance' roundly informs Bech of her opinion of American Jewish writers: 'I hate the "pity me" in all your books,' she remarks acidly. We may surmise that more than one non-Jewish reader has felt the same.

Human nature being what it is, and literary fashions now being subject to more rapid changes than ever (the New York and Chicago Jewish phase supplanted the Southern phase, after all), it can scarcely arouse surprise that the consecration of any movement should produce some stirrings of impatience and revolt. Such stirrings are doubtless healthy and necessary in order to prevent complacency and stagnation. The establishment of the American Jewish literary genre was not, of course, solely the work of Saul Bellow and Bernard Malamud, but the consequence of an upsurge of gifted authors and critics, including numerous lesser figures like the tragically short-lived Edward Lewis Wallant or outstanding, marginally Jewish writers like Nathanael West, who was also cut off in his prime.

Still, it was Bellow and Malamud who can be said to have 'made it' both as Jewish writers and as central figures of general intellectual importance and literary merit, with whom any self-respecting reader of fiction must needs be acquainted. According to Philip Roth, it was they who were important for other writers, too, including himself. Norman Mailer, on the other hand, though extremely influential as a dazzling cult figure, as advocate and incarnation of a bold life style, does not fit so readily into any scheme; and he belongs with those writers whose claim to attention is to some extent subordinately or obliquely Jewish in character. By reaction, his Hemingwayesque prize-fighter's stance betrays the avowed urge to be anything except 'a nice Jewish boy'.

Without adopting a tough guy persona, Philip Roth has evidently been motivated by a similar desire to escape that label, and with it, its hint of the prim and the prig. And now, in an essay entitled 'Imagining Jews'[1] he has renewed his sharp analysis of his Jewish confrères, linking it with a somewhat disingenuous apologia for himself. This essay is plainly connected with the concerns of his latest novel, *My Life as a Man*[2].

Of all the Jewish writers who have won fame in recent years, Philip Roth, no mean wielder of the word, is perhaps the most acutely self-conscious, as American, as Jew (vis-à-vis American society, American Jews, and the Jewish state), as *littérateur*, in an intellectual milieu where literary and personal self-awareness and self-questioning are dominant qualities. Some years ago, in a much-quoted essay, he wrote that the American writer has difficulty trying 'to understand, and then describe, and then make *credible* much of the American reality', so fantastic and appalling did it appear to him. And he went on: 'It stupefies, it sickens, it infuriates, and finally it is even a kind of embarrassment to one's own meagre imagination.'[3] With the loss of the wider social and political scene ('the community') as a theme, he envisaged that the writer would be obliged to turn inwards to the self, which might become his subject or even the impulse for his technique.

This prophecy is amply fulfilled in Roth's new novel, which offers not only two highly personal stories by a Jewish novelist named Tarnopol, concerning a Jewish novelist named Zuckerman, but Tarnopol's own 'true' account of his ghastly marriage, divorce and unsatisfactory affairs, together with comments upon the stories from different angles by various characters – the whole, of course, being the work of a Jewish novelist named Philip Roth. The turn towards the self after the failure of high political hopes and dreams was, it will be remembered, the path followed by many nineteenth-century Romantics, some of whom likewise employed a self-conscious, Chinese-box, narrative technique.

Maybe Philip Roth should have been a literary critic, suggested one American critic, Irving Howe, author of *Politics and the Novel*, in a recent none-too-friendly survey of Roth's work (in *Commentary*, December 1972). Frequently, though, Roth's novels may be regarded as a form of literary criticism. The six hundred pages of squalor and misery of *Letting Go* may be seen (and have been seen by Norman Podhoretz) as a rejection of what Roth called the 'bouncy style' and the unearned euphoria of Bellow's *The Adventures of Augie March* and *Henderson the Rain King*. The brilliantly sustained moan of *Portnoy's Complaint* may be regarded as a satire on the theme of suffering in the Jewish novel (particularly in the work of Malamud) and its abuse. 'Do me a favour, my people, and stick your suffering heritage up your suffering ass – *I happen also to be a human being!*' cries the unspeakable Portnoy.

As for Roth's current anti-hero, Tarnopol, he is the esteemed author of a novel on a 'Serious Jewish Moral Issue', about 'a retired Jewish haberdasher from the Bronx who . . . nearly strangles to death a rude German housewife in his rage over "the six million" '. (This pathetic scenario will not sound entirely far-fetched to anyone who has done a stint as a fiction reviewer in recent years). Moreover, *My Life as a Man* offers a critique not only of the moral and life-enhancing assertions of literature itself, but also – more startlingly – a critique of the Camus-Faulkner axis, the humanist tradition in general, of which Bellow and Malamud may claim to be leading contemporary representatives.

In his essay, 'Imagining Jews', Philip Roth raises some thorny questions which are of central importance at the present moment, and far from easy to resolve. I am not concerned here with what I have called the 'disingenuous' aspect of his personal apologia. It seems hardly likely that he could seriously have expected to be received with the reverence accorded to a master, after the outrageous defiance of *Portnoy's Complaint*. One does not address the creator of a virtuoso of masturbation as 'cher maître'.

As a novelist who had taught English and creative writing at various American universities, and who certainly knew all the drawbacks and the misconceptions associated with a novel written in the first person singular – indeed, he once significantly remarked that the modern writer's concern with personality could sometimes be a form of 'literary onanism' which limits the fictional possibilities – Roth can scarcely be taken at his word when he grumbles because a novel in the guise of a confession was judged by some as a confession in the guise of a novel. He knows perfectly well that the novel, while not a literal confession, is nevertheless an imaginative and oblique projection of the author's innermost responses as a man, an American and a Jew, which in his case issued forth as a part humorous, part agonizing cry of frustrated rage.

The point Roth makes about the *succès de scandale* of *Portnoy's Complaint* is, however, a valid one, which certainly does not affect literature alone. It involves the ancient and unresolved problem of 'the image of the Jew' in the mind of both the Jew and the non-Jew – as well as the image of himself and his correligionists that the Jew (rightly or wrongly) supposes to be buried in the mind of the non-Jew. For, as Roth observes, neither his Jewish nor his non-Jewish readers were expecting an outwardly respectable and liberal Jew like Portnoy to confess to sexual perversions or to offend against the widely admired institution of the Jewish family. Scarcely a quarter of a century after the ravages of Nazi propaganda, the Jew was certainly not supposed to be pictured as an aggressive, unrestrained, vulgar, lustful slob. Besides, Roth notes, the Jew is thought to violate the code of respectability 'at his own psychological risk, and perhaps at the risk of his fellow Jews' physical and social well-being. Or so history and ingrained fears argue.'

And this is indeed the heart of the matter. Have times and circumstances and mentalities changed, or have they not? Is the New World better than the Old, so that traditional hypersensitivity is misplaced? At a time when candour was all the rage among some American writers – doubtless under the shadow of Mailer – there suddenly arose, as it were, an intangible barrier to be crossed at the author's peril, and at the peril of the Jewish community in general, as though one might be candid up to a certain point, but no further. One might be free to tell the truth as one saw it, but not if that truth concerned what some felt to be a demeaning 'image of the Jew', whether as one who desired fame and financial reward, or as one who was obsessed with sexual prowess of a certain sort and with sexual revenge through non-Jewish partners. In short, the vile traditional caricature of the Jew as a man who preferred his ducats to his daughter, or as a moral and sexual defiler, secretly continued to prove an inhibiting factor, at a time when a number of writers were revealing a lot more daring than some of their (Jewish) readers were prepared to allow them.

This is not the place to discuss the merits or demerits of Roth's literary criticism in his essay, though it is tendentious in the sense that he singles out and emphasizes those elements in his contemporaries which reinforce his argument, while for the most part blithely overlooking those features which do not (for instance, the place of the temptation of violence in Bellow's work, the role of the Jewish exploiter in Malamud's, and the theme of lust in the stories of Isaac Bashevis Singer). What concerns us here is the argument itself, which he illustrates chiefly from the work of Bellow and Malamud (the former receiving rather more guarded and respectful treatment than the latter). Two points in Roth's argument, which firmly puts the ball back into the lower court from which Bellow and Malamud had largely sought to remove it, stand out and demand consideration.

The first is his insight into the way Bellow's heroes tend to appear as Jews when they participate in dramas of conscience, and as non-Jews (or only remotely Jewish) when they are governed by appetite. Thus, of the repeated cry, 'I want!', uttered by Bellow's Hemingwayesque figure, Henderson, Roth observes wryly: 'In a Bellow novel only a goy can talk like that and get away with it.' (Mailer, who does treat themes of libido and aggression, is, however, according to Roth, widely regarded 'as a writer *period*', a proposition of which I am by no means convinced.)

The second is Roth's insight into the nature of aggression in Malamud's work. Roth points to the element of 'punitive redemption' at the end of *The Assistant*, when the young Gentile, Frank, takes upon himself the burden of the wretched Jewish grocer's shop and is painfully circumcised. The creator of Portnoy also perceptively notes the element of 'violent pornography' in *The Fixer*, with its accumulation of horrible assaults upon the body of the innocent Jew, Yakov Bok, 'by the sadistic goyim'. Bok may dream of killing the Tsar, but he cannot shed blood because to do so is 'not in my nature'.

Thus, Roth's main challenge to the content of the work of his major Jewish contemporaries lies in the fields of sexual appetite and violence at a time of unprecedented social upheaval, not only in the United States but elsewhere. Recent years have witnessed a widespread relaxation in codes of sexual morality, in what is tolerable or tolerated in society or in literary and dramatic representation. It is unlikely that Jews would have escaped this wave, and indeed, many will have encountered instances of the break-up of family life, through divorce or the revolt of children, which would have been thought singular in an earlier generation, but which now elicit little surprise. Roth therefore takes issue with the literary view that the Jew remains as depicted in the Ethics of the Fathers, a figure noted for self-discipline, restraint and renunciation. This is his private King Charles's head.

As regards the field of aggression and violence, Roth's passionate strictures seem to me to be more strikingly significant. He objects to the proposition that Jews are always 'aggressed *against*' – an objection which has since received confirmation in a searing image, that of an enraged mob at Bet Shean in the act of burning the corpses of three Arab terrorists. For a subtle modification has taken place in 'the image of the Jew' which, as far as I know, has scarcely been reflected in fiction by Jewish writers (though it has appeared in work by non-Jewish authors in the shape of the Wiesenthal-like vengeful pursuer, a modern variation on the vindictive Shylock with his demand for his pound of flesh). This change has been wrought by cataclysmic events concentrated into a very short space of time, between thirty and forty years.

First, there was the Jew as innocent victim of the Nazis and of Nazi genocide – a view amply explored in current literature written by both Jews and non-Jews of varying degrees of talent, and with varying artistic success, the theme being virtually intractable in art. (So intractable was the theme of the holocaust that it led to the questioning of the value of art itself and its ability to interpret life, and ultimately helped to contribute to the depreciation of literature.) The image of the Jew as innocent victim was followed by that of the Jew precariously on the defensive, one who attacked only in self-defence, and (despite the outrages perpetrated by the Irgun and the Stern Gang) it largely prevailed in public imagination until after the Arab-Israeli War of June 1967.

Between the victory of June 1967 and the trauma of the War of October 1973, there emerged an 'image of the Jew' whose actions were not in accord with his words, the deeds of a victorious occupying power being incompatible with the words of a defenceless victim. This contradictory phase apparently went unremarked in literature – or at best received oblique expression. And now, in the period after October 1973, everything is again subject to question: old and terrible possibilities, thought to have passed for ever, recur, possibilities whose consequences for the morale of the Jewish people as a whole, to say nothing of its physical survival, would be dreadful to contemplate.

The last phase, of which Philip Roth seems well aware in his essay, does not cause him to modify his argument, which is essentially rooted in the phase of 1967 to 1973: that is, the period of the tendency to overlook the paradox of the victor-victim, or the aggressive urges which were attaining satisfaction yet remained concealed beneath a certain self-righteousness. This, surely, is what he is pointing out when he notes ironically in the work of his leading Jewish contemporaries the distinction between Us and Them, between Jewish victimization and Gentile vengeful aggression, between Jewish dignified survival and Gentile gloating triumph, between Jewish renunciation and Gentile excessive desire, 'except the excessive desire to be good and to do good' demonstrated by Jews. This, too, is surely what he has in mind when he remarks sardonically upon the fact that it is supposedly not in the nature of the Jew, whether Malamud's Bok or Bellow's Herzog, to commit violent deeds or to shed real blood.

It was such unsubstantiated claims to higher morality and right conduct, such vain superiority, such self-righteousness as a cover for narrowness or aggression or racialism (towards blacks and other supposed inferiors) that Roth satirized in Portnoy's dreadful mum. Her complacent words, 'Maybe I'm too good', will not be easily forgotten. Thus, it is not primarily the work of Bellow and Malamud itself which provides his target – their work is simply a convenient source of illustrative material which saves him the trouble of writing an abstract essay. His target is rather a set of attitudes common among Jews as a result of two thousand years of faith and solidarity, of religious and racial persecution which culminated in the Nazi holocaust, attitudes unmodified by more recent momentous upheavals.

Now the picture Roth himself gives is essentially that of modern man living beyond his limited authentic means or seeking to draw moral funds from a spiritual legacy which is exhausted, or meaningless to him, or to which he is not entitled by his secret thoughts, his conduct and manner of life. If, in Bellow's *Herzog*, the comedy lay in the gap between the vast intellectual purview and pretensions of the protagonist and his thoroughly confused and unsatisfactory personal life, in Roth's *My Life as a Man* the humour lies in the gap between the lofty literary-cum-moral purview and pretensions of the narrator and his messy marital and extramarital affairs. Indeed, it is largely because of Tarnopol's absurdly excessive literary and moral aspirations, his grotesque wish to savour in actual life a profound moral dilemma, of the sort Henry James explores in literature, that he is tricked into marrying a woman he does not even like. Where Bellow offers the irony of high comedy, Roth offers the disgust and rage of satire – satire not in the gentle, humane code of a Cervantes, but the bitter, savage, cloacal mode of a Swift or a Céline.

Of course, Roth's satire is not confined to the Jews but extends to the larger American scene. There, he finds a contradiction between claims to moral idealism and actual deeds, such as the killing of students at Kent State University and the My Lai massacre in Vietnam. This last inspired some telling pages in *Our Gang* (1971), a satire which, though over-long and diffused, had the measure of Tricky E. Dixon's power-complex and gift of linguistic obfuscation before the Watergate Scandal broke. *Our Gang* was consequently in advance of its time in striking a Swiftian and Orwellian blow in favour of the proper use of language as the foundation of truth and justice.

The core of Roth's satire seems to lie in the detestation of the self-deception caused by unearned moral superiority, and in the belief that the self-deceiver who likes to think he is acting from the highest motives frequently does more harm than good to others. Paradoxically, therefore, in a certain light, and despite his savage double-edged criticism, Roth may perhaps be regarded as the most high-minded, atavistic American Jewish moralist of them all.

Probably what he would really like is freedom from the given (as Irving Howe suggests) – the ability to be defined solely in terms of the human, without any of the additional qualifications of birth, birthplace, conditioning, heritage, and the heavy burden and responsibilities these entail. Discussing in 1959 Roth's painful early story, 'Defender of the Faith' (where three unlikeable Jewish recruits try to take advantage of the tribal sympathies of a Jewish sergeant, who exacts disproportionate revenge on the ringleader, and then has to live with his own vindictiveness), the noted critic, Alfred Kazin, remarked:

> 'In punishing the soldier so severely, Sergeant Marx was affirming his own – not altogether admirable but candidly mature – acceptance of his own raw human limitations... This is a note that Jews, in writing about other Jews, do not often strike; the appeal to raw human nature, to the individual in his human complexity and loneliness as a mere human creature, is less common than the grand collective themes of Jewish life, of Jewish solidarity in the face of oppression... The unusual thing, Mr Roth's achievement, is to locate the bruised and angry and unassimilated self – the Jew as individual, not the individual as Jew – beneath the canopy of Jewishness.'

This insistence on raw human nature was found in the second part of Portnoy's outburst (quoted above): *'I happen also to be a human being!'* Regarded purely as a human being, the Jew, acculturated or not, would be indistinguishable from any other person. The end of the American Jewish genre – and its counterparts – would be in sight.

But the question remains: what is the likelihood of sloughing off the unwished-for skin? Roth acknowledges that *Portnoy's Complaint*, along with Bellow's *The Victim* and Malamud's *The Assistant*, 'are largely nightmares of bondage, each informed in its way by a mood of baffled, claustrophobic struggle'. The goal of freedom as simple human being remains unattainable unless the writer chooses to leave the Jews and their history or martyrology out of it; unless he draws upon his acculturated sensibility alone (as indeed, many American Jewish writers, including Roth, have in certain individual works).

For clearly we are dealing here with writers who are aware that they are not very Jewish in any positive religious or other sense, and who consequently cannot help feeling that Jewishness (the claim of family, tribe, sentiment, history, negative experience) is a burden. Where Malamud would consciously take up the burden, Roth revolts against it. For Roth, giving expression to this kind of tormented sensibility in his denial of Malamud's view that 'All men are Jews', even the men who are Jews are not sure they are Jews. He seeks to reverse Malamud's proposition by saying 'All Jews are men' – and by insisting that this must include vulgarians, lechers and crooks as well as suffering martyrs. But all he does is produce the dark instead of the light – not the far more complex and subtle mingling of shades and tones which makes up the common human lot.

The trouble is that when writers seek to examine raw human nature, their emphasis all too easily falls upon the 'raw'. This is certainly the case with Roth, who understands by 'human' everything squalid, mean, and sometimes downright revolting. For him, 'life' means foul actuality unredeemed, and in his work he veers between extremely skilful literary artifice and untransmuted experience. All too often, like the good disciple of Céline that he is, he seizes the reader by the scruff of the neck, as if the unfortunate fellow were a dog who must be taught to mend his ways by having his nose rubbed in his own mess. That is why Roth has no patience with those literary colleagues who exalt human dignity and who strive to proclaim that, despite everything cruel and evil, the human spirit must prevail. Ultimately, therefore, whether as Jews, as Americans or as human beings, his characters are seldom allowed to make a good impression – and this unrelenting harshness weakens any case he tries to establish.

Since many people tend to think in stereotypes – it is so much easier – the difficulty concerning 'the image of the Jew' remains. As Roth himself remarks in his essay:

> 'In an era which has seen the... Americanization of millions of uprooted Jewish immigrants and refugees, the annihilation as human trash of millions of Europeanized Jews, and the establishment and survival in the ancient holy land of a spirited, defiant modern Jewish state, it can safely be said that imagining that Jews are and ought to be has been anything but the marginal activity of a few American-Jewish novelists...
> 'For the Jewish novelist, then, it has not been a matter of going forth to forge in the smithy of his soul the *un*created conscience of his race, but of finding his inspiration in that conscience that has been created and undone a hundred times over in this century alone...'

Since he wrote those words, we have seen the survival and destiny of the Jewish state, and consequently that of the Jewish people, again questioned in the comity of nations, in a way no other independent state has experienced in modern times.

If we could be sure that the debased image of the Jew as the symbol of motiveless evil, rancour, vengeance, subversion, money-grubbing, and so forth, had vanished along with his embarrassing and ambivalent compensatory saintly counterpart, we might be more ready to fall in with Roth's argument. Perhaps we should not attribute too much significance to such incidents as those described in Edgar Morin's *Rumour in Orleans*, which reveal the survival of anti-Jewish mythology in a highly civilized Western democracy. Perhaps we should not pay much attention to occasional remarks by blinkered military leaders on insidious Jewish influence, and by old-fashioned members of the Catholic clergy on the Jews as deicides or creatures eternally condemned.

On the other hand, we should be foolish to overlook them altogether, to ignore the fact that the very existence of the Jews is a stumbling-block to a number of diverse interests, and to suppose that centuries-old preconceptions can vanish from the non-Jewish collective unconscious overnight. After all, preconceptions have not vanished from the Jewish collective unconscious, as Roth rightly points out in his work. Possibly we should be more ready to sympathize with his desire to avoid giving comfort to a certain complacent and unthinking Jewish public, if we could be sure that he were not giving satisfaction to an even more unattractive readership.

Still, despite my misgivings, I suppose the writer has to take his chances. Either he can say what the public wants to hear or does not mind hearing – or he can say what it would rather not hear, because it is unpleasant, or might offend, or might give comfort to a potential enemy. If literature is ever to return to a position of esteem, if it is once again to occupy a place of central importance as the touchstone of society and its values, the writer must have his freedom – and that includes his freedom to annoy, to outrage, to defy, to take risks to provoke the reader into self-inquiry. Despite all that has happened during the last fifty years – perhaps even because of it – self-inquiry is even more essential. Self-deception may prove disastrous, and never more so than in a time of crisis.

Maybe, as writers or readers, we are more free than we think we are. At least, to act as if we were free would surely be a sign of maturity. The same freedom of judgment and expression – however painful (and it is both painful and perilous) – is going to have to be extended to all, for already there are signs that it will eventually be seized by all, whether one likes it or not, as we move out of the immediate post-holocaust decades. All we can hope – alas, in an age of mounting barbarism, we cannot be sure – is that, *pace* Mr Roth, human decency will prevail.

1 *The New York Review of Books*, 3 October 1974.
2 *My Life as a Man*, by Philip Roth (Cape).
3 'Writing American Fiction', *Commentary*, March 1961.

1975

Recollections of a Bookworm

RAFAEL SCHARF

To spend one's life away from one's native tongue – commonplace as this has become in our day – is a condition which fragments personality and stunts development. Man cannot remain whole when the most vital link with his own past is disconnected.

The transfer and absorption into the new language can be effective and even rewarding; the new language can form a polished surface over which one is able to glide comfortably enough. But such mastery as is attainable will come from the brain and not the bowels, it will in most cases lack the subterranean connections, the multiple layers of associative fabric from which words draw their full meaning and resonance.

As the native shore recedes in the distance, can the sieve of memory dredge up from the books read long ago the authentic blend of one's formative years?

Some of the fondest memories of my childhood are of being in bed but not very ill, claiming all mother's attention and turning it into reading time. She read me little verses of young love and broken hearts of mermaids and sunsets, of diamonds and pearls, but only much later did I realize, like some latter-day Monsieur Jourdain, that they were *poetry*, mainly from Heine's *Buch der Lieder*. After that came the folk-tales of the Brothers Grimm, witches, dwarfs and giants, Rapunzel, and Rumpelstitzchen and princesses married to frogs. For a different mood the subtler and disquieting inventions of Hans Andersen: the boy with the splinter of the devil's mirror in his eye, abducted by the Snow Queen; the red dancing shoes and the sea-nymph who, for love, changed her fishtail for human legs and whose every step was like the thrust of a sword ... The stories were endlessly repeated and I knew them by heart but would not allow a single word to be skipped. (There was, however, a total embargo on stories about orphans; the loss of a parent was a thought too painful to endure even in make-believe.) Having the stories word-perfect and following the lines (wasn't that how Moses Mendelsohn, through the *Bi'ur*, taught the German language to his coreligionists?) made it easy to learn to read and I became independent long before school-age, an accomplishment soon demonstrated as I spelt out the lettering on the spines of books on the eye-level of the lowest shelf in the bookcase.

That bookcase was a massive mahogany piece, matching the fortress of the sideboard and the plateau of the dining table with its surrounding ramparts of chairs, in the style of middle-class households in the first decades of the century in Cracow, Poland.

It had a tall central section and two lower wings, somewhat like an altar, each section behind cut-glass bevelled panes. The process of growing up was for me calibrated by new rows of bookspines rearing into view. Prolonged acquaintance with each row had scooped its own groove in my memory, bringing what seems like total recall of titles, bindings, illustrations – a lump in the throat and havoc in the remembering.

The left-hand side was my Father's and it contained 'seforim' which means not mere books but *the* books. Worn from much use or long transit, in mottled brown covers, the brittle pages yellowing unevenly all round the edges, they exuded their own smell of beeswax and fish-glue; and from the way they were handled, the caress, one knew they were holy. Bending over an open volume my father would slowly turn the pages, as if feeling his way through an embarrassment of riches and then, with a familiarity which breeds contentment, he would settle down to a study of a chosen passage. He was no scholar – growing up in a household of fifteen children he was pushed out early into the world in search of a livelihood and he was, I suspect, quite unable to make his own way through the solid columns of text, buried in the undergrowth of commentaries and sprinkled with the poppyseed of glosses. But no matter, he was not looking for solutions to problems or rulings of law, but seeking to wash away the triviality and harshness of everyday existence in the waves of the eternal. He believed, simply, that the book contained the truth and that it was good to touch it.

He wished to persuade me to share this outlook but he knew it was too late in the day to arrest the slide and that an argument with a precocious know-all only led to an aggravation of spirit. Only once, I remember, he exploded when I asked him 'What is all this *for*?' 'What is this *for*, fool? The whole of life is for *this*!'

He saw his role at home as that of breadwinner, and even though he genuinely felt that all he had aspired to was done for our sake, the bringing up of children would not have been a part of his conscious concern. What little modicum of success he had as a merchant and small-time manufacturer was brought about by ceaseless hussle and total immersion in the task at hand. He would provide for all the needs – and be the sole judge of how these were defined.

While spending of money on books was grudgingly approved, there was much pursing of lips and shaking of head. Novels, in his eyes, were *naarishkeiten*, foolishness and frivolity. How could adult men and women give serious attention to imaginary misfortunes of non-existent people! Whilst I had argued that they nourish the sources of feeling and imagination, open the door to experience beyond one's personal orbit and give a glimpse of the many faces of truth. Where else would knowledge of the ways of the world come from? Were not the scandalous infidelities of Mrs G. next door made comprehensible through the reading of Madame Bovary and didn't our cousin Hymie, with his frenetic and perpetually misfiring schemes step out straight off the pages of Balzac?

My father understood perhaps more of these matters than he thought fit to concede. He and I maintained a brittle truce which lasted till just before the outbreak of war, when I left home and hearth for a foreign land. I never saw him again: he died in 1942, felling trees in the Arctic Circle in Russia. I can but hope that he was somehow aware of my love and respect.

My mother reigned over the centre section of the bookcase. The volumes were all in German, reflecting the preponderant cultural influence in that part of Galicia. Imperial Vienna was a magnet, thought to embody everything that was civilized. Her perspective was the Vienna of Freud, Schnitzler, Hugo v. Hofmanstahl, Gustav Mahler, Max Reinhardt, Theodor Herzl, Josef Popper-Lynkeus, Karl Kraus. (As Stefan Zweig put it: 'Nine-tenths of what the world celebrated as Viennese culture was created, nourished and promoted by Viennese Jews.')

Cracow was a satellite, catching some of the reflected glory. It gave itself airs as a cultural capital, pretensions which were a source of derision to Warsaw, Lodz or Lwow, which saw the worthies of Cracow as self-satisfied, small-minded and provincial. Beautiful Cracow – in retrospect, a foolish place to have chosen for one's birthplace . . .

The language in my mother's home was naturally German, but she learned Polish in childhood, at school, from her nursemaid and friends. She did switch effortlessly from one language to another; she would gabble and joke in Yiddish with my father's populous clan, but with the children only Polish was spoken. As it happened this facility proved her life-saver. Combined with 'good looks' (meaning lack of semitic features) it enabled her to pass as an Aryan, when under the Nazis the shibboleth of pronunciation (using the word, for once, in its true biblical meaning) was a matter of life and death. The Gestapo found that their preconceived image of a Polish Jewess did not accord with a woman who spoke German fastidiously; whilst the hawk-eyed Polish informers and blackmailers, sharp to Jewish speech-habits, were put off when every tricky, give-away consonant was uttered with precision in a deliberately high-flowing or vulgar turn of phrase, not expected from a mere Jewess.

The pride of place in the bookcase was held by the classics: Goethe, Schiller, Lessing, Heine – in those popular editions without which it seemed no Jewish middle-class home was complete. Their circulation must have been vast. I have seen odd volumes in the familiar gold and purple mock-leather on bookstalls all over the world; clearly, these were the books which the refugees carried in their knapsacks, token of faith in another Germany. On the shelf beneath there was Ludwig Boerne, to whose *Letters from Paris* I was, profitlessly, directed by a friendly editor as an object lesson in polemical writing, when it looked as if I might become a journalist.

Magisterially stood Theodor Mommsen with his Roman History, mighty volumes quite beyond my reach. Only much later, a professor under whom I studied Roman Law and who revered

Mommsen was able to convey to me something of his towering stature and achievement in the field of Roman inscriptions, constitutional law and criminal jurisdiction – an example of German scholarship in excelsis.

Next, there was a profusion in cloth of the volumes of the fierce and bewhiskered Björnstjerne Björnson. I have not read him and know of no one who has. I thought warmly of him nonetheless when, in 1945, I found myself with a small 'Intelligence' unit at a remote forest lodge in Tromsö, at the northern tip of Norway. We had come for no martial purpose, but to observe the Aurora Borealis. Despite a vast supply of Aquavit, the eerie twilight which passes there for night made us shiver. In the corner of the room was a bookshelf and in serried ranks the books of none other than B.B., the local lad. We kindled a small flame in the fireplace and – bowing to the inevitable – dismembered the case for firewood. Then, somewhat shamefacedly, but not sufficiently so, we fed the volumes one by one into the fire and watched the petals of charred paper flying up the chimney. As the embers died we shook our heads with regret – that the venerable B.B. had not been even more prolific. *Habent sua fata libelli* ...

I recall that a whole shelf in our bookcase was in the grip of a 'Northern glacier': Selma Lagerlöf's *Gösta Berling*, Knut Hamsuns's renowned *Hunger*, Sigrid Undset's *Christin Lavrans' Daughter* and others. I cannot say wherein lay the power of this strain of Scandinavian writing, that despite its chilling earnestness was so widely popular.

More heartwarming, a topic of conversation and adolescent gropings were Maeterlinck's *The Blue Bird* and *The Life of the Bees* – shadowy philosophy and fanciful speculation. A slim volume entitled *Home and the World* by one of an improbable name, Rabindranath Tagore, is remembered solely for an awe-inspiring photograph of the author. Then there were the pairs – Kipling and Galsworthy, Anatole France and Romain Rolland. *Stalky and Co.* was taken to be an exact model of contemporary English school-life, in the same way that *The Forsyte Saga* was understood as a clinical description of English town-life. It was somewhat anticlimactic to find, on arrival in England, that already in the late 'thirties both models, on which one thought to rely for the savoir-faire were totally obsolete, depicting vestigial phenomena. Galsworthy's colourful canvas had captured the middle-class in the act of worship at an altar over which there is the motto: 'What will it profit a man if he save his soul and lose his fortune?'

Of Anatole France I recall little except those intriguing titles *Gods are thirsty* and *The Revolt of the Angels*. But I sampled Romain Rolland, not through the inhibiting dimensions of *Jean Christoph* (life seemed too short), but through the wise and warm-hearted *Colas Breugnon*.

What brought all these to rub shoulders on our shelves? Sheer accident? It now comes to me that, beginning with Mommsen, they were all winners of the Nobel Prize for literature. They must have come to us by subscription to some precursor of a book-club.

Following this clue I have looked up the complete list from Sully Prudhomme in 1901 to Odysseus Elytis in 1979 and am saddened to observe the transience of acclaim and the ashes of reputations.

Did you know that the 1904 prize was shared between the French poet Frederic Mistral and the Spanish dramatist José Echegaray? Have you read Karl Gjellerup and Henrik Pontoppidan, joint holders for 1917? Did you know of Benavente y Martinez, Grazia Deledda, Ivan Bunin? Frans Emil Silanpää? Haldòr K. Laxness – where art thou! Sure enough the fiery Björnstjerne is among them, for the year 1903. And the Poles Henryk Sienkiewicz and Wladyslaw Reymont. Also, of course, Thomas Mann – but that's another story.

The Magic Mountain had a special place. One of my schoolteachers (they were all – even the games-master – called 'professor', but this one really deserved the appellation) had translated the book into Polish and in a literary 'study-circle' he read us pages from his version as it progressed. The long 'snow-chapter', the dream poem of rapture and terror at the heart of the book, enacted in the timeless no-man's-land between life and death, with its beatific vision and a glimpse of hell, made a lasting impression on us. In retrospect, however, Hans Castorp, who is a kind of ringmaster in an ideological tournament, hardly appears as a figure of flesh and blood. His musings upon the nature of life have the illusory profundity of adolescent polemics, riddles without answer. The examination of society through debate between the Jesuit Naphta 'luxurious and spiteful' with his ascetic fanaticism and the humanist Settembrini 'for ever blowing on his penny-whistle of reason', takes place in the hermetic isolation of the sanatorium, an artificial laboratory – and it remains suspended in a vacuum. In the end the great and important truths sound, as perhaps they must, platitudinous and insubstantial, some vague commitment to kindness and love and liberal values. In that respect a magic mountain seems to have laboured to bring forth a magic mouse. Nonetheless, no other work of fiction captures so well the illusive nature of time – perhaps the author's prime object.

And now for a cluster of books with a great family resemblance, by my mother's favourite writers: Jakob Wasserman, Arnold Zweig, Franz Werfel, Stefan Zweig.

Of the many solid, craftsmanlike novels by Jakob Wasserman, full of strange characters, complicated plots and psychological insights, the one best remembered is *The Case Marizius*. Based on an actual event of a man pardoned after serving eighteen years in prison for murdering his wife, Wasserman shows how a seemingly simple case under the surface discloses a morass of uncertainties, and how the notions of guilt and innocence are perplexingly ambiguous. Wasserman is, of course, identified with the pathetic credo of the Jewish German: 'I am a German and a Jew, each as completely as the other; neither can be separated from the other.' He spoke sonorously for the species, which was to suffer so rude an awakening. Mercifully, he himself died in 1934 having seen only the writing on the wall, before the total collapse of his 'world of illusions'.

Sardonically, Arnold Zweig himself wrote of the 'Insulted and Exiled'. His *Case of Sergeant Grischa*, which secured his fame, tells of the conflict between the Prussian military caste represented by Schieffenzahn ('The State makes the Law – the individual is but a louse') and the Jewish writer Bertin who fights for justice. It was the shape of things to come. The judicial steamroller crushes the innocent Grischa, but it becomes clear that he will not be the only victim.

Werfel is also preoccupied by the theme of brute injustice. His *Forty Days of Musa Dagh* deals with the Armenian persecution, and specifically with the story of the 5,000 who organize themselves into a resistance group, go up the mountain and endure for forty days an ever tightening siege. I found *The Class Reunion*, one of his lesser works, strangely affecting. Here the magistrate Sebastian finds that an accused brought in front of him resembles, or indeed is, one Franz Adler, with whom he shared a bench at school and whom – he now painfully recollects – he had grievously hurt and humiliated. Reviewing his past life he recognizes his guilt in another man's undoing, but it is too late to make amends, for the accused, on second sight, proves to be a stranger.

Stefan Zweig was the even-tempered voice of reason and imagination, the master of *vie romancée* (Mary Stuart, Joseph Fouché, Marie Antoinette), a genre in biography practised with success also by Emil Ludwig and André Maurois amongst others, concerned less with the accuracy of historical data than the intuitive reconstruction of an inner truth. In his cosmopolitan culture, his breadth of vision and unflinching adherence to humanistic values Zweig epitomized what he himself described in the *World of Yesterday*. When these values succumbed he found life unendurable and committed suicide, as did Werfel, and for the same reason.

As my mind hovers over the place in the bookcase occupied by my own books, the focus becomes sharper. The texture of things past is made up of printed pages; books stand at the crossroads of life's journey; the train of thought shuttles between quotation marks. There was a time when even that other enchantment was subordinate and girl-friends were chosen not for their comeliness and compliance but for their ability to talk books. The appetite for reading matter was constrained only by the meagreness of supply. We had our private lending libraries with their few score of shelves, and many a book was read to the end in those less trafficky days, on the way home across town. Imagine my incredulous delight on arrival at being introduced in London to the public library, with virtually any book obtainable on request. It was a good omen for the love affair with a new language and a new country.

Among juvenilia on my bottom shelf, known and loved by youngsters everywhere in Europe except, it seems, in England, was Edmondo de Amicis's *The Heart*. Perhaps it was the title that kept the English schoolboy away. It is written in the form of a Turin boy's diary and is interspersed with letters from his father, with praise or reproach. Didactic, though wise and touching, it so vividly depicts daily life at school that at a distance of more than half-a-century I still recall the *primus* Derossi and the tall, magnanimous Garonne, and the new boy from Calabria. Sandwiched in between are his teacher's monthly readings – self-contained short stories portraying some selfless or heroic deed of a young boy. Amicis speaks unblushingly of love of his country (another love that dares not speak its name?) and it is, possibly, this unfashionable patriotic note that gave the book a dubious name. Some while ago I loaned the book to a young friend, a brash Israeli, in Hebrew translation, for bed-time reading. Next morning he confessed, sheepishly, that the book had kept him awake till the early hours and that he had had a good cry over it. I was glad to hear it.

Regretfully, I admit to an early addiction to Karl May. I had a few selected volumes in an illustrated edition, in stiff blue covers, with a colour frontispiece behind tissue – a horse and rider falling over a precipice (a common end to villains, this) or Kara-ben-Nemzi (Karl the German, you see) on his incomparable Rih (a horse into whose ear he must nightly whisper a Sura from the Koran!), with his sidekick Hadj Halef Omar streaking through the desert. These were possessions equal in prestige and power to a real leather football, and to lend a volume was to bestow a matchless favour. I recall a period when, to the virtual exclusion of all else, I read the opus de capo al fine and yet again. The phenomenon of Karl May calls for an explanation (but not from me): why these simplistic, black-and-white, totally inauthentic yarns (or, rather, the same yarn endlessly rehashed), with the invincible writer-hero 'Old Shatterhand', who can – and does on every page – fell an adversary with one blow of his fist, with his Apache soul-mate Winnetou (the 'Redskin Gentleman'!) at his side and with an admixture of religious sentimentality have retained their unflagging appeal to succeeding generations.

I am told that the complete works of Alexandre Dumas *pére* were issued by Michael Levy Frères in 277 volumes – and I seem to have had most of them in a pulp edition. It started with *The Three Musketeers* and *Twenty Years After* and *Vicomte de Bragelonne* and expanded, unstoppably, into *Joseph Balsamo-Cagliostro* and *Ange Pitou* and *The Queen's Necklace* and *The Black Tulip* and others, all part of some jumbled historical sequence for which one cared not a sou, except for the marvellous convolutions of the plot and mischievous intrigue. But my favourite by a long margin was the incomparable *Count of Monte-Cristo* which I would still back against any adventure story and to which

I returned periodically, long after such fare was considered proper for a youngster with aspirations.

What about this bundle of stories by Jack London, perhaps the most popular American writer available in translation, *The Call of the Wild* and *White Fang*, the autobiographical *Martin Eden*. The apocalyptic anti-utopian *Iron Heel*, foreshadowing urban battles between a fascist oligarcy and city slum-dwellers was riveting. It surprised me to discover that Jack London was rather less regarded in England and I feel sure that my impression of him as a major writer will one day be vindicated. He served, in a way, as a bridge between the tale of adventure and the socially committed writing, onto Silone's *Fontamara*, Upton Sinclair's *The Jungle*, Dos Passos' *The 42nd Parallel*.

Then came our feverish though short-lived enchantment with Aldous Huxley. *Point Counterpoint*, fresh from the translator's desk (some six years after publication – such was the usual lag) was a revelation. The author's encyclopaedic knowledge and voracious interest, his intellectual virtuosity and weary cynicism, it all seemed oh, so adult, fine grist to one's own busy little mill. And what sophisticated English society, how infinitely desirable when contrasted with the provincialism of our milieu!

A special place was taken by a batch of pacifist books, works conceived in the trenches during the First World War and reeking of the mud as men gained or yielded a few yards of ground: Barbusse, Renn, Remarque, Glaser, Sheriff, Hemingway.

Barbusse's *Le Feu* is an indictment of the folly of the slaughter, the misery and exploitation of the common soldier. It has never been surpassed, though, of course, Remarque's *All Quiet on the Western Front* exceeded it in popularity. The impact of such writing seemed to make it incontrovertibly clear to my generation that the 'little man' would never again be persuaded to rise against a fellow creature. Till the next time, that is, and the one after that.

When human behaviour becomes unendurably absurd perhaps the only fit comment is an obscene joke and gesture. Hašek follows the Byronic dictum: 'If I laugh at any mortal thing, 'tis that I may not weep' and in *The Good Soldier Švejk* he created a foul-mouthed imbecile in private war against pompous authority, a speck of humanity fouling up the cogs of the mindless machine. Max Brod, who was right about Kafka, predicted that Hašek would stand alongside Cervantes and Rabelais – an acute judgement. Hašek's masterpiece has won the final accolade: Švejk has entered every language and tongue.

Doubtless, since Auschwitz and Hiroshima, this writing of the First World War has taken on an air of unreality and irrelevance, as if history there described belongs to 'the good old days'.

I try to recall what there was on display of specifically Jewish writers and subjects. Not untypically, I regret, there was but little. One had, of course, read Mendele and Sholem-Aleichem, Bialik and Tchernichowsky and even studied the history of Dubnov. But all this, and a good deal more was crammed into the school curriculum, the so-called compulsory reading, and as such was not supposed to give pleasure. For a long time it remained in a different layer of memory, separated from the free, extracurricular reading.

Meanwhile there was the inevitable and ubiquitous Graetz, an institution rather than a book, the many thousands of pages yellowing, one might have thought, from grief of neglect. But as I discovered, on a casual dip, ours was not a virgin copy and the previous owner had filled the magins with critical notes. There is great fascination in deciphering such glosses, a sort of *obligato* to the main theme, and here an anonymous but clearly no mean scholar was relentlessly pursuing the master and getting his claws into him from the flank. Inconsistencies were sternly noted, purple passages ridiculed, rhetorics deflated. Graetz's references to Hasidism, to the 'fossilized Polish talmudists', his contempt for Yiddish ('ridiculous gibberish') brought the glossarist to a frenzy of question and exclamation marks. Empty spaces after end of chapters were covered with precise, snappy phrases, pointing out the one-sidedness of treatment of this *Leidensgeschichte*, the neglect of Poland and Russia, the omission of economic and political factors. *Le style est l'homme même* – I formed a distinct picture of this 'writer on the margin', took a liking to him and felt in his debt for this early lesson in irreverence towards authority.

Cheek by jowl with Graetz there lived a few large de-luxe bookalbums, bound in white parchment with gold blocking, with beautiful endpapers, half-empty pages and blinding black-andwhite illustrations and vignettes by E. M. Lilien. The biblical figures, patriarchs, heroes, lovers, angels, impeccably precise in the *Art Nouveaux* manner reminiscent of Beardsley, were viewed by us with piety, as if they were a sort of Jewish icon. There were among them some idealized panoramas of the Holy Land with the word 'Zion' forming the sun, but also a number of quite realistic and excellent etchings of Jerusalem, among them the most popular and frequently reproduced 'Wailing Wall'. Among the biblical compositions, one was startled to see that Moses looked increasingly like Herzl – and Herzl, in turn, like Moses. In the imagination of Lilien the two figures became interchangeable and it was fortunate for him, indeed, that the Founder was so marvellously, imperiously decorative (no artist could have attempted similar play with, say, Jabotinski). A copy of *Altneuland* carried a famous photograph of Herzl leaning over the bridge in Basle, which, if memory serves, was also posed and taken by Lilien.

We come to Achad-Haam. The four volumes of essays *Al Parashat Derachim* ('At the crossroads' – a title which is guaranteed to remain forever topical) commanded enormous – in retrospect one would say excessive – respect. His use of Hebrew was a revelation – a decisive proof that the holy language will serve naturally, gracefully and without strain in daily intercourse and that it can be used to describe and discuss secular matters lucidly and without ambiguity. His style, which set the standard, proved more durable than the contents, which however, had appeared to us original and profound. In his criticism and opposition to what seemed the wild and unattainable objectives of political Zionism, Achad-Haam turned out wrong in most respects, but his error was understandable: he saw problems which in his sober view could not be overcome – no man of entirely sound mind believed that they would be. His naturally sceptical temper and a pragmatic approach demanded aims which were more modest. One recognized in him the paradigm of the familiar ambivalence between a deep emotional attachment to ancient tradition and an unflinching rationalism. He sought to uncover values in tradition with which the Jewish intellectual could identify without selling the pass – and if he did not resolve the issue he remains in that respect in good company.

'The Polish connection' looms large on the horizon. The ambivalence of belonging and exclusion, of acceptance and rejection by the country of his birth, often gave the young Jew a heightened love for its language and literature, to which access was free. The intoxication with poetry could be heavy and durable.

I cannot explain why, through the years, the words of Juliusz Slowacki castigating the Polish nation on the site of Agamemnon's tomb send a shiver down my spine, or why the stilted pathos of his patriotic dramas, obscure and remote, still quickens the pulse. Why when I walk the Sussex Downs should the inner voice ring with the Crimean Sonnets of Adam Mickiewicz or why should this semblance of the landscape of childhood tug with the lines from his 'Pan Tadeusz' (where, to add to the puzzlement, the shores recalled are not even those of the Vistula, but of Niemen!).

Stanzas, lines, rhymes from Kochanowski, Krasicki, Konopnicka, Asnyk, Wyspianski long ago embedded themselves in the subconscious and at odd moments come up to the surface, surprising and welcome.

Nothing read in later years, in any language, compares with the rapture in the lyrics of Julian Tuwim, the unsurpassed and untranslatable magician. Had he written in a language accessible to a wider public he would doubtless have been acclaimed as one of the finest lyric poets of his time. As it is, having direct access to him is an exclusive privilege. As with Heine, with whom he has affinity in all his moods, it is an irony that the most exquisite master of his native tongue should be a Jew, and that this fact should be found so galling to the so-called patriots.

Two books to engage my sceptical attention I always carefully kept back-to-front, with the title on the spine hidden from view. They were Renan's *Life of Jesus* and D. F. Strauss's *Life of Jesus – critically examined*. My father would have found their presence offensive, particularly in proximity with *his* books and would have been perturbed to find that I concerned myself with the unmentionable. They were important to me in that they put the subject matter in a rational perspective. Renan showed Jesus as a man within the setting of his time; Strauss, with his disbelief in the supernatural, analysed the sources of faith with scientific rigour. They cleared the air of incense and taboos which the hostile religion was pressing upon a budding seeker after truth.

Once, a very long time ago, our maid-servant took me with her to church confronting me with that human figure stretched on his cross, nails piercing hands and legs, droplets of red paint oozing from open wounds. She whispered urgently: 'This is God-Jesus and he loves you, though you are a Jew and your forefathers crucified Him and – and you mustn't tell your mother about it.' I was overcome with nausea. On coming home I sobbed inconsolably but would not let on why.

Perhaps this experience left me with my lifelong interest in theology. Many years and many volumes later, with the clock ticking ever faster, I remain an unregenerate agnostic, thank God. (This serves me reasonably well by day, if not so well by night.)

On first returning to Cracow after the war I avoided the street where we lived. But with time the scar-tissue corrugated and on my last visit I had an irresistible impulse to glimpse the family home – would the old furniture be there, would Napoleon be still retreating from Moscow in the incongruous canvas by Kossak? And the bookcase, would it be standing now, in the same place?

The house stood overlooking the girdle of parks which are the pride of Cracow, in what used to be the more prosperous Jewish quarter – now, judging by the peeling façades, greatly down on its luck.

I walked into the cavernous entrance hall, heavy with the sour smell of poverty. Striking a match I deciphered from the list of tenants – a police requirement this – the occupiers of flat number 4. As I steeled myself to mount the stairs and thought how to apologize for my ghostly intrusion, a door opened on the ground floor. A man loomed over me, immediately cross and aggressive, as is the custom of the land: 'You lost something? There's nothing here for you!'

Yes, I thought – that about sums it up.

Chaim Superman Gazes Down on His Nigh Perfect People

BARNET LITVINOFF

I can now be absolutely frank, declared Chaim Superman as he alighted on a remote star in the celestial galaxy for one of those close encounters which had made him famous even while a mortal on Earth. I can now be absolutely frank, because having been transmogrified into a spirit, it may be assumed that I have ceased being a member of the Jewish race, or people, or nation, or what-have-you.

Chaim was one of the super-intellectuals invited to participate in a symposium, under the general heading of 'The Individual and his Environment'. Papers had been read by Superliberated Women, Superhomosexuals, Third World Supermen. Now it was Chaim's turn as the final speaker, before they adjourned to a Superbar afterwards, for a less formal interchange of views.

I have also ceased to be a British subject, he informed his fellow-Superpersons, and therefore need no longer grieve over the performance of Leyland Motors, and Britain's placing in the Great Power League, and the cataract of high art issuing from The Best Television Service in the World. I may now, if I wish, give the Jews my undivided attention, and so propose to share with you a few ideas that have crept into my rarified mind about the lifestyle pursued by me and my people on Earth, and about our condition in general.

The Jews are an upstanding, generous, law-abiding, industrious, talented people, Chaim averred by way of introduction. I know this because the *Jewish Chronicle*, that splendid weekly newspaper, regularly told me so as we were suffused every Friday night in the glow of our Sabbath candles and the all-round goodness produced by the mystical practice of imbibing chicken soup. And I would be fortified in my belief as to the excellence of my people by the striking headline periodically appearing in the *Chronicle*: 'Peer Praises Anglo-Jewry'.

Not a laser beam broke the pattern of his supernatural thoughts as Chaim developed his theme. It was touching, he said, at a time when the flames of republicanism were licking at the edges of the British Constitution, how my people retained their affection for the House of Lords. Naturally, we preferred our peers to be hereditary, but we did not totally scorn the life-peers, recognizing as we did that standards everywhere were falling. Indeed, we were prepared to admit that we ourselves were affected by the general lowering of those standards; even on Friday evenings certain family defaulters were known to absent themselves from those gatherings dedicated to nourishment, spiritual and material. How un-Jewish of them to prefer a West End disco, or the Moonies, or, strangely enough, the baize tables in the Mayfair area of London where people played, not prayed!

Some anti-semitic newspapers would actually publish the names of the latter, when the premises were raided by the police. It was therefore comforting when a courageous peer spoke up to describe us as we truly were.

Chaim contemplated the purport of this statement for a timeless moment and then continued: As I steal a backward glance to my brethren nestling in the more temperate climes of Mother Earth, I realize how tolerant we were, even towards people who did not keep winning Nobel prizes. This applied also to those of us redeemed, ingathered, and fulfilled in a Free Jewish Life in the State of Israel. We demonstrated this particularly when a Prime Minister of South Africa wished to travel abroad, and no other country would invite him in – except perhaps Paraguay – yet he was given a most cordial welcome in the Jewish State. The Israeli newspapers were most warm, explaining that, contrary to the biased reports elsewhere put about, he was not anti-semitic and pro-Nazi during the Second World War; he had merely worked for Britain's defeat.

Endowed as I now am with supernatural faculties I can illustrate our advanced civic-sense by stating how many Mayors we produced for Cape Town and Toronto: 103, in fact, counting the deputy Mayors. Our *Jewish Chronicle* was particularly zealous in following their fortunes. And this, mark you, in cities where the Jews were a small minority. Of course, we refused to monopolize the limelight, and perhaps that's why, in the city where we were for about fifty years almost the majority, New York, we have only recently taken on the responsibility of Mayor for the first time, leaving the glory in the main to the Irish and the Italians, more or less alternately.

We endowed numberless colleges and medical institutions (I have the figures, but won't tire you with them). Our passion for good works was finely tuned to accord with our patriotic sense. Hence our monuments in Israel – forests and the like – bear the names of kings, queens and world statesmen (not, I might say, of General de Gaulle, for he anticipated his rank of superstatesman prematurely). All this brought us no end of goodwill. We found room in our charitable activities to support the arts, and we kept our children off the streets. Our youngsters frequently achieved this for themselves, when they developed spirituality on the highest level and made off helter-skelter for a distant ashram, in India perhaps or Peckham Rye. Sometimes their elders would hasten them on their way, by arranging an extended pilgrimage to the Hebrew University or a kibbutz. This path was the more desirable, of course, as there was always some generous Zionist body nearby to cover most of the expense.

How devoted we were to education! How strong our humanitarianism! We were as near perfect as a people can be, living our respectable minority lives in our modest little homes, enjoying our modest little Barmitzvahs, engaging in our modest little businesses. Why we should be criticized at all I could not understand. But indeed, anti-semitism was everywhere – you could find it in a Butlin's holiday camp if you searched hard enough. A generation after Hitler and we still tracked anti-semitism down, among journalists, public figures (some of whom went so far as to believe the Arabs actually had a case), the BBC. This prevented us from securing a fair share of the good things in life. There would, no doubt, have been lots more Jews at Oxford and Harvard and in Beverly Hills, and in Winnington Road North West Eleven, and running property empires, and working down the coal-mines, if we hadn't to wrestle with the disadvantage of being a misunderstood minority. We had a terrific struggle merely to survive.

In my day, Chaim emphasized to the impressed Superpersons who now made a respectful supercircle around him, we were great ones for fair play. If only the same could be said for our neighbours! I speak now without inhibition, for I am, in the literal meaning of the term, a has-been. As a minority ourselves, we felt close to all other minorities, whereas everyone else seemed to be down on them. Our brothers in America refused to drink Californian wines because of the exploitation of the Mexicans at work in the fields there. They welcomed the blacks almost, though not quite, into the Jewish neighbourhoods of Queens and Westchester, New York. (*You* put your life-savings into an air-conditioned duplex and see how *you* would feel as you watched its value deflate.)

In Britain too we Jews fought hard for the rights of oppressed peoples. We pioneered the enrolment of Philippino girls as au pairs in St John's Wood. In my young days – those good old days – we would turn up en masse at demonstrations for the release of fighters for freedom incarcerated in some colonial prison, not to mention Sacco and Vanzetti. Swarming over the East End of London, a copy of the *Daily Worker* in one hand (it had a useful list of weekend dances in aid of good causes in their Saturday 'What's on' column) and the latest Upton Sinclair novel in the other, it was self-evident to us that all men were born equal. But the message had somehow not penetrated to the rest of the world, and so we were for revolution heart and soul.

Man, like Superman, does not live by bread alone, Chaim pointed out, and in my time our native genius enriched literature, the cinema, the theatre. We had a lord of our own, a particularly good man, who reminded us of this whenever he came to address one of our tribal meets. Strange that his praise for our great contribution only appeared in the *Jewish Chronicle*, to be read by those who were already persuaded. I don't recall his having alluded to this aspect of our character in the national papers, where the ignorant could be informed. Perhaps our lord had great difficulty in getting any statement of his published in the national Press. I trust the good man is awaiting a suitable opportunity to raise the subject in the Upper Chamber.

It may well be that his Jewish trait of modesty prevented his proclaiming all this to the outside world. In our humble way we often eschewed collective glory, as by revising our names. Hence the many Einsteins among us who had very little to do with the theory of relativity would take the precaution of becoming something else, like In stones. Conversely our Wingates would hasten to deny, if asked, any relationship with the hero who founded the Palmach and led the Chindits. We had Kayes and Conways by the hundred, all branches of that great creative trunk the Cohen family, but they never dreamed of vaunting it. Doubtless they took the view, laid down by our forefathers and enshrined in our tolerant religion, that being born a Cohen was enough, there was no need to wear the label on one's sleeve.

Ah yes, our religion. No dogma, no superstition. No sterile rituals. Brotherhood all round. If it was more difficult for Mr Cohen's prospective daughter-in-law Miss O'Connell to convert to the Jewish religion than it was for a Sikh to enter Potters Bar Golf Club, well, there was valid reason. It was because we wished to conserve our purity – no, what am I saying, God forbid! Chaim Superman corrected himself. I'll put that another way: if it was difficult for outsiders to embrace our religion it was because we wished to ensure that each and every convert would keep its tenets as faithfully as we did ourselves, and not join for reasons of convenience, or merely to ensure that their children, poor bastards, would not be classified as *mamzerim* should they desire to emigrate to Israel. In that country religious tolerance was enforced by the Cabinet, I might say with an iron hand.

Education? We were mad about it, and so we coaxed and pressed and changed names and amended the list of Jewish holy-days and banged our fists against the doors of the very best schools until the headmasters of St Paul's and Haberdashers and Harrow (not necessarily in that order) eventually opened up and let our little ones in, under or over their quotas, secret or otherwise. We would drive our children across London every day, and even into the country, to be sure that they were ensconced fresh in the class-room, not worn out in advance from a laborious journey by train.

It was all to achieve the finest possible general education for our children. Now *Jewish* education was something else. The only requirement we insisted upon in the Hebrew Sunday School was that it shouldn't be too far away. We weren't too inquisitive about their head-teachers, who rarely saw us, and in any case we couldn't really tell whether our kids learnt anything or not. We ourselves had attended a similar Sunday school in our youth, when it went by the olde worlde name *Cheder*, and where we learnt little and remembered less. No harm befell us in consequence. Funny places, Hebrew schools, said Chaim with a twinkle, they were always complaining about not having enough qualified teachers. But where do you learn this kind of stuff and still remain a teacher?

We had rabbinical colleges too, yet they seemed to produce anything but rabbis. I am not a bit surprised that so many university dons and distinguished jurists were stumped when they had to recite a brief prayer in Hebrew, even at a funeral. After all, they could reel off complete epics in Latin and Anglo-Saxon, and deliver unerringly on subjects like Gnosticism and the Albigensian heresy. Mortal men cannot know everything.

Now, announced Chaim as the others reached for the door-handles of their spacecraft, a few concluding thoughts on the burning topic of the Intellectual and his Jewish Identity . . . *Chugger-plunk, chugger-plunk, chugger-plunk.* What's this, all disappeared in their spaceships? There we are, even here in the Outer Void! Anti-semitism again.

ASPECTS OF ISRAEL

The Arab Image in Israeli Fiction

J. B. SEGAL

I have had the good fortune, by accident rather than by design, to spend a prolonged period in the Yishuv at the beginning of each decade between 1931 and 1971. On each occasion the advance of the Hebrew language has been a source of wonder and delight. But it is particularly during the past ten years that, to my mind, Israeli Hebrew has taken breathless strides forward. One could scarcely have foreseen the malleability and the buoyancy of the language today – while it has lost little of the rich music of the Bible. The spectacular expansion of vocabulary is most evident, of course, in the new terminology needed for the sophisticated processes of twentieth-century living, from soapsuds to space travel. Words have been coined with wit and easy ingenuity. More remarkable are the subtle turns of phrase, the nuances and idioms of a society that is Western in outlook and Oriental in speech. And the development has come about with such apparent naturalness that I doubt if the average Israeli realizes how rapidly his linguistic apparatus has grown.

Nowhere is this range of language shown in fuller play than in works of fiction. They are of a variety and adroitness that would have been inconceivable a generation ago; they reproduce the vibrations of this strangely self-assured, self-critical community.

Among novels of the past few years we have had the ebullience of Bartov's *Whose Child are you?* with its inimitable gallery of country folk; the studied sarcasm of Shamir's *The Border*, reminiscent of Evelyn Waugh at his most caustic; the whimsical skill of Aharon Megged's *The Living on the Dead*; the fine closing volume of a trilogy (*The Life of Eliakum*) by Tammuz; the introspection of Oz's *My Michael*; Orpaz's *Daniel's Trials*; the fastidious word-patterns of A. B. Yehoshua and Appelfeld. I have compiled the list at random and obviously it is incomplete, for it does not include the names of Burla and Hazaz, of Yizhar, Kovner, Amir, Shaham and many more.

Omitted, too, is the illustrious name of Agnon, the Grand Old Man of Hebrew letters, whose last two works have appeared posthumously. Agnon's strength lay in his familiarity with Jewish tradition. His style, like many of his characters, belonged to a past that has become archaic – and embarrassing, almost distasteful, to many Israelis – the townships and villages of pre-war Europe transferred to the Yishuv, Jews with the mentality of the ghetto. True, he represented continuity and reaffirmed the links of Israel with the Diaspora. But while Agnon may not have been regarded by Israelis with affectionate respect, he has found virtually no imitators among Hebrew novelists. They prefer freedom from nostalgic memories that, to them, have the smell of helpless tragedy.

In most countries the danger of parochialism is held in check by intercourse with foreign neighbours. Here Israel's position is peculiar. Geographically she is situated in a region occupied principally by Muslims, but her access to the adjacent Arab states is barred. The difficulty, however, is apparent rather than real. Israeli Jews are today in contact not only with the Israeli Arab minority but also with Arabs in the occupied territories. Whatever the political future of the area, this contact is virtually certain to continue.

How do Israeli novelists view the Arab? It is fascinating to trace the treatment of the theme at the hands of successive generations of writers. It is important, too, for this reflects with fair accuracy the attitude of Israeli Jewish society towards the Arabs. Seventy years ago many Jewish settlers in Palestine were in daily congroves and on the farms, in contrast to the Socialist *kibbutzim* based solely on Jewish labour. Both situations are represented (as

Bartov pointed out to me) in Hebrew literature of the time. The stories of Mosheh Smilansky (born 1874) have a mawkish, paternalistic flavour, not far removed from the writings of white settlers in southern Africa or the plantation-owners in the deep south of the United States. Smilansky observes with kindly sympathy the emotional stresses of the poor Arab villager, of the Negro freed-slave, of the old man who pines away because his Ottoman flint-lock failed to kill the jackals. Like Smilansky, Bar-Adon (born 1907) and Burla (born 1886), who served as interpreter in the Turkish army in the 1914–18 war, and Shami (born 1889) write of the Bedouins rather as Fennimore Cooper wrote of the Red Indians – of the hardships of their life, of their rigid moral conventions. Only Mosheh Stavi (born 1884) describes with insight the customs of Arab villagers.

A principal exponent of the other, left-wing school was Brenner (born 1881). For him, as for Smilansky, the Bedouins (who 'make their camels kneel, as did Abraham's servant in his day'!) have a remote fascination. Like Smilansky, too, Brenner implicitly subscribes to the folksy hypothesis that the Arabs are brothers, or at least cousins, of the Jews – and why should fellow-Semites quarrel? Less romantic, if not more practical, than Smilansky, Brenner believed passionately in the doctrines of social equality and the dignity of labour. It was there, he felt obscurely, that lay the key to mutual understanding between Jew and Arab – not, he urged in an essay published after his death, by playing politics, but by discharging the 'sacred duty' of cultivating the Arabs and their language.

> 'A few steps further... there jumped out behind me from one of the groves an Arab –... a young workman about 13 or 14 years old. He asked me something in a ringing, rather clamorous voice but with clear, precise enunciation. To my regret I could not answer him because I had not taught myself to speak Arabic. I then put a question to him in a single word, "From Sulaima?" (that is, are you from the nearby village Sulaima?). He answered me, "No, from Nathan", that is, he was from the orange plantation here, and he went on speaking. Then I asked him with a gesture of the finger, "Effendi?", that is, does this plantation from which you are coming and where, one may assume from your words, you work, belong to that effendi sitting there at the entrance to his courtyard? He replied in the affirmative and went on to tell at length and quite naturally that he, the boy, had not father or mother, they had died during the war years, he was an orphan... This I understood from stray

words of his, and even more from his gestures and grimaces. He also understood my question, "*Qadesh?*", that is, how much did he receive for a day's work? He answered ... "*Tamanya grush*", that is, eight piastres. "Not good," I said. For a moment he was surprised and could not understand what I meant by "Not good", far too little or too much. Then he explained to me at length and with great emphasis that some receive 15 piastres a day and even 20 ... adult workers ... and he had little sisters ... and one must eat, make a living ... and he gets eight ... everything is from Allah.

At the moment I blamed myself for the serious fault of not teaching myself Arabic. Here was ... an orphan worker ... a young brother! Whether the theory of the scholars is right or not, whether you are related to me by blood or not, in any case responsibility for you rests on me. It was for me to enlighten you, to let you taste human relations. No, not making a revolution in the East on the spur of the moment at the order of some Committee or on the instructions of the representatives of some Socialist political movement. No, not politics. Perhaps it is not this that is specifically our task, and perhaps indeed it is in spite of ourselves that we are engaged in it, from despair, because there is no alternative. No, not this! But contact between people ... from today ... and through generations ... for many days ... and without any precise objective ... without any deliberate aim except that of a brother, a friend and a comrade ...

"Goodbye, sir." The lad withdrew from me swiftly, seeing apparently that I was troubled and the conversation was over. But in his parting greeting one could see all the same his great satisfaction that he had been able to engage unexpectedly in a worth-while conversation with an adult, and to speak with as much good sense as an old man used to these occasions.

"Goodbye, my friend," I whispered and I pondered on about him and me. I continued my wandering in the darkness of the evening.'[1]

But on the most sensitive and influential section of the Arab population, the Muslim *effendiyah* of the cities, Hebrew writers of this period are silent. But we have a disparaging account by Yerushalmi (born 1900) of a self-indulgent Hebron youth:

'When Jamil (a member of one of the families who were hereditary guardians of the Cave of Machpelah) grew up the influence on him of the capital was strong, and it could be discerned in all his ways and habits; together with the French language, the son of the sheikh acquired also European dress and all the other habits of the Franks. Through efforts from above, Jamil was accepted as a dragoman in one of the important consulates at Jerusalem, and by this means he had an opportunity to frequent European society; and he was also greatly exalted in the eyes of his acquaintances who from this time appended the title Effendi to his personal name. His outward appearance was very pleasant and engaging; his dark oval face was always well shaved, his moustache trimmed and well curled; over his high forehead fell a gleaming black lock, always smeared with oil and perfume and pressed in a sensuous manner to his head under the edge of his *tarbush*. When he returned to Hebron for the festivals and holidays he used to boast in front of friends of his own age that he had already succeeded in seducing several fair daughters of the Franks, and particularly the youngest and most innocent.'[2]

Jamil pursued the daughter of a Haham of Hebron whom he had placed in his debt; it was only with luck and in the nick of time that she escaped his lascivious embraces in the dark streets of the ghetto. And Barash (born 1889) writes of an Arab woman with a veneer of education:

'She spoke German almost faultlessly. From her childhood she had been a servant and had been brought up in a family of "Templars"; and she had even been a pupil for one and a half years in their school in the Colony. When she grew up she married an Arab from Nazareth who did not know even a word of German. And then she returned to her place of origin. Her five children were also Arab children in all things; the soiled shirts, the locks of hair, even the chronic eye ailments were not missing. She scarcely went to the German Colony; her husband forbade her to go there.
The main business (in the shop) was in her hands . . . The Jews used to buy from her with pleasure, because they could speak to her in a "human" language.'

But when she is angry with her brother she pursues him brandishing a melon knife and screaming 'Let me kill him!'

'When I related the incident to the wife of my friend the writer, she said, "And so what? Don't Jewish women quarrel with their brothers? Obviously he had made her very angry."
"Yes, but the knife? And these (screams of) 'Murder'?"
"'Murder!' I tell you, if only there were more like her among us (Jews)!"'[3]

The evaporation of British authority in the Middle East was in no small measure the result of lack of sympathy with the Arab intelligentsia. The Jews were to pay no less a price for their neglect of the culture and traditions of educated Arabs.

The withdrawal of the Turks from Palestine and the thirty years of British Mandate – the 'interlude', as Israelis call it – did nothing to draw Jews and Arabs together. The political ferment of those days and the shadow of Nazism gave Jews little time or inclination for a direct – far less a sympathetic – approach to their Arab neighbours.

This gulf is also reflected in the Hebrew literature of the period. Even human relations cannot withstand political pressures. A volume of extracts from Hebrew prose on Arab themes edited by Yosef Arikha includes two charming stories of love between a Jew and an Arab girl. In one, by Burla, the daughter of a *fellah* from Silwan is willing even to accept Judaism and to become the junior wife of her Jewish lover. In the other, Shalom (born 1905) tells of the love of the teacher of the *moshavah* for Lina, the plump little daughter of a village sheikh who works in the office. Her lips and her eyes are always laughing.

> 'Lina always speaks Hebrew. All the Arab girls in the *moshavah* speak Hebrew. And when they are aware that (the teacher) is near them they raise their voices, and are careful about the purity of their language in order to display the depth of their knowledge.'

Lina is to be married to a fellow-villager. 'I shall teach him to be like you,' she says to her Jewish friend. For marriage between the Jew and the Arab girl, the story declares sadly, is out of the question. They could not live together in Palestine, and a Jewish teacher would not forge papers to take them abroad. They were caught in the snare that lay between their two peoples.

> 'A wall is beginning to divide us, an ancient wall standing in an obscure place and worn away in a remote corner of Jerusalem, the holy city; (this Western Wall) entangles bloodshed with bloodshed, it sows the seed of hatred between us, it beats ploughshares into swords, kindles fire in the tents of the tranquil, and still its hand is stretched out, stretched out.'[4]

The stress of this period affected everyone. In his *Golden Dunes*, Tammuz (born 1919) describes an encounter between the child who had run away from home and an Arab.

> He must have dozed, because he found himself waking to the voice of a man singing to himself and striding up behind him. It was an Arab. His stick was upon his shoulders, and the skirts of his dress were rustling and rolled back. The Arab came close to one of the goats and scratched its back affectionately.
> 'Yours?' asked the Arab.

'No,' answered the child and laughed.

A feeling of gratitude for the Arab welled up inside him, because he had spoken to him and treated him like a grown-up and had assumed that he owned cattle.

'Whose are they?' asked the Arab.

But before he could answer, a sound of anger was heard from the direction of the twins' house, and a bearded man came out from the shadow of the veranda and stood near the fence. The Arab left the goat and went on his way with rapid strides. The man with the beard looked at the child as though he did not know whether to leave him to go away or to drive him away.[5]

However, in his admirable description of Arabs and Jews meeting casually in the train, even the sanity and humour of Tammuz are not proof against the bitterness of the times. Jews and Arabs exchange cigarettes and unite in cursing the British.

'But this united front is suspended over an abyss. Both peoples know that once every seven years or so incidents will break out; on the border of Jaffa a Jewish carter will suddenly be slaughtered and in distant Hebron a mother will be raped in front of her daughters, and a house will be set on fire over the heads of its occupants, and the English will proclaim a curfew and arrest Jews for carrying arms without a permit.'[6]

Shamir (born 1920) tells, with the expertise of a Somerset Maugham, of the killing of an old Jewish farmer by the Muslim bailiff, half-Negro and half-Circassian, whom he had dismissed under pressure from his Jewish neighbours. Steinberg (born 1874) has a picture of an elemental, symbolic figure of an Arab watchman with beetling hatred of the Jewish settlers.

I strode forward . . . I felt fine. I took hold of everything afresh, my motherland and the night. My eyes looked ahead, towards the mists that raced diagonally across the expanse of the universe. They seemed, these living mists, like desires that had taken shape . . . And suddenly for a moment I curbed myself. I encountered the (primeval) Foundation stone. The form of the old man, emerging from the paleness of the thin mists, seemed extended across (my path) . . . I could not loiter, so I made my way around the stone . . . And suddenly his staff struck . . . I stopped walking and I saw the old man straighten himself in a trice, angrily. He moved, his coat in disarray, took a few steps towards me, and stopped; his staff began striking the earth with great rapidity, and for a moment a torrent of snorting . . . spilt out from the watchman's throat in my direction. I knew that he was cursing me, but I stood there without moving. Suddenly he rolled up the skirts of his coat over his body and began to go towards the hill of sand. I looked at him trembling with both astonishment and understanding. The understanding that comes at times with the swiftness of lightning when the enigma of events is too great passed over me in a rush as the Haj gradually disappeared in the mist. I knew that he, like me, wanted to take hold of the motherland afresh. I pressed upon him, night, night; I filled the air with strange longings. He could muster no strength; now he was fleeing, his form whirling, wrapped in the mists, now he appeared hunched up on the sloping hill; he seemed to go down to the depths of the earth, only his dog emitted in my direction a muffled bark.[7]

With the withdrawal of the British and the declaration of the Jewish State the picture changes dramatically. 1948 and the years immediately following are notable for Hebrew fiction expressing a hatred of war as deep-seated as any in the West. Yizhar (born 1916), Tammuz, Orpaz (born 1923), Koren and others exposed its indiscriminate cruelty with skill and savage wit – and with courage at a time when tempers ran high. Yizhar portrays brilliantly the evacuation of an Arab village; he contrasts the sullen fury or the resignation of the villagers with the reactions of the Jewish troops, some dismayed at the inhuman demands of victory, others indifferent, others contemptuous of an ineffective enemy. ('No one asked [the Arabs] to start this war . . . ; let them eat what they have cooked.') Orpaz has a simply-told narrative of a soldier who, almost by accident, had captured an Arab armed with an old Turkish rifle. As he conducts him to the H.Q. for interrogation, the soldier grows attached to his prisoner. Both, he discovers, had lost their girl-friends to other men.

> After all, what is the difference (between him and us)? Probably it is that you think for yourself and raise objections. He comes to terms and submits and believes that everything is from Allah. If they would stand on his feet, and lift up his head, straighten his back, and slap him on the shoulder and call him *haver*, possibly he too would begin to think for himself (like one of us) . . . Suddenly you realize that there is another difference between you and him. You have hope. As long as you are established on your soil, you nourish your hope. What is his hope? . . .

But the end is sudden tragedy.

> 'The Arab?' asked Shmulik.
> 'He is there,' pointed Musik. 'Died on the spot.'
> 'I told you to bring him here and not to finish him off.'

'Who finished him off? You told me to bring the prisoner. So I prodded him to go. Yankele came with the rifle. The prisoner took fright, and began to run away. Yankele fired at him. That is all. So what is the tragedy? . . .'

. . . In the car in front of us were lads singing. 'We have brought you peace.' And I was looking at the ground in which was buried my friend Ibrahim.[8]

Tammuz recounts a tale in similar vein. As a boy the narrator had stayed with his mother in an Arab house in the country. He had raced against an Arab in the pool and had been beaten. Years later he finds himself with Israeli troops attacking the same house. Among the Arabs who surrender is his friend of the swimming race, and before the Arab is led away with the prisoners he challenges him to try to beat him in another contest in the pool. But soon afterwards he hears a shot.

> The officer shouted, 'Who fired, in the name of the devil?'
> One of the lads shouted, 'One of my bullets slipped out.'
> The officer saw me approach and said, 'Hell, we have lost (our source of) information. They have killed your Arab.'
> 'We have lost,' I said.
> And then I went up to the body of 'Abd al-Karim and turned it over . . . His face was not that of a man who had lost.
> Here in the yard, I – yes, all of us – had been beaten (in our hour of triumph).[9]

In these stories the theme is war rather than the Arabs. There are semi-political allegories by Koren and Yehoshua. But there is little attempt to enter into the feelings or the motives of Arabs. Aharon Megged (born 1920) has an exciting description of an Arab returning to his former village furtively by night to recover a cache of money; the story is marred by waspish and unpleasant innuendo. There are fleeting glimpses of Arabs in, for example, Shamir's *The Border*, with its portrait of the Jordanian representative on the Truce Commission. He was a villager who had made his way up by his own talent and energy.

> A young Arab, clever and also cultured and, what is most important, able to distinguish between what is primary and what is secondary . . . He had been a boy in his village when the refugees came streaming from the *Shephelah*: he had scarcely reached manhood when the talk against the Jews became, as though casually, talk against Israel, and he

was conscripted into the National Guard in the difficult days when the Israelis replied to the destruction of houses with the destruction of villages and to the killing of single persons with the killing of tens of people. But none of these things was as challenging, as inflaming of hatred, as the lights of the young state below at night, decking itself out, blossoming, winking, full of enticing secrets, and showing contempt for those who looked at it from above by the very insolence of throwing its light towards them.[10]

Two full-length novels revolve around personal relationships between Arab and Jew. Hemda Allon's (born 1925) delightfully impulsive Jewish heroine falls in love with an Arab fellow-student. He is later arrested for helping his brother, the member of an espionage network, to escape from Israel, and with tact and affection releases the girl from her attachment to him. This is a fine work: its excellently drawn characterizations of Jews and Arabs reflect the tensions of traditions and conventions that separate their two societies. Less convincing is a novel by Miriam Schwarz in which a Jewish girl is rejected by her *kibbutz* because the father of her unborn child is both Arab and Communist and melodramatically she meets her death on Yom Kippur.

When one considers the swift efflorescence of Hebrew fiction after 1948, the number of works in which Arabs appear is meagre in the extreme. Nor has there been much change since the events of 1967. Arabs emerge briefly again against the background of war. The emotions described in that remarkable chronicle of reactions of *kibbutzniks* to the 1967 crisis, *The Seventh Day* – unhappily fact, not fiction – are echoed in Tischler's *Last to hold the Ridge*.

> Refugees. We came across them in the morning . . . A sight that you struggle to push away, but it floats up and pierces you. The sight was familiar to me and my friends from history lessons, from the writings of Jewish authors, from the pictures of Jewish artists.
> This time they were not Jews. They were Arabs, Arabs in their thousands. All the street was full of Arabs – with their families and their suitcases and their parcels tied in sheets, in *kefiyas*, in *abayas*.
> We were told that at dawn the Arab notables had announced the intention of the inhabitants to evacuate the city. The operational command agreed to an orderly evacuation. The inhabitants were ordered to tie up their bundles in haste. All the inhabitants of Lod were gathered in the great mosque and the square around it.

'Have they all left their houses?' we asked a soldier...
'All of them,' he said with a smile. 'They gathered like sheep.'[11]

Characteristic is the hatred of killing. In a novel by Orpaz, his hero, returned from the war, is haunted by the memory of a corpse lying in the sand.

> 'Look,' said Daniel, 'it isn't because I'd never seen a dead man at all before, or that it was all sudden and the first dead man that I saw was my own dead man whom I had killed. It isn't that, it's not only that — how can I explain it to you? It also isn't at all important whether he was an Arab or a Jew or a Hottentot, not that that isn't important, but in this case somehow or other this really isn't important... Look, he was wearing a sort of white trousers and a light khaki shirt, and that suited the sea shore and lying in the sand, and he lay in the sand on his back, one hand under his head and the other at his side, in absolute rest. He seemed to be resting or dreaming or sleeping. Don't laugh at me, but he lay there just like you or me.'[12]

And where fiction describes the years of peace there is little place for Arabs. Bartov's vivid account of life in a *moshavah* as seen through the eyes of a child has few allusions to Arabs – and these are, for the most part, associated with heat, dirt and flies.

It would, I think, be over-subtle to ascribe the absence of the Arab in Israeli Hebrew fiction to some guilt-motif; Israeli writers have not, on the whole, been reluctant to touch on a topic because it may be embarrassing or disagreeable. Indeed, Oz's *My Michael*, the analysis of a middle-class intellectual couple of Jerusalem, provoked considerable controversy with its reflection of the traumatic role of the Arab in Israeli Jewish emotions. Across the curtain of the heroine's subconscious appear the figures of Arab twins who had been her childhood playmates. Now their father is a refugee, their villa a Government clinic; and they appear and reappear in her nightmares as commandos with whips and handgrenades.

A thoughtful and well-documented survey of the attitude towards the 'Arab problem' in Israeli children's books up to 1967 was presented by Menahem Regev a few years ago (*Akhshav xxiv*, 1968, 209). In this type of literature, Regev concludes, the Arab is frequently – though not by any means always – the 'baddy'. Invariably the writers know Arabs only at secondhand. Their descriptions follow a stereotyped pattern; they write of villagers or

Bedouins; they portray colourful clothing and marriage practices that have a simple exotic appeal. Their work is not the result of understanding or research.

Ignorance of Arabs and of Arab traditions is not confined to authors of children's books or of Hebrew fiction in general. But these, as is so often the case among prose writers, reflect an attitude common to the bulk of their public. The Arab areas under Israeli occupation are, with the exception of East Jerusalem and certain tourist centres, unfamiliar to most Israeli Jews – and so are their inhabitants. It would be surprising if this were not so. Terrorist activities do, after all, still occur. Refugees and refugee camps seem to belong to another world – although Gaza is at walking distance from the Israeli frontier and only some eighty kilometres from Tel Aviv itself. More serious is the extent to which many Jews are strangers in the Arab enclaves that Israel has administered for nearly a quarter of a century; some Jews would feel more at home in a foreign country than in their Arab neighbourhood.

The attitude of almost neurotic suspicion of Arabs, the product of the blind course of history, cannot be removed by the wave of a wand – or by governmental decree. But there is one field in which a partial remedy may be sought, the field of language – and here writers certainly have a role to play. Many of the early Jewish settlers of Palestine learned Arabic to talk to their Arab employees. Members of the *kibbutzim* were, like Brenner, aware of the need for a cultural rapprochement with the Arabs. But the urgency of the revitalization of Hebrew left little time for Arabic. A generation grew up to whom the study of Arabic seemed almost irrelevant.

In a charming description of life in a *moshavah* at this time, Hedda Bosem writes of her childhood:

> We were invited to a wedding feast in the village. The great copper bowls, which were used for washing in the yard, were full of food. The horses' hides were glistening with sweat, and they tramped with their hooves. My father spoke to all of them in Arabic with a pronounced Russian accent. My mother thanked them for the food, standing to one side and not touching anything. She said that what they ate was dirty. The children shouted and laughed. I stood by myself.
> ... On the boundary of the *moshavah*, on the Third Hill ... lived a tribe of watchmen. One Shabbat we went to visit them, the yellow dogs

barked and circled around us angrily, and Amer came to meet us on the slope of the hill, tall and thin, his moustache black and shining ... Beside the tents a fire was burning, and on it stood a black, steaming pot ...

My father spoke to them and they laughed. The children gathered around the tent and looked at us with great inquisitive eyes. I did not go out to play with them. The smell of the *tabuns* and the smell of the spices hung in the air. It hangs to this day in the new white *skikkunim* that have been built on the Third Hill; ... only the yellow dogs seem to have died in the course of time.

Later, tensions grew more urgent.

> Yusuf came to see my father. They sat on the wooden bench beside the house and talked and talked.
> Yusuf was already an old man, and he had authority over the Third Hill and over the watchmen ... Now he sat and spoke in a whisper to my father while the white mare tethered to the eucalyptus tree tramped with its hooves and made whinnying noises. In the *moshavah* they said that soon there would be trouble, and that Yusuf did not love the people who lived in the village. My father entered the room and said that they would be loyal to us, and when I asked to whom he made no answer.
> ... In the *moshavah* they began to build the main roads and the newspapers appeared with black borders. At night they went out on guard, and many orange groves were cut down and nails were scattered on the roads. On the streets of the *moshavah* was heard only the sound of the steam-rollers and there was a sad silence. The sellers of vegetables and eggs disappeared ...
> ... I came back in the holidays. The (Arab) housemaid hugged me and expressed surprise at how I had grown, and went on washing the many dishes in the sink. I wanted to tell her about everything that had happened ... but I could not speak Arabic ... Ahmed had disappeared, and in his place Fawzi worked in the yard. He spoke fluent Hebrew, curled his moustache, and did not love us.[13]

True, on the establishment of the State, Arabic was declared one of the official languages of Israel. Israeli schoolchildren are required to learn some Arabic in the lower classes. Most, however, abandon Arabic in favour of other subjects of the syllabus before they have made much progress in the language. Nor has the influx of Jewish immigrants from countries of the Middle East produced a wider knowledge of Arabic. Among them are a number of young intellectuals who have made a notable contribution to Orientalist studies in Israel. But the vast majority of these newcomers have little affection for the official speech of the Muslim authorities under whom they had once lived as a tolerated minority.

The need for the study of Arabic by anyone living in the Middle East is self-evident. It is demanded by the political facts of life. To Jews the use of Hebrew is an article of faith. But for Arabs a no less powerful function is exercised by Arabic. They are more surely a linguistic than an ethnic or a religious entity. They are united by pride in their speech and in their literature; in these are enshrined their achievements over thirteen centuries. One cannot understand Arabs without understanding Arabic.

Without understanding among Arabs and Jews of the traditions and the points of view of both groups, not even a formal peace treaty, countersigned by the Great Powers and all the member states of U.N.O., will be worth much. With it, the cultural renaissance of the peoples may well inspire the moral and physical regeneration of the whole region. In this, Hebrew novelists, who can direct as well as mirror the ideas of their contemporaries, can act with vision.

1973

1 Y. H. Brenner, *'Mi-pinqas'* (pub. 1922), *Collected Works*, 1958.
2 N. Yerushalmi, cited in Y. Arikha, *Sippurim 'ivriyim mi-hayye ha-'Aravim*, 1963, 151.
3 A. Barash, *'Shafiye ha-notzriyah'*, *Works* ii, 1952.
4 S. Shalom, cited in Arikha, *op. cit.*, 207.
5 B. Tammuz, *Holot ha-zahav*, 1967.
6 Tammuz, *Sippur Anton ha-Armeni*, 1964, 113ff.
7 Y. Steinberg, cited in Arikha, *op. cit.*, 113.
8 Y. Orpaz, cited in Arikha, *op. cit.*, 336.
9 Tammuz, *'Taharut sehiyah'*, *Sippur Anton ha-Armeni*, 31.
10 M. Shamir, *Ha-gevul*, ch. 6 ii, 8v, 1967.
11 Y. Tishler, *Aharonim 'al ha-rekhes*, ch. 16, 1970.
12 Y. Orpaz, *Massa' Daniel*, ch. 5, 1969.
13 H. Bosem, cited in Arikha, *op. cit.*, 348.

The Israeli Image in Arab Literature

SHIMON BALLAS

Dr Shimon Ballas was born in 1930 in Baghdad where he received his education. At an early age he began writing stories and literary criticism in Arabic and, after emigrating with his family to Israel in 1951, continued writing in Arabic and contributed to the Arabic press in Israel. He wrote his first novel in Hebrew in 1964 and published an Anthology of Hebrew translations from the works of Arab-Palestinian writers. At present he teaches Arabic literature at the Haifa University.

Forerunners of the literature of conflict, the Palestinian writers were the first to introduce the Israeli character in the Arab novel and short story. At first the Israeli was seen not as an individual but just as belonging to the mass of the enemy army and his behaviour towards the Palestinian civilians only served to stress the brutality of the oppressor. At a later stage he was indeed fused into the stream of the story yet without being individualized. Thus he still is a superficial and hostile being, the very incarnation of the enemy. The third stage presents a slightly more individualized Israeli who stands out by his character and his milieu. Yet, he almost invariably remains a soldier.

The novel of Ghassan Kanafani, *What You're Left With*,[1] is the most striking example of this attitude. The drama that is taking place in the desert between an Israeli soldier and a young

Palestinian stems not only from the conflict between the two nations, but from a mutual misunderstanding as well.

Hamid is running away from his miserable life in the Gaza refugee camp to join his mother in Jordan. On his way through the desert he encounters an Israeli soldier. In the darkness of the night, the soldier walks towards him without noticing him. Hamid catches him unawares, throws him to the ground and seizes his machine gun and his bayonet. The soldier thinking a friend is playing a joke on him, shows no resistance; he only shouts and curses. He realizes his situation only when Hamid orders him in Arabic to shut up. At this point, the drama takes on a new aspect. The two foes who can neither see nor understand each other try to peer through the darkness, and wonder how they can possibly escape the absurdity of such a situation. The soldier has become a prisoner and the fugitive can knock him down at any moment. However Hamid has second thoughts about killing him and running away, for he is afraid of falling into the hands of the Israelis; yet he tries to wring out of him some information about the way and to get to know his name at least, but in vain; there is no way to communicate. The silence of the desert night wraps them up in deep anguish, and Hamid realizes that he has become prisoner of his own situation. He has reached a deadlock, everything seems blurred; he derives no advantage from his superiority; both he and the soldier are victims of their own fate.

Dawn scatters the stifling darkness yet without scattering the gloomy misunderstanding which separates the two antagonists. On the contrary, under the biting heat of the sun, Hamid's anguish keeps growing; he is aware that the drama will have to unfold in full daylight. He searches the soldier's papers, tries hard to decipher his name but can only make out the word 'Jaffa' stamped in Latin characters. Jaffa is the town where he was born. Once more he tries to speak to the soldier, but the latter is deaf to his entreaties though Hamid has a feeling that he understands his words. Hatred gnaws at his heart. Now he is ready to knock him down. As he hears voices and sounds of barking coming close he makes up his mind and thrusts the bayonet into the soldier's heart.

Kanafani has based this novel as well as his earlier one, *Back To Haifa*,[2] on the idea of the deadlock, namely that hostility and lack of understanding can only result in tragedy. Yet, more than the language barrier, it is the very silence of the soldier that nipped in the bud any attempt to reach a mutual understanding. This silence seems indeed exaggerated!

In *Back To Haifa* the deadlock does not stem from the lack of communication. The father, filled with disappointment and indignation during his visit, comes to the conclusion that the conflict can only be settled at the point of the gun. Once more Kanafani expresses this deadlock, by presenting the Israeli in uniform. Dov, a foundling, was brought up by an Israeli family since he was five months old. He has every reason for being different from his adoptive parents, yet the writer did not even think of presenting him as a student or just a worker. Besides, we are told that his adoptive father was killed at the front in the 1956 War.

Kanafani is not the only one to nurture the prejudice that Israeli society is a military society with whom no agreement is possible. Thus the Israeli is not only a stranger, but a being who must be killed wherever he might be. This is what emerges from the short story of Yusuf Jad a-Haqq, *If I Had Killed Him*.[3] At London airport the narrator meets a man for whom he feels an immediate aversion, yet out of sheer politeness he offers to listen to him. The stranger tells him about his adventures during World War II while he was fighting with the British Army. The narrator listens with indifference, eager only to get rid of him in order to resume the reading of his novel. When the loudspeaker announces the plane for Tel-Aviv, the stranger picks up his suitcase and holds out his hand to him. Dumbfounded, the narrator looks at him with hatred and does not move. Then the stranger gets the point and goes away. The narrator sums up the episode thus:

'If I had killed him what would have happened? What would have happened does not really matter, what matters is to give vent to the hatred of a nation on the odious representative of the Zionist band of usurpers. It might well have been of no consequence, yet it would have enabled me to make my voice heard to the world outside this bustle of ours, to let the world hear this voice which claims that I am living with the hope of getting my revenge.'[4]

In this short story as well as in Kanafani's two novels the purpose of the writer is to show the enemy as a stereotype and not as a character capable of developing This is a purely political technique; it seems that the enemy as a human being is of no interest to the Arab writer.

Jad a-Haqq expresses his instinctive dislike of the Israeli without even knowing his identity. On the other hand, Kanafani presents him from two different angles: both as the soldier keeping a stubborn silence up to his death, and as the soldier delivering speeches smacking of the eloquence of the media. The former is an enigma, the latter a foe incarnating hatred and disdain.

The same attitude is found in *Flower of Blood*,[5] a play by Suhayl Idris. Here the writer tries to present a somehow subtler image while still keeping within the confines of his plan which consists of showing the enemy as a stereotype. He first shows the Israelis so frightened of Arab terrorism that some of them even consider leaving the country. One of the characters, Rachel, describes this state of mind when she tells an officer: 'Their bombs explode among us, behind our homes, under our cars, in our camps. Their ghosts are turning our dreams into nightmares. Can't you see how our people go home early in the evening, how empty the streets, the cafés, the night-clubs are, how the towns and villages are deserted? My neighbour Lulu told me that she often wakes up at night with a start, feeling two hands gripping her throat.'[6]

The officer is overcome by a feeling of helplessness when faced with the recrudescence of sabotage acts. In a grotesque scene he is shown full of confusion, giving vent to his anger against the 'services'. The following dialogue develops between him and his subordinate private:

OFFICER (*getting hold of the phone*): Hello, yes, you don't say! Which ammunition store? On our side one soldier and two civilians? What about them? Only one?[7] Of course, if they go on like that... Well, thank you. (*He hangs up, muttering to himself.*) I don't understand what we got out of this lightning victory! Is the Six-Day War really over? It seems to be going on endlessly! I wonder where these devils come from?

THE PRIVATE: From their land, sir!

OFFICER (*angry*): Shut up! I haven't asked you anything!

PRIVATE (*withdrawing*): I'm sorry, sir, I thought you had asked me a question.

OFFICER (*calming down*): I see! I wonder where our army is! (*Knocking on the table.*) Where are our defence forces?
PRIVATE: Scattered all over the place, sir.
OFFICER (*starting up*): Shut up! Have I asked you anything?
PRIVATE: I'm sorry, sir. I thought you had asked me a question.
OFFICER (*resuming his monologue*): How can we face such a situation? Do we still have to live another twenty years worrying only about equipping ourselves and begging our friends to supply us with money and war material? Why can't these dogs let us live in peace?
PRIVATE: Sir...
OFFICER (*springing up and thrusting his fist under the soldier's nose*): You're going to shut up, aren't you?
PRIVATE: Excuse me, sir, I thought...
OFFICER (*imitating him*): I thought you had asked me a question. Shut up, and tear up all these reports.
(*The soldier is ready to comply.*) What are you doing you fool?
PRIVATE: I'm going to tear up the reports as you've ordered me to, sir.
OFFICER: Did I order you to do this? Did I?...

In another scene the author lets his imagination run wild: a Palestinian girl fighter is raped in the officer's office; more dialogues like the above are invented. There could be nothing further from reality: a soldier with the mentality of a peasant who keeps calling his officer 'sir' simply does not exist in the Israeli army. The relations between officers and soldiers are in fact completely different.

When the play was performed in Cairo the Egyptian critic Faruq Abd al-Qadir wrote: 'If we refuse to overestimate the role of the Resistance Organizations it is because we refuse to fool the people. Nothing is more dangerous than to infuse this soporific in the minds of the people, this pleasant dream of a victory won on paper (or on the stage), but not in reality... Once more we are faced with the hackneyed cliché: the Israeli men are pimps and their women whores.'[8]

Idris assigns to Rachel the same role she assumes in Bsiso's works.[9] On the one hand, she is her commander's mistress and on the other hand she tries to seduce the *fedayin* in order to get information. Suayman Fayyad also tells of a little act of seduction: during a raid on a kibbutz the *fedayin* comes upon a woman lying stark naked in bed, in a shelter. 'She invites him to lie with her, but he kills her on the spot. Then he finds a gun under her pillow.'[10]

The Israeli woman is also the very incarnation of the perfidy of her society, in the case of Nadya-Nathalya-Natasha in Alfred Faraj's play, *The Fire And The Olive Tree*.[11] In the play, Fathi, nicknamed Abu Sharif, who was born in Haifa, enters Israel to visit his father's grave. On his way he goes past his old house and knocks at the door hoping to find a Palestinian family. A young Israeli girl opens the door. Astounded, he is on the point of turning back when he recognizes the girl. It is Nathalya, the daughter of his old Jewish neighbour. The surprised Nathalya is very happy to see him and they speak of their childhood, in particular of the general strike during which Nathalya's father had sent her to Arab neighbours to shelter her against the possibility of anti-Jewish riots. All the while, Nathalya seems delighted to have met her childhood friend, but her attitude changes completely as she goes behind the partition to dress up before going out with him. Fathi tells her that he has no papers and she, behind the partition, apologizes for having to wear a khaki uniform. The astounded Fathi wonders if she is really a soldier while she reassures him that he is quite safe since he is with her. Yet within a few minutes she has undergone a complete metamorphosis; once she is in uniform her smiles are replaced by hostility.

Bewildered, Fathi tries to remind her of their conversation, but Nathalya's only answer is to thrust her gun under his nose and order him to put his hands up ... Then she lifts the phone and gives him away to the authorities.

A. Faraj presents the girl soldier as the most contemptible character. She is living in the house of her neighbours who had become refugees; she is disloyal and ungrateful to her friend Fathi; finally she deceitfully gives him away to the police. She is by far more devilish than the two Rachels, although she is not a whore.

Al-Sharqawi, who has tried to diversify the Israeli male characters of his play[12] has done nothing of the kind where women are concerned. He indulges in quite a number of hints about the frivolity of women in the army. He also gives details on the profanation of the holy sites, as depicted in the following scene:

SLAMSKY (*kissing girl soldier*): I remember the first time we danced together, the beginning of our love. That day I danced only with you.
GIRL SOLDIER 1: It was the day of the liberation of Jerusalem, we danced till dawn (*flirtingly*): I danced and danced... Oh! I'm so embarrassed... then we felt free to do anything!
SLAMSKY: We were so happy at the corner of the Al-Aksa mosque.
GIRL SOLDIER 1 (*flirtingly*): Please, don't talk about it, I'm so embarrassed! We'd better forget what we did behind the golden altar of the church.
SLAMSKY: I've been looking for you ever since, my dove, where can I see you? Can we make love only in Jerusalem?

In another scene taking place in an officers' mess in Tel-Aviv, the writer shows Israeli women inciting men to rape Palestinian women. The servant announces the visit of Abu Hamdan (a Bedouin working as an Israeli agent against the *fedayin*) accompanied by a young girl.

GIRL SOLDIER 1: Here I am too busy, but let's have a date in Jerusalem. When can we have it?
SLAMSKY: I'll go back to Jerusalem next week.
GIRL SOLDIER 1: Then I'll meet you at the cradle of love, in Jerusalem.[13]
SLAMSKY: Is she pretty? Show the Arab girl in!
JACOB: According to regulations we are to behave respectfully to the women even if we are the guests.
GIRL SOLDIER 1: What would our enemy have done to us if they had conquered Tel-Aviv?
GIRL SOLDIER 2: All victorious armies lay hands on the women! Have we forgotten the Allied troops in Europe?
JACOB (*to servant*): Show the old man and his daughter in.
GIRL SOLDIER 2 (*going on*): I was fifteen then.[14]
GIRL SOLDIER 1: They didn't force you, did they?
SLAMSKY (*laughing*): Nor was it out of anti-semitism.

GIRL SOLDIER 1 (*sneering*): Wasn't it the first time?
GIRL SOLDIER 2 (*going on*): Yes, it was. I had nothing to eat the whole day! I did not love him but he gave me food, wine, cigarettes and a bed.
SLAMSKY: So you had a taste of happiness!
GIRL SOLDIER 2: It was war-time. But with the U.S., we ran the danger of losing all this with peace.[15]

Throughout the play, the woman is reduced to a sex object, a being incited to evil, whereas man undergoes an important development. The most notable is Marcel's. He is a Jew of French origin, who fought against the Nazis and now he has settled in Israel. On the eve of the war he joins the army as a military correspondent for a foreign daily determined to 'shake the world's indifference to his country' (p. 40). It is while fighting that he finds out how far he has been fooled. In Sinai he witnessed 'the slaughtering' of Egyptian fellahs (p. 103). He sums up thus:

'In the war I have betrayed all the values that have conferred on me my self-respect, in Sinai I disavowed my past, I have been a stranger defiling a foreign land, other people's land. I who fought in Paris against the ignoble Nazis, I have become a monster! There must be many men and women in Egypt who curse me.'[16]

The awareness of his situation shakes his belief in the future of Israel. He dares tell his friends assembled to celebrate the first anniversary of the victory that none of them has any right to live on other people's land. What then is the just solution of this drama of bloodshed? It is that all the Jews should go back to their countries of origin:

'You, Jacob, you come from France, (*to a girl soldier*) you are German, (*to another*) you come from Warsaw, you from Rumania, you from Switzerland, you from Tunisia (*goes on pointing*) you are Hungarian, Austrian, Swiss, Finnish, Australian, Canadian, Australian, Colombian; you are Mexican if I am not wrong, you are Dutch and you Italian, you also come from Rome, don't you? You are from Berlin and you immigrated to London, you are English and you American and you, where are you from?
GIRL SOLDIER 3: From the heart of Brazil, I still keep its warmth in my heart.

MARCEL (*to an officer*):   You've also come from America (*going round them frantically*) you are from Hamburg, from Oslo, from Colombia, from Oran, from Dublin, from Geneva, you are French, Danish, American, you are German, you are from Budapest, you are Russian, Iraqi, Egyptian, Turkish, from Brussels, Prague, Athens. My God, a gang of barbaric conquerors!'[17]

Yet, in this wild gallery, in this ethnical medley, someone is conspicuous by his absence; it is the Israeli-born Jew.

Just as in the case of *Flower of Blood*, here too an Arab critic points out the partiality of the author:

'Our view of the Israelis rests on the out-dated slogans according to which all Jewish women are whores and all men fools. They make love in the yards of mosques and churches... Three out of five Israelis are shown on stage conscience-stricken at having come to Israel, a fourth (invisible) joins the Fedayin and the fifth is the very incarnation of rudeness and phoney chauvinism. How can I help asking: if the Israelis are indeed so, how did they manage to defeat us?'[18]

A. Faraj has managed to avoid this pitfall due to the quasi-documentary structure of his play. In order to create coherence he has made use of two methods: on the one hand he shows on the stage characters from political life, on the other hand he animates historical episodes by using official documents and quotations from Hebrew periodicals. Israeli leaders appear successively on the stage, each one expounding his point of view on the relations with the Palestinians. Though their presence is not connected to the episodes of the play, it serves to outline their expansionist strategy. This technique could have been effective had the author not added scenes illustrating the cruelty of the Israelis, such as soldiers obeying their commander's order ('Kill the men and undress the women'), pilots bombing centres of population, the episode between Fathi-Nathalya, etc....

However, the use of official documents and periodicals does give the play a documentary tinge. In order to show the soldiers involved in the massacre of forty-nine civilians at Kfar-Kassem in 1956, the author refers to press reports published at the time of the trial of the accused. He quotes from an article by an Israeli correspondent, Boaz Evron, condemning the operation and those responsible for it (p. 86). He also quotes another Israeli journalist,

Amos Kenan, who took a stand against the demands of the expansionists wishing to apply Israeli law in the territories occupied since June 1967. Yet it seems that the author misrepresents Kenan's sarcastic tone, for he includes him among the expansionists!

Faraj refrained from creating characters who are up against oppression, but through Boaz Evron he has brought to light a contestant standing out from the crowd (the shouts and uproar that he causes). Yet this contestant represents only a very negligible minority. As to his intervention, though it might be quite impressive it does not contribute to any change. That is why one of the aims of the *Fedayin* is 'to liberate the Jew from his aggressiveness and from Zionism and to restore his human traits.'[19]

Faraj also deals with the problem of the relations between the various communities. He draws two portraits of the Oriental Jew: on the one hand, the beggar in Jerusalem and the song of the poor deploring the power of the Ashkenazi, and on the other, the pilot who stands out by his understanding of the mentality of the Arabs and by his ties to his homeland.

As a rule the Oriental Jew is viewed sympathetically by the Arab writers: he is presented as more understanding towards the Arabs and as sceptical of the policy of the Ashkenazi leaders. Muhammad al-Hurayji grants this aspect of the problem a very peculiar importance. In his novel, *Ripe In Pink Dreams*[20] he quotes (in the form of letters) four soldiers narrating events that happened in their regiments. Whereas Ezra, of German origin, expresses his hatred of the Arabs: 'We must exterminate them all, for the best solution is that which will rid us of all the Arabs of the world,'[21] Adnan (sic), a Lebanese, and Ben Yehusha, a Moroccan, are seized by doubt, complain of their position of inferiority in the army and toy with the idea of going back to their countries of origin. However, they remain passive and bear their lot in silence.

The Iraqi writer Dhu-I-Nun goes further; he endows his Israeli characters with more precise dimensions. In his novel *Before The Crossing and After*,[22] he tells of a group of *Fedayin* who crossed the Jordan River on the Israeli side after their rebellion against King Hussein had been crushed in September 1970. He tells of an episode in which a soldier of Iraqi origin finds among the captured fugitives a man who will be his benefactor. During a clash with Israeli forces, Ismail comes upon a wounded soldier who asks him for some water. He gives him a drink of water, and, surprised by his excellent Arabic, he asks him if he is an Arab. 'Yes,' answers the Israeli Jewish soldier. In the Israeli truck he tells Ismail his story. As a militant communist in Iraq, he always considered himself an Iraqi and never thought of emigrating to Israel, but the authorities of the monarchy expelled him handcuffed.

'In Iraq we were happy until Hitler's curse reached us. Most of the Iraqi Jews became convinced that their salvation depended on emigrating to Israel, but the intellectuals among us were quite aware of what was going on. They understood that the oppression aimed at forcing the Jews to leave and therefore they chose to fight against oppression by joining the ranks of the democratic parties: the socialist party and the communist party.'[23]

Ayyub does not only quote these words which are true, he also calls his soldier Yusuf Zalkha. Yusuf Zalkha was actually one of the leaders of the communist party in the forties and one of the founders of the 'Anti-Zionist League', some of whose supporters were Jews.[24] He was arrested and some years later expelled to Israel.

At this point the author engages in mere fantasy. As the soldier tells his life-story to Ismail and his friends, he states that he never stopped considering himself an Arab and has not even learnt Hebrew. 'If all Israelis were like me, Israel would have disappeared long ago. But there are hardly a thousand people like me.'[25]

All this is supposed to be taking place in the truck driving the *Fedayin* to prison and in the presence of other Israeli soldiers. However there is still more absurdity to come: the very same Yusuf Zalkha, the private who speaks no Hebrew and feels alienated from the country, promises Ismail to arrange for him an interview with Moshe Dayan. Indeed a week later he informs him that the minister is inviting him to his home! In this imaginary interview the minister and his guest engage in a passionate discussion and drink to each other's health!

The works mentioned here have not managed to describe convincingly any real Israeli character. This is not surprising, since there is neither an Arab nor a Palestinian hero who carries conviction either.

Indeed the Israeli character has not yet found his place in contemporary Arab literature.

1. 'Ma tabaqqa lakum', dar al Tali'a (Beirut, 1966). Kanafani, born 1936 in Acco, one of the most outspoken representatives of Palestinian writers. He edited several newspapers, wrote some novels and plays. Died in July 1972 by a bomb explosion in Beirut. Was an active member of the PLO.
2. A'id ita Hayfa', dar al-Awda (Beirut, no date, 91 pages).
3. 'Laww annani qataltuhu', in 'sanaltaqi dhat yawm', dar al-Katib al-Arabi (Cairo, 1969), Yusuf Jad a-Haqq is a writer and journalist, resident in Egypt.
4. Ibid., 46.
5. 'Zahra min dam', Adab (March 1969, 7 November 1959, 1963). Suhayl Idris is a Lebanese writer. Studied in France where he received his doctorate in Arabic literature. For the last 25 years editor of 'al-Adab', one of the most important Arab periodicals.
6. Ibid., 55.
7. There are always more victims on the Israeli side.
8. 'as-Masrah', May 1969. In his answer ('al-Adab', August 1969, 66–69) Idris re-asserts his thesis and accuses the critic of provocation. We should mention that the play ran only six days. (See Muhammad Barakat in 'al-Adab', September 1969, p. 74.)
9. 'Shamshunwa-Dalila', a play in verse, al-Hay'a al-Misriyya (Cairo, 1971, 160 pages). Moyen Bsiso, born in Gaza, lives in Egypt.
10. See 'al-Insan wa-l-ard wa-l-mawt' ('al-Adab', March 1969, 14–16, 107–112). Suleiman Fayyad, an Egyptian playwright, leaning towards the nationalist Left.
11. 'Al-nar wa-l zaytun', Haya al-Misriyya (Cairo, 1970). Alfred Faraj, an Egyptian playwright, leaning towards the nationalist Left.
12. 'Watani Akka', a play in verse, Dar-al-Shuruq (Cairo, 1970). Avad al Rahman Al-Sharqavi, a noted Egyptian writer, author of novels, short stories and verse plays. His most important work, depicting village life in the twenties, was also published in an English translation, 'The Egyptan Earth' (1962).
13. Ibid., 71.
14. At the time of the play, she must be thirty-eight, which is far too old for a girl soldier...
15. Ibid., 117–118.
16. Ibid., 104.
17. Ibid., 128.
18. See Sabri Hafiz, 'al-muqawama al-filastiniyya bayn al-sathiyya wa-l-tajrid', in 'al-Adab' (June 1970, 21).
19. 'Al-Nar', opusc. cit. page 60.

20 'Tashaqquqat fil-ahlam al-wardiyya', in 'al-Majalla' (September 1971, 84–88). Muhammad al-Hurayji is a young Egyptian writer.
21 Ibid., 85.
22 'Qabl al-Ubur wa-badahu', in 'al-Adab' (December 1971, 7–12). Dhu-I-Nun, one of the older Iraqi writers, wrote novels and short stories of pronounced social content. In the 30s and 40s he belonged to the underground Communist Party, now is counted among the Nationalists.
23 Ibid., 9.
24 See W. E. Laqueur: 'Communism and Nationalism in the Middle East' (Routledge & Kegan Paul, London, 1955, pp. 335–336).
25 'Qabl al-Ubur', 9.

1977

Judaism in the Jewish State

ERWIN I. J. ROSENTHAL

What strikes the Jewish visitor from Europe so forcefully in Israel is the apparent normality and obvious naturalness of life in town and country. Outside Israel, thinking Jews must constantly prove to themselves not only that they are Jews and as such distinct and distinguishable from their fellow-citizens; they must also define in what their distinctiveness in a non-Jewish world consists. No matter how much or how little of our tradition we observe as individuals, it is precisely this tradition which is the rock of our survival as Jews in a non-Jewish world, and which bestows upon us our distinctiveness. It is our way of life which distinguishes us from our neighbours, which makes us 'different' from them, although we share with them many ideas and ideals. But this tradition must be re-assessed in the light of modern life and – and this is important – of the experience of daily life in Israel: without both a living Judaism is not possible.

On the other hand, Israelis take their Jewishness for granted. To ask them what their Judaism consists of betrays the origin of the questioner; he is a *Galuth*-Jew and his question is born in, and of, the *Galuth*. It would be the same if one asked an Englishman to define his English character. It is not a problem needing definition, not something the existence of which must be proved, defended, asserted. Many a young Israeli does not understand the question at all. He fought for the State, he works for the State, he is prepared to give his life for the State if need be, the State *is* his Judaism, or rather, the State of Israel is for him what Judaism is for the Jew in the Dispersion.[1]

For us Judaism is not only a synthesis of the religious and the national: religion permeates every sphere of Jewish life. Naturally, the young Israeli brought up on the Bible and Rabbinic literature – Talmud is taught in 'secular' schools – recognizes the religious character of that body of literature. But for him it is in the first place the literature of his people, the reflection of the national culture. The faith enshrined in the Bible can be and actually is recognized, but it has not necessarily any relevance for his own person. He can appreciate the religious fervour of the prophets, he can recognize that their whole being is devoted to God who dominates their every thought and action, and yet he does not see any compelling reason that he himself should also believe in the God of the Bible. What is relevant is the attitude of the prophets to the social problems of their generation which is seen to have a direct bearing on contemporary social life in the State of Israel. The religious origin of the teachings of the prophets is of less interest to the non-religious pupil of a secondary school than the message as such and the people of Israel to whom it is addressed. The young generation feel themselves heir and successor of this people. The Bible is to the young Israeli a living book whose pages come to life when he wanders in the Judean hills or in the Jordan valley, identifying Flora and Fauna of his country, the Land of the Bible. His daily speech is full of the language of the Bible with its rich associations of formative ideas which must impress his mind.

I am confirmed in this belief by the lively interest of the pupils, especially in the non-religious schools (co-educational), in the historical books of the Bible, for example. I listened to a discussion on the relative merits of kings David and Solomon and was impressed by the manner in which the boys and girls reacted to the teacher's suggestion that David was a good king and Solomon was a tyrant. Arguments for and against were hotly debated and when the teacher, in defence of his contention, pointed to Solomon employing slave-labour in the copper mines at Etsion Geber, as we know from Professor Nelson Glueck's excavations, one of the boys declared spontaneously that he would go into the mines, in the service of his country. 'Very well,' said the teacher, 'but you would do so voluntarily, where Solomon forced the people.' The boy thought that slave-labour was the natural thing in those days, and no proof that Solomon was a tyrant.

What matters in this connection is, I think, the relevance of past history for the present generation. Moreover, since this history is told as the unfolding of the Divine plan and man's reaction to the Divine will, this attitude, so characteristic of Jewish thought throughout our history, cannot fail to make a lasting impression on young minds, even though they may sooner or later be taught that same history from the Marxist angle. While I would not draw definite conclusions from what I experienced to this Marxist approach – or for that matter from my experiences as a whole considering my short stay in the country – it is quite clear to me that 'Marxist' requires a precise definition. For I would say that their approach to Jewish history, including the Bible, though clearly materialistic, resembles more a blend of the scientific approach at the turn of the century and the sociological method of today. I would, however, reiterate with emphasis that the important thing – to me at least – is this awareness of the relevance of our Bible which permeates all strata of Israelis of school-age. Where else is the Bible the foundation of the education of a whole generation of Jews moulding their thoughts and expression, and binding together children from so many different cultural and social levels as the result of their ethnic origin?

In the State of Israel, as in every State, the key to the emergence of a situation favourable for the pursuit of the higher values of a truly human life is education. The Hebrew University, notably in its Judaistic Institute, is doing fine work in most difficult, trying conditions. It provides the future teachers with a scientific knowledge of Judaism, taught according to a well-balanced plan remarkable for its depth and breadth. The younger members of its staff are graduates of the Hebrew University and men of ability and promise.

The Unified system of education is certainly a great improvement over the previous party-systems and owes much to the previous Minister of Education, Professor Dinur.

The *Kibbutz* movement has its own Institutes for the training of teachers, manned by excellent teachers whose ability is matched by their enthusiasm. It is here that I found deep understanding for the religious value of Biblical and Rabbinic literature rather than an ideological bias.

Jewish tradition is growing in importance as can be seen, for example, in the *Pesach Haggadah*. Compared with editions of earlier years, the approximation to the traditional *Haggadah* is becoming ever more marked, despite variations from *Kibbutz* to *Kibbutz*.

What strikes those of us who are used to the long-established *Seder* Service when we take part in such a *Seder* in a non-religious *Kibbutz*, is the absence of the blessings over wine, *matza* and *maror* although the prescribed four cups of wine are drunk, *matztot* are eaten, and *maror* and *charoset* are on the table. The *Haggadah* used at the *Seder* I enjoyed in one *Kibbutz* near Jerusalem contained much of the traditional material, from both Bible and Midrash with additions from the *Song of Songs*, sung by a choir, and from Bialik's poems. The mood was festive and the atmosphere happy, joyful and naturally dignified. Although I found it a little incongruous being bereft of its religious, ritual character, I sensed the feeling of elation, of a holiday that pervaded the whole *Kibbutz* and its many guests. It was a distinctly Jewish atmosphere and I would not agree for a moment with those who almost see a *hillul haShem* in this kind of *Seder*, so largely traditional and yet not religious in the accepted sense. It was certainly not a profanation, and yet, one could not be sure whether the passages from *Exodus* were read in their literal meaning, that is to say, whether reading the Divine Name aroused any consciousness of God, or whether these passages were read simply as history, national rather than religious-national history.

The same applies, though undoubtedly in a lesser degree, to a still stranger phenomenon: the celebration of *Bar Mitsvah* (and *Bat Mitsvah*) in non-religious *Kibbutzim*. At first sight, it seems to have nothing in common with the age-long institution but the name. The celebration has certainly not a trace of religion in it, the boy is not called up to the reading of the *Torah*, he does not become a full member of the *religious* community with all the rights and duties that this membership entails. Yet, in one important point of substance there is a resemblance: this entirely secular ceremony celebrates the maturity of the boy. Just as the *Seder* is becoming more and more traditional, so this specifically Jewish form may take on more of its traditional character as time goes on. Education is spreading knowledge of Jewish forms and ceremonies systematically in ever growing volume, and even where stress is laid on the customs of the Jewish people as the nation from which the present generation stems, the religious character is undeniable which their form in origin and observance represents. Is it not natural that such composite festivals as, say, *Pesach* and *Shavuot* should take on a new significance in the land of Israel and should therefore be celebrated there differently than in the Dispersion, where their spiritual significance is stressed equally naturally? Time is needed to redress the balance and to restore the equilibrium. Consciously and more often unconsciously manifestations of a religious spirit are discernible, especially where tradition is more and more taking the place of innovation, improvisation or a vacuum. Generally speaking, there is a stirring abroad in Israel in all strata of the people, especially the young, comparable to that in the world at large, where, after all, a religious urge is spreading, often unconnected with and even in opposition to organized religion.

Daily experience in face of the many problems besetting the young State and an as yet heterogeneous Society of Israel will inevitably lead to modifications and adaptations of the *Halakhah*, so largely developed and often hardened in the Dispersion. Openminded, searching study of the *Halakhah* may indeed be the only key to much-needed adjustments in the reality of political responsibility in a modern State after centuries of the dichotomy between private and public life in the Dispersion. Without faith there can be no religious observance today.

To assess correctly the religious situation in Israel today would require a much longer stay and a much more extensive inquiry than I had in Israel. Many more visits to many more people and places; many more conversations with individuals and groups of people of all and no ideological viewpoints would be needed, together with a sympathetic study of the growing literature on the spiritual problems, including the specifically religious ones, before a Jew not living in Israel and not experiencing the strains and stresses of a surprisingly normal life in abnormal circumstances could dare make a prognosis, leave alone sit in judgement.

If I were to venture a guess from which quarter the impetus to a renewal of a living Judaism was mostly to come I would point to the religious *Kibbutzim* of the Hapoel Hamizrachi and their spiritual leaders, men of deep religiosity, open-mindedness and a sense of civic responsibility. Only those who stand to the *Halakhah* as the Jewish way of life will have the power and the means to move the religious authorities to action; only those who accept Divine sanction for tradition, and at the same time realize the necessity for change in a spirit of tolerance and sympathy will gain the ear and the support of small religious, though not 'orthodox', groups and individuals.

The stirring of minds, a sign of spiritual malaise, of which I spoke earlier on, is by no means confined to a particular group of definite religious or political outlook. It is abroad everywhere, not least in well-established *Kibbutzim* of Mapai who, one might say, have achieved their material goal. For them the question, 'what next?', in a spiritual sense is most acute, not least, for the sake of their children and children's children. What makes this stirring appear so hopeful for the future of Israel and the Dispersion is that the fundamental questions of human existence, of the meaning of life, both individually and socially, are asked and their answer is being attempted on the purely human plane, unencumbered and undistorted by the specifically Jewish questioning vis-à-vis the non-Jewish world which is our lot in the Dispersion. It seems to me that only on this purely human level is a meeting of men and women with contrasting and opposing viewpoints possible. Until this happens – and nobody can be sure of its happening at a definite point in time – both Israelis and ourselves must do our best not to drift apart, or I should say, drift further apart. For I realized very soon after my arrival in Israel that there is an urgent need to explain not only Israel to the Diaspora, but also the Diaspora to Israel. This applies particularly to people born and bred in Israel who often lack any understanding of the life and the problems of Jews living outside Israel. Very little is being done to remedy this situation and it will not be easy to find a quick cure. The language difficulty is the least of the hurdles, but it is the first thing to be eliminated – only to find out that, although we speak Hebrew, mentally we speak a different language. A generation growing up in freedom, without the 'Jew-non-Jew' complication, seems unable to grasp our position and our problems in the Dispersion. I found that even many of my former compatriots experienced great difficulty in understanding our problems after 15 or 20 years' life and work in the *Yishuv* as free human beings. Here is a field for concerted thought and action, and we must set about it without delay.

The moral values which we claim as Jewish, are today put to the acid test in an independent Jewish State. For those who want to learn and see there are manifestations and signs in abundance of humanity, of moral integrity and watchfulness. Let us, from the safety of our homes and the security of our position, nurse the tender seedlings to bloom and fruit by strengthening those groups of practical idealists who want to put into practice our Hebraic heritage by remaining in touch with them and by making known their work.

1 This statement needs qualifying: There is no 'Standard Israeli' any more than there is a 'Standard Frenchman or American'; there is not even an 'Average Israeli'. For the 'Ingathering of the Exiles' has resulted in such a *Mizug galuyot* (an intermixture) of Jews from different countries with different traditions and customs and levels of culture and civilization, that one cannot generalize.

1956

ART AND ARTISTS

Towards a Definition of Jewish Art

CHARLES SPENCER

Researching for his book, *The Jews*, Chaim Bermant, the charming and ubiquitous chronicler of contemporary Jewish experience, sought from me a definition of Jewish art. We did not agree. Like many who seem to have little understanding of the visual arts, and less respect for modern experiments, Chaim pursues the limited theory that nationalism or racialism in art can only be defined concretely by its subject matter.

Such a theory, logically concluded, would assign a local landscape by Turner as English art, whilst claiming a different label for a view of the Swiss Alps by the same artist. Clearly this is ridiculous. Anyone who has looked at an Italian panorama by the French painter Poussin knows this is not the work of an Italian artist; that, in fact, there are not merely differences of character and temperament between every two men, but also different national characteristics, which inevitably contribute to individuality.

National character is complex, almost indefinable, yet, as we all know, recognizable, whether in the delicate curiosity of a great novelist (of course Proust could only have been French, but equally he could only have been a French outsider, fascinated by a world of which he could never feel wholly a part) or in the vulgar caricatures of the music hall. Both images, in fact, are true – in varying degrees; the caricature may even be truer, if crueller, because its exaggerations are based on carefully chosen, recognizable features. Thus when Fagin is presented with a hooked nose and wringing hands, we Jews may object, but our pain is directly related to the recognition that at one stage of Jewish history, such images were predominant.

There are group characteristics which give rise to pride, and others to shame, fairly equally distributed amongst all peoples. But such qualities have their roots and causes, some of which can be traced, although the interaction of history, religion, climate, social conditions, and numerous environmental processes makes it very difficult. To return to Chaim Bermant, who, as an entertaining novelist and journalist, makes a poor art critic; to dismiss Modigliani as 'oversold' is insensitive, and to assume that Chagall, after Picasso, is 'the greatest artist of the century', smells of what I call the Cecil Roth-*nachus*-syndrome, compounded by ignorance of the achievements of Malevich, Kandinsky, Matisse, Klee, Brancusi, Mondrian – all in my view of greater universal importance than Chagall, without denigrating the latter's own genius. Measuring Bomberg as inferior in talent to Gertler is another example of Bermant's simplicity. Of course he has a right to preferences and personal prejudices, but this is no substitute for informed judgement.

More serious is a naïve confusion of subject matter with fundamentals; the great painter Chaim Soutine (as worthy of honour as Chagall), we are informed, revealed 'nothing in his subject matter, nothing in his utterances or writing to suggest anything Jewish in his work'. As though the basic experiences and instincts of a man will necessarily be revealed in such superficialities. I prefer to view Soutine's undoubted Jewishness in the terms of an anonymous critic in *The Times*, some years ago: 'certain characteristics of mood and style which a great many Jewish painters seem to have in common . . . love of hot, rather hectic colour, and a nervous agitated line, which are used to portray mankind or landscape charged with an intense often sombre and melancholy emotion . . .'

Let's take another comparison; in Bermant's terms Wesker is obviously a Jewish playwright, whilst Pinter is not. Wesker's work has all the necessary concreteness, chicken soup and barley, East

End Jewish radicals, yearnings for kibbutz-communality. Certainly they represent aspects of contemporary Jewish experience, but in this respect Wesker is similar to the lesser Jewish painters of *l'Ecole de Paris*, where the repetition of symbols over-simplifies the experience. Mané-Katz is a typical example; what eventually is more Jewish in his work is not the Chassidic fiddler and the Menorah lamp, but those characteristics of colour and line detected by *The Times*' writer.

In Pinter's work there is none of this obvious symbolism, and few references to Jews, except in the early play, *The Birthday Party*, but all his writing is saturated with themes of family relationships, feared aggression from outsiders, the conflicts of localized, tribal loyalties. No play more clearly reveals these obsessions than *The Homecoming*, where the situation of an intellectually gifted boy of a working-class family is accentuated by the arrival of his alien wife, an American in this instance, but really the classic *shicksa*. Whilst personal to the writer, it represents a problem and a theme common to his background; indeed Wesker also wrote on the subject, in *Roots*, but from the opposite angle, the effect on a rural English family of their daughter's infatuation with a Jewish intellectual. Both Pinter and Wesker come from similar East London *milieux*, descendants of emigrant Jews, children of parents whose inheritance was strongly alien-Jewish, tempered by different English qualities, apart from the all too recent experience of the cultural transplantation of the older generation, and the contemporary rise of Hitler and his English imitators. That generation clung to aspects of ghettoism (still part of the Anglo-Jewish environment), or sought salvation in political panaceas. The children of that generation, in the form of Pinter and Wesker, accurately mirror the fears and hopes of their parents, as well as their own attempts at stability.

Bermant seems anxious to squash any possibility of linking Jewish experience expressible in artistic terms; does he not think there are common factors to Jewishness, or is he dismissive of the visual arts in comparison with the literary ones? He states, 'There is little in the work, say of Chagall, Modigliani, Soutine and Pascin to suggest a common style or even a common subject matter.' My quotation from *The Times*' critic undermines such narrow terms of reference, but one only needs to consider Turner, Constable, Hogarth, Moore, Ben Nicolson, Hockney to ask whether Bermant's inability to trace a common style or subject matter in any way invalidates the fact that all these artists are English, and recognizably English, demonstrably different from their contemporaries, whether in America, France or Italy. We are not talking of measuring rods of quality or achievement, but merely national differences.

An indication of Bermant's confusion is revealed in the case of Mark Antokolsky, the famous Russian-Jewish sculptor, the first artist, one might say, to emerge from the ghetto to national fame. The problem here is that Antokolsky abandoned Jewish subjects for Russian themes; Bermant therefore quotes the approval of Ahad Ha'am that 'an insistent search for spiritual beauty of internal form is surely a Jewish trait if ever there was one'. 'Surely' – what nonsense! So weak a cliché can be applied to all creative effort, and would willingly be adopted by any nation or race. Even more absurd is the treatment of Jacob Epstein, who was not only a most distinctive Jewish personality (born in New York of immigrant parents), but accentuated by deciding to live and work in London, and indeed by choosing so many Christian subjects. (Chagall, incidentally, also painted Crucifixions.) There can be no denying that without reference to specific Jewish themes, Epstein's bombastic, emotional, expressionistic art is completely different from any other English sculptor's, and so, perhaps, it is reasonable to suppose that this difference can partially be ascribed to his Jewishness. To overcome the paradox of Jewishness without Jewish symbols, Bermant falls back on Epstein's own view that his Jewishness is revealed 'in the human rather than abstract implications of his work'.

This is unacceptable. One of the basic features of Judaism is, indeed, abstraction, of which the injunction against the creation and worship of images is a corollary. The only way the overpowering concept of God or creativity could be envisaged was as something beyond human description, indefinable and limitless. That surely was the revolution in spiritual and mystical thought of the ancient Hebrews, what made them different from the idolators who needed physical evidence of the indefinable and from the Greeks and later the Christians who could only relate to God as man. How, therefore, can Epstein's abandonment of his splendid early, cubistic forms, for increasingly ugly, sentimental, humanistic ones be described as Jewish?

MARC CHAGALL (*lithograph*)
b. 1887
Illustration to Abraham Sutzkever's 'Siberia'

MANE-KATZ
1894–1962
The Drinker
Private Collection

EL LISSITZKY
1890–1941
CHAD GADYA – Which
My Father Bought
Me 1919
*Annely Juda Fine Art,
London*

CHAIM SOUTINE
1893–1943
Self Portrait c. 1918
*The Henry Pearlman
Collection, New York*

ALFRED WOLMARK
1877–1961
Self Portrait c. 1918
Belgrave Gallery, London

MARK GERTLER
1891–1939
Rabbi and Grandchild
1913
Southampton Art Gallery

WILLIAM
ROTHENSTEIN
1871–1945
Reading the Book of
Esther 1907
Manchester City Art Gallery

DAVID BOMBERG
1890–1957
Hear Oh Israel 1955
The Tate Collection

JAKOB KRAMER 1892–1962   The Day of Atonement 1919
Leeds City Art Gallery

JACOB EPSTEIN 1880–1959   Doves c. 1913
The Tate Gallery

ISAAC ROSENBERG 1890–19
Self Portrait 1915
National Portrait Gallery

BERNARD MENINSKY
1891–1950
The Cockney Girl 1924
Belgrave Gallery, London

JANKEL ADLER 1895–1949
The Priest 1942
Sacerdoti Collection

JOSEF HERMAN b. 1911
'Old Miner and Child' 1956
Oil on Canvas
National Museum, Montreal

LEON KOSSOFF b. 1926
Portrait of Father No. 3 19
Fischer Fine Art, London

FRANK AUERBACH
b. 1931
Head of J.Y.M. 1969
*Marlborough Fine Art,
London*

It is a common error to attempt a definition of Jewishness in art as mere humanism. Solomon J. Solomon (1860–1921) was the leading Anglo-Jewish artist when, in 1906, the Whitechapel Art Gallery held the first Jewish art exhibition in the country; he recorded in his memoirs:

> 'That the proper study of mankind is man, especially applicable to the Jew, shut out, or I should say shut in, as he has been for ages past... This thought pressed itself upon me when I was engaged in hanging a collection of paintings by Jewish artists a few years ago at the Whitechapel Art Gallery. One was naturally on the look-out for some special characteristics of Jewish art, and the human note so almost universally adopted was a fact which struck me most forcibly.'

The central fallacy to this argument is that all art is a study of mankind; it simply cannot be anything else, and that study can take any form, and is as potentially useful whether it contains a human figure or not. For my part, I still prefer the definition in *The Times*.

When the American Jewish painter Mark Rothko died in 1970, I wrote an obituary for an art journal. Born in Russia in 1903, Rothko was taken to the United States at the age of 10, where later he studied under the important Jewish painter Max Weber, who, with Soutine, influenced his work. Rothko was one of the founders of the American Abstract-Expressionist school, in my view the most important visual expression to have emerged from America. A number of Jewish painters contributed to the movement, notably Kline, Barnet Newman, Reinhardt, and Gottlieb who with Rothko once signed a letter to the *New York Times*, outlining their aesthetic creed: 'We favour the simple expression of the complex thought.' Now that has a true Biblical ring to me. Rothko, indeed, was probably the most religious, in a mystical sense, painter of the century, as I wrote in that obituary:

> 'Rothko used large surfaces, which are meant to be viewed close up, so that they absorb and envelope the viewer. This, in fact, is the very opposite of decoration; it comes near to the original role of art as an instrument of religious activity. Rothko's paintings, with their powerful single image, are in fact meant to cast an effective spell on the viewer. It is this religious character of Rothko's work which I find of special interest. I do not think it can be dissociated from his Jewishness ... It cannot be denied that in a profoundly irreligious age, secular modern

art has taken on, for a significant number of people, both artists and spectators, something of the character of religious involvement and satisfaction. For a Jew the falling away from traditional religious practices is a fundamental experience which often leaves undisturbed "the enduring myths of the race as a source for the most profound and universal emotions" (to quote the critic Barbara Rose). It is surely no coincidence that, whereas artists like Toby and Pollock found their symbolic equivalents in gesture and calligraphy, in influences from the more subtle, diffuse, less moralistic philosophies of the Orient, Rothko and Newman came forth with a positive presence, more puritanical and moralistic, perfectly representing the monotheistic archetype of Judaism. It is not surprising that in a joint statement Gottlieb, Newman and Rothko spoke of the "impact of elemental truth" (another Biblical phrase). They also asserted that "there is no such thing as a good painting about nothing" and that "the subject is crucial and only that subject matter is valid which is tragic and timeless". These were not the aesthetic yearnings of Mediterranean hedonists!'

In England we have the opportunity to experience Rothko's timelessness. The murals he painted for a restaurant in the Seagram Building, New York, were rejected as sombre and sacramental. In 1967 Rothko presented one of the paintings to the Tate Gallery, expressing his love of England and the paintings of Turner. Three months before his death Rothko agreed to the request of Sir Norman Reid, Director of the Tate, which resulted in the remaining eight panels coming to London.

The more serious the art, the greater its bearing on all mankind, the more it is truly reflective of self; self, indeed, is the only factor the artist has to work on, and it is the quality of self, mysteriously tempered by environment, expressed through the mastery of techniques, which establishes the quality of art. And perhaps most magically of all, the self, in this creative sense, can be greater than the individual, since artistic self, paradoxically, also includes wider national and human extensions. Surely we Jews of all people have no difficulty in accepting this; the people who assumed that mere mortals could be inspired by God to superhuman roles – Moses and the prophets, Solomon and the Kings! That is what ordinary mortals mean by being inspired, being capable of deeds outside their normal range.

The self, however, must have roots, must come from somewhere; whilst at the same time it can only be of its period, reflective of personal as well as common experience.

It is not by chance that England has not produced a major

religious artist; anti-Catholic iconoclasm was a contributing factor, but even that had roots in local character. The fascinating secularism of Shakespeare is a national strain. Indeed climate and culture seem to have undermined visual talent, so that when the court could afford art, foreigners, like Torrigiano, Holbein, later Rubens and Van Dyck, had to be imported. The English have never achieved an artist on the grand, idealistic scale of Michelangelo or Rodin. The reverse of the coin, a realistic scepticism of human nature, is to be found in the works of Jonson, Swift, Hogarth, Byron and in our healthy democratic traditions. Perhaps the rejection of God and man led to the worship of nature, as seen in Wordsworth, Constable, Turner, Gainsborough and the English watercolourists.

English materialism is balanced by a mild mysticism, tempered by suspicion of idealism, social panaceas, political dogmatists. Common sense, one might call it, a dangerous counter-factor to the qualities which produce great art. Shakespeare may be the exception which proves the rule; we have no playwright to compare with Chekhov, Ibsen, even O'Neill, no composer to equal Mozart, Beethoven, Verdi, no novelist to list with Balzac, Flaubert, Tolstoy, Dostoevsky. The mere statement and the questions it arouses, are enough to point to not merely different national characteristics expressed in art, but the fascinating effect of environment on individuals.

Obviously the same genetic, environmental patterns apply to Jews,[1] and the artistic expressions they have adopted. We all know that religious injunctions impaired the early development of visual artists, and that in the Dispersion Christian dominance of training and patronage held back talented Jews willing to escape from traditional fetters. As European civilization itself broke from religious fears and controls, so, in the more advanced countries, Jewish artists began to emerge, some, by the 18th century, as prominent as Zoffany. Emancipation had two notable effects: on the one hand a group of Jews prospered and were able to patronize artists from within their group, concerned with national or racial symbolism – what has been called Viennese-Jewish regionalism, which treated Jewish nostalgia or reality in a Rembrandtesque style, as diluted by the Dutch painter Josef Israels, which for some curious reason was acceptable as a Jewish manner. The result was a group of charming, genre artists, Moritz Oppenheim, Maurycy Gottlieb, Leopold Horowitz, Isidor Kaufmann, Yehuda Epstein. No one could possibly exaggerate their gifts or achievements; nostalgia soon degenerated into sentimentality, and the limitation of subject stifled real experience, or the kind of marriage between self and technical experiment which makes Rembrandt unique, or even the search for truth which makes Israels a minor but considerable artist.

The second result of emancipation in the 19th century was the willingness of the art world to accept Jewish artists, even when they preferred Jewish subjects; and a further development was the determination of some artists to be judged solely as painters, which often resulted in their adoption of Christian or social themes. The Veit brothers in Germany are typical; grandsons of Moses Mendelsohn, they nevertheless became leaders of the famous Nazarene movement, with its inspiration from the Gospels and revolutionary simplicity, which in turn influenced the Pre-Raphaelites. In England we had Solomon Alexander Hart who combined an academic career with Jewish themes; Simeon Solomon whose homosexuality drew him to the ambiguous world of Burne-Jones, Beardsley, Wilde, Swinburne; and Solomon J. Solomon who, like William Rothenstein, maintained a worldly sophistication. Then, by the end of the century, two major artists emerged, Camille Pisarro in France, Max Liebermann in Germany, who fully justify the claim that without religious, social, political and environmental hindrances, it is likely that Jews would have produced many more painters of genius.

The explosion of brilliant talent which has occurred among Jewish artists in the 20th century, notably those who emerged from Eastern Europe, is partially explainable by social conditions and freedoms, but deserves deeper analysis.

The first 'artist of the ghetto' to achieve national fame, as we have seen, was Mark Antokolsky, born in Vilna in 1843, 44 years before Chagall's appearance in Vitebsk; he is therefore more of the generation of Pisarro (1831) and Liebermann (1847). But in contrast to those comfortable, middle-class, emancipated young men, Antokolsky's creative gifts could only find expression in carpentry and carvings for wooden synagogues. Chance patronage by a local gentile resulted in his elevation to the St Petersburg Academy. Intensely Jewish, he has been repeatedly criticized for abandoning Jewish subjects for Russian nationalist themes.

This fails to appreciate that the Slavophils in the mid-nineteeth century turned to Russian themes – in art, literature, music – as a direct criticism of the Imperial regime which rejected anything Russian as inferior, boorish, vulgar. Even Glinka's operas were described as music for coachmen. Antokolsky was therefore making a courageous stand by identifying himself with this movement, which in time, under the influence of William Morris, sought inspiration in the past, in craft work, in functionalism. This very nationalism was to be an inspiration to Jewish artists; two of Antokolsky's students were Ilya Ginsburg, who in 1919 founded a Jewish Society of Creative Jewish Art, and more importantly, Boris Schatz, who in 1906 formulated the Bezalel School of Art in Jerusalem, devoted to the creation of Jewish national and folkloric art. There were similar manifestations in many Jewish centres, such as the establishment in London of the Ben Uri Art Society in 1915 (also named after the legendary designer of the Biblical Tabernacle), through the enthusiasm of Leon Berson, from Poland, for the purpose of promoting Jewish Decorative Art.

The example of the Russian Slavophils, and the fame and prominence of Antokolsky, proved that nationalism could inspire art; and indeed it might be suggested that it affected Zionism and the desire for a homeland.

Certainly out of Eastern Europe there soon poured a flood of Jewish talent; Levitan and Serov as part of the Slavophil Movement, and their younger friend Bakst, who was to achieve wider fame through the *Ballets Russes*, and whose orientalism is a form of nationalism, on occasions particularized in costumes for Jewish dancers, combining Chassidic with Biblical motives. He was, in fact, born on the Lithuanian border, and equally revealing is the fact that when Chagall failed to gain entry to the St Petersburg Academy he turned to Bakst – just as Bakst had turned to Antokolsky years before – so that one finds personal, as well as racial, links between three generations of Russian Jews. Alongside this Russian nationalism which a few privileged Jews could enter, there was the vibrant, throbbing, enclosed Jewish-Yiddish nationalism, bound by Judaic formulas and accumulated folk customs, but now influenced by new social and political ideas. Within its confines it was the only complete Jewish nationalism since the second exodus; religion, language, social custom, a culture which ranged from food to dress, expressed in poetry, stories, songs, dance. The visual arts were inevitably the last manifestation of this experience, and except in ritualistic crafts, the communities provided no possibility for development or training, even when they did not positively oppose it.

There were two lines of escape; the first, headed by Chagall, who reached Paris in 1910, leading a voluntary movement of young artists who hailed Paris as the Mecca of Art, the means of escaping the ghetto, religious and social restrictions. It is fascinating to list their ages. Chagall, born 1887, was 23 when he came to France; Soutine b. 1884, Kremegne 1890, Kisling 1891, Kikoine 1891, Georges Kars 1885, Mintchine 1898, Mané-Katz 1894, Maurice Blond 1899, the sculptor Lipchitz 1891. It is not insignificant that three other artists of the same generation, Sonia Turk (Delaunay) b. 1885, Louis Marcoussis b. 1883, Henri Hayden b. 1883, are not identifiable with this 'Jewish' group, because they came from well-to-do backgrounds, in which Polishness or Russianness had diluted their nationalism. Two other major Jewish artists of the Parisian school should be mentioned, Modigliani b. 1884 and Pascin, from Bulgaria or Romania, b. 1885.

The second line of escape was the enforced migration of poor persecuted Jews, refugees from the pogroms, seeking shelter in the United States and Britain. It is, again, the same generation; in America, Abraham Wolkowitz, born 1880, Webber 1881, Lozowick 1892, Rattner 1893, Cropper 1897, Shahn 1898, the twins Moses and Raphael Soyer 1899, and three sculptors, Jo Davidson 1883, Zorach and Nadelmann, both 1887. Their successors include Joseph Hirsch 1910, Hyman Bloom 1913 and Jack Levine 1915.

Anglo-Jewry produced a similar crop of artists: Wolmark 1876, Epstein 1880, Bomberg 1890, Isaac Rosenberg 1890, Meninsky 1891, Kramer 1892, Gertler 1892; one can add Jankel Adler, born 1895, who came from Poland at a later stage, and, as representative of the next generation, Josef Herman. b. 1911.

In Russia itself, coincident with the revolutionary period, a Jewish Art Movement emerged, including Lissitsky 1891, Ryback 1897, Altmann 1889 (and Chagall when he briefly returned to Russia); the same generation includes the two Pevsner brothers, Antoine 1888, Gabo 1890.

What does all that prove? Certainly that as a result of national experience, in its widest context, there emerged this astonishing parade of artists, most of whom shared historical and cultural experiences which were recognizably expressed in their work, as recognizably, say, as any comparable group of French or English painters.

Of course, successive generations share a diluted Jewishness, related to their own environments and experience, but as we see around us, in an increasingly unstable world and disintegrating civilization, there is a nostalgic yearning for the past. In Jewish terms Israel satisfies much of this need in contemporary Jewry, but Israel is another nationalism and its art will eventually reflect that special experience. Younger Jewish artists and their work are more difficult to analyse in Jewish terms, although as I hope I have indicated in references to Wesker and Pinter, the basis for such analysis exists. In current English art there is no doubt in my mind that most Jewish practitioners reveal a significant difference from their contemporaries; not necessarily superiority, of course, but forms or manners which reveal their origins. Perhaps a special pair of examples are the painters Auerbach and Kossoff, the former born in Berlin, the latter in London, who shared a common influence from David Bomberg, and paint in heavy impasto subjects limited to their intimate personal and physical surroundings. They are virtually unique in the English art scene, quite alien from typical English expression. I have no doubt that what makes them different is their Jewishness.

Let me end with two conflicting quotations which, I hope, will strengthen my argument. Firstly, that the evidence completely refutes Bernard Berenson's assertion (in his book *The Visual Arts*) that 'Jews have never revealed any originality, nor expressed anything recognizably Jewish', a pathetic example of Jewish self-denigration, in the mistaken belief that internationalism, universalism, is ipso facto preferable to recognizable localism. And, lastly, from Edouard Roditi's essay on 'The Jewish Artist in the Modern World' (from *Jewish Art*, edited by Cecil Roth): 'Jewish styles of painting, it seems, are originally a product of an acute conflict, in the consciousness of individual artists, between the cultural traditions of the Western world and the familiar background of orthodox Judaism from which they are breaking away, if only as a consequence of their choice of a career in the figurative art, a choice that still seems to inspire occasional feelings of guilt . . . a Jewish style of painting imposes itself only as a synthesis in this conflict . . .'

Whilst there is much in that statement I agree with, it is unnecessarily masochistic. Beyond the historical conflict that Roditi describes, Jewishness, both in a positive sense or as a form of inescapable 'nationalism', continues to inform the work of Jewish artists in every field.

1 In his article in *The Times* on 6 January 1978, Bernard Levin produced a useful definition of such patterns: '... we all act in accordance with our heredity, our upbringing, our genes, our traumas, our general psychic make-up, our relation with our parents, even (it is said) our toilet-training and our very birth — it has long seemed to me astonishing that a belief in the unpredictability of our own actions is so often matched with a fanatical denial of the unpredictability of the universe.' The very contradiction Levin objects to seems more likely to be accepted by someone who has inherited Jewish historical experience.

1978

The Modern Artist in Modern Society

JOSEF HERMAN

... 'A writer must of course earn a living to exist and be able to write, but he must in no sense exist and write so as to earn a living ...
... 'In no sense does the writer regard his work as a means. They are ends in themselves; so little are they means for him and others that, when necessary, he sacrifices his existence to theirs and, like the preacher of religion, though in another way, he takes as his principle: "God is to be obeyed before man"...
... 'The writer who debases it (his writing) to material ends deserves as punishment of his intrinsic lack of freedom, the extrinsic lack of freedom, censorship: better yet, his existence is already his punishment.'

KARL MARX
Debating the Freedom of the Press, 1842

Our present day society is scientific and technologically orientated. It favours utilitarian ideas. It favours the scientist and the engineer. Some scholars even claim that the greatest works of art of the 20th century are to be found not in the museums but in the streets, in engineering, in the constructed bridges, in the designs of aeroplanes, in the designs of roads, etc. This way of viewing art is purely formal and functional but it confirms that art in the sense of image making is on the fringes of our society and not at the heart of it. Many seem to think that society can well do without it.

The mere number of people directly involved in the existence of art, the artists, the connoisseurs, the museums, the dealers, the private collectors, the critics, etc., is indeed very small. I doubt whether they amount to more than six figures in the whole of the Western world including the Americas.

Art today exists not because society depends on it but because by some freak of nature artists still exist and they impose themselves and their works upon existing societies.

The artist todays stands alone. Not unlike the philosopher who stands alone for a long, long time in our history. Today if we ask an artist: 'for whom do you work?' his answer will invariably be: 'for no one'. He may rhetorically add: 'for whom does the philosopher do his thinking?'

No longer working for a tribe, for a church, for a patron, for a bourgeois Maecenas, the artist, again, not unlike the philosopher, believes that in one way or another his labours are not parasitic, that they do add to man's intellectual effort to get to know himself, change himself, civilize himself. On this basis there still exists an interaction between the artist and society. In a purely cultural sense the images done today by artists still work, to use a utilitarian expression, for some purpose, and not a purely decorative one either.

No longer a maker of symbols of magic or myth, no longer a maker of icons of religious significance, his images in a functional sense, have taken over where religions have left off; the artist's images today are a personalizing force in parallel to the depersonalizing science. The equilibrium of the total man makes him as much depend on art as on science. Science is man's armoury in face of a hostile nature; art is his quest towards a spiritual wholesomeness. Science is for the facts of life; art is for the experience of life.

For a time the scientific pressure on all spheres of life was such that even artists thought they had to adjust art to the condition of science. They thought that now was the time to forsake art's own autonomy and to link up with the applied arts which have always been nearer to the utility of science.

The artist in front of an easel, working on an image nobody asked for, was thought of as a figure of yesteryear, an anachronism in modern times. It was suggested that the NEW artist 'sits in a clean overall, white or blue, bent over a drawing-board, and works on a design for immediate use, designs for a stove or a suit functional to its use' – wrote the Russian constructivist Tatlin. 'The art of the future' – wrote Frans Mark – 'will be formal, an embodiment of our scientific convictions.' Poets of the time were just as explicit: 'The progress of an artist' – wrote T. S. Eliot – 'is a continual sacrifice, a continued extinction of the personality... It is in this depersonalization that art may be said to approach the condition of science...'

Significant though this mood may have been it was by no means the prevailing mood of all or even most of the artists. Neither a Picasso nor a Braque nor a Matisse nor a Rouault, nor the German, nor the Flemish Expressionists shared his view. The artist, the image maker, remained and is still with us, he still works in front of an easel and apparently nothing can deter him.

True, the images he is now making are different from the images of former times and former cultures. It is in the content of these new images that there lies also the answer to the question of the function of the artist in modern society. But first let us see in what way the present day images differ from the images of the past. Whether in painting or in sculpture the present day images differ in two main aspects: they do not belong to any single tradition, and they are free of rules, so that individual expression is of a variety and a degree not known in previous history.

Now the artist has a free choice of pictorial sources, techniques and forms, derived from many traditions, according to the needs of his individual temperament. In works of a 20th century artist we are likely to meet with traces of traditions as far apart as that of ancient Mexico and Tribal Africa, ancient China or Archaic Greece.

Every effort, even of a purely aesthetic nature, at establishing some sort of general rules has failed. Whether they were the rules of colour of the Fauves, of the Cubists, of form and space, of movement and dynamics, of the Futurists or the Suprematists rules of design, each had a short list of followers and existed for a short time, but eventually proved unacceptable to most artists.

To a number of art historians this variety of means seemed an embodiment of chaos. Well, what may seem chaos was in fact the embodiment of the spirit of social democracy. Capitalism for its own selfish ends established the rule of freedom of the individual. From this rule society as a whole profited. It began to mean also freedom of expression and of organization. Without this rule trade union movements could not exist let alone grow in strength. Nor could anti-capitalist, socialist movements grow. To the artist freedom of the individual meant also a free choice of artistic expression. Freedom of the individual became one of mankind's most treasured possessions. We may as well get used to the idea that uniformity of artistic styles belongs to the past.

However, in the arts two general attitudes did emerge from our great variety of strivings: one an expression through means of absolute abstraction, the other an expression through more realistic means, figurative means. These two attitudes will most probably go on growing into the foreseeable future. It is these two attitudes that I now propose to consider.

Abstract art is an art which makes no reference to object or subject, an art without a definite iconography or image. Its surface is its content: colour, shape, design somehow unified and somehow holding together. It can be intellectual as with Mondrian, that is to say, calculative in its effect; or it can be emotional as with Kandinsky, that is to say, unpredictable in its effect. It can be harmonious and pleasing or disturbing and vaguely spiritual but at no time can it be physically exact in its pictorial definition. In this limitation it comes nearest to decoration and ornament.

How the notion of abstraction became a workable theory is clearly explained in the writings of both Kandinsky and Mondrian. 'I steadily absorbed impressions' – writes Kandinsky – 'until I trained myself to overlook objects' ... 'Observing sea, sky, and stars' – writes Mondrian – 'I sought to indicate their plastic function through a multiplicity of crossing verticals and horizontals' ...

Now, because we usually see colour connected with matter and shapes connected with objects, abstracting can only become second nature through the effort of the intellectual will. Kandinsky also asserts that he had to strain his mind to the utmost 'until the realm of art drew farther and farther apart from the realm of nature'. Mondrian, as we have seen in the earlier quotation, had to go through the same process.

Having reassured themselves that such a process was possible at a later stage, their experiments no longer needed any reference to nature. In this lies the great difference between abstract art and its forerunner, the Cubists: the latter's pictures are still linked with nature no matter what the degree of abstracting they were committed to. The Cubistic method was one of interpretation, not denial.

Since Kandinsky and Mondrian, abstract artists contributed a vast variety of designs, textures and imaginary colours but basically it remained as stationary and repetitive as naturalistic art after the 17th century. Nevertheless it is still too early to give up the ghost. Other unexpected inspirations may still produce unforeseeable results. After all, who could foresee the sudden appearance of the Abstract Expressionists in the United States in the forties? Thanks to the works and talents of a Rothko or a Barnet Newman the Abstract Expressionists discovered new facets of abstract possibilities, particularly in their effort to assimilate subject matter.

In spite of the present day bias in favour of abstract art, the modern figurative contribution may prove the richer in imagination, more varied and less prone to monotony. Whether it is inclined towards fantasy (Chagall), religious compassion (Rouault), Mysticism of Nature (Nolde), social realism (Kollwitz and the Mexican muralists), peasant epics (Permeke), romantic idealisations (Modigliani), or dramatic hallucinations (Beckman) and so on and so on, it is not short of painterly ideas and in their formal quest does not give way to any of the abstract painters.

Covering the same historical period modern figurative artists have, of course, some points of contact with the masters of abstract art: they share with them the same freedom from academic tradition and aesthetic rule; they, too, put experience of reality above the materiality of things whether of nature or of man-made artifacts. And like the abstract artist so the figurative owes more to the primitive imagination than to the naturalistic or classical. Inevitably, like abstract art modern figurative art is recognizable at a glance as being of our times. But in essence it differs from abstract art: it communicates its spirituality through recognizable forms, no matter what the individual approaches to objects and subjects are. But above all, it is humane in the same degree as the art of Renaissance was humanistic, though instead of being preoccupied with muscles it is preoccupied with human existence. The German sculptor Barlach puts it this way: 'What man suffered and can suffer, his greatness and his various concerns (including myth and dreams of the future) are the things I am committed to.'

With the figurative artist the aesthetic emotion is linked to the moral, and both have an equal place in their art. But their main contribution to the arts of all times lies in their success at establishing in serious art a new popular image at once social and spiritual. This needs some further clarification.

The 20th century is in many ways a prolongation of ideas which were already active in the 19th century, in particular in the field of iconography or subject matter. The umbilical cord which held art to the antique past was strongest in the so-called 'eternal subjects'. In the 19th century this umbilical cord was cut. Lionello Venturi put it this way:

> 'To understand why this has happened it is necessary to go back to Goya, Daumier, Cezanne and Van Gogh in order to remember that in the 19th century moral beauty was identified with the lot of the common people as a reaction to physical beauty, which by tradition has been identified with the upper classes. This finding of the salvation of the soul in the lower classes, in the simplicity of life, in the subverted sublime, was the claim of 19th century painting, one of the greatest contributions to art of all times.'

In this shift of class sympathy lies the meaning of the words 'popular image'. Thus 'popular image', by implication as well as in practice, is an image of the ethos of our every day. Stylistically, too, it comes nearer the folk arts. It tends to make no concession to prettiness nor idealization of the Appollian kind.

When all this is said about both abstract and modern figurative art, we need not be surprised to see the same artist practising both types of art. For instance de Kooning, Picasso, Moore and many others are equally distinguished in their figurative art as in their abstract art. A 20th century masterpiece like Picasso's Guernica or some works by Leger could not have come into being without a cultural climate which accommodates both abstract and figurative attitudes.

If I did stop at greater length at explaining the nature of modern figuration it is because too many writers have too often claimed that only abstract art is representative of our century. I wanted to illustrate that it simply is not so: *there exists a figurative tradition which in every sense is just as modern as the abstract tradition.*

In this review of the artistic situation of the 20th century I aimed at a general image rather than detailed analysis: thus under abstract art I had in mind all those movements which for one theoretical reason or another departed from object, such as Plasticism, and Neo-Plasticism, Constructivism, Suprematism and the like.

With figurative art things are rather different. Here we are likely to deal with individuals rather than with groups, though here also I had in mind the Fauvists, the Expressionists and the Mexicans who called themselves 'Artists of the Revolution', and also some of the Surrealists. The groups which appeared after the Second World War, like Op, Pop, etc., produced no men of genius to back up their postulates and therefore belong to a different aspect of the art of our century.

Art cannot be discussed in terms of seasons, or even decades. I tried as objectively as I could to discuss here the two mainstreams of our century which have both produced men of genius, and are of immense historical significance.

1978

Absence and Echo

GABRIEL JOSIPOVICI

On looking at Vermeer's 'A Young Woman Standing at A Virginal' in the National Gallery.

– Tell me. Tell me.
– What?
– What is she doing? What is she doing now?
– Standing.
– Just standing?
– She's looking round. Her hands are on the keyboard.
– She's playing?
– No. She's finished playing.
– Finished?
– For the moment. Or perhaps she's about to start.
– Why has she stopped?
– Like that.
– What do you mean like that?
– She just has.
– Oh.
– Perhaps she's listening.
– Listening?
– To the music fading. Or to a noise, a whisper, outside. Or perhaps she's just turning. Looking in this direction.
– Is she alone?
– Yes.
– And she's still standing? Listening?

– Light enters from the window behind her. The room is filled with light. Her hands rest on the keyboard.

– Can you see through the window?

– No. It is only the source of light.

– Go on.

– She waits. There is the trace of a smile on her lips. She turns towards us.

– She is smiling? At us?

– No.

– What else is there in the room?

– There are two paintings on the wall behind her. There is a chair between us and the keyboard.

– Describe the paintings.

– Near the window, in a golden frame, there is a small landscape. The sky is very blue.

– Go on.

– The other is behind and above her. It hangs exactly in the middle of the rear wall. Her head bisects the left hand bottom corner so that the ebony frame encloses her face as well as the picture.

– What is the subject?

– It is a Cupid. A naked boy holding a bow in his right hand, facing the room. In his left hand he holds aloft a card or little book.

– A card?

– It is impossible to be more precise.

– Is she aware of the Cupid?

– No. She turns her head away from it. She looks towards us.

– Us?

– Perhaps she is not smiling. But she is not sad either.

– What is her expression then?

– She is turning. The light catches the right side of her face, her neck. It rises off the chair, the wood of the instrument. Perhaps she is listening.

– Listening?

– To the music. To her memory of the music. Perhaps.

– What instrument is she playing?

– A virginal. It is delicately marbled. The strings are just visible. On the lid, which is laid back, a landscape is painted. She stands in front of the instrument, her back to the window.

– What is there outside the window?
– Nothing. It is the source of light, as I have said.
– And she has still not moved?
– She half turns. Her body faces the painted landscape on the lid of the instrument. Behind her, on the wall, the Cupid stands upright.
– Why is he there?
– He is an echo.
– An echo?
– Of the music. As the painted landscape is an echo of the trees and meadows outside the window.
– And us? She cannot hear us? She is not aware of our presence?
– Who knows? She listens. For a moment her body listens. To the fading of the music. To the light. To the picture behind her.
– She thinks about it?
– No. It echoes.
– Will she move away? Will she come towards us?
– No.
– Then what will she do?
– She does not belong to the world of doing. Though her body listens to the echoes of the upright Cupid.
– You mean she will do nothing? Even if she discovers us?
– She will not discover us. She does not belong to our time.
– But when the echoes are stilled? When she grows tired of standing?
– She belongs where she stands.
– She is not real then? She belongs to mythology?
– She is no nymph. We know who she is. But for a moment which lasts for ever she cannot see or hear us.
– Even if we intrude upon her? Will she not see us then? Not hear us?
– We cannot intrude upon her. She exists within the cube of light which is the room. We are outside.
– We cannot go in? We cannot call out to her?
– No.
– She exists outside time? Outside our time?
– She has made time her own. It no longer has power over her. She is time, Cupid and echo.
– And we? What are we?

— We are divided where she is single. We flee from time. And from Cupid too. They have us in their power.

— And now? What is she doing now?

— Nothing. She stands. The notes are played. Or will be played. The music is completed. For a moment she hears it all.

— She remembers it?

— Her body remembers.

— And she will not talk to us? She will not tell us what she feels?

— No. We belong outside. We can talk to each other but not to her.

— Is there no hope for us then? No hope at all?

— Perhaps. Perhaps when we turn away the echo will remain. The echo of her face, the room, that cube of light. As for her the echo of the fields outside, of the music, of the painting on the wall behind her.

— All we have to do then is turn away?

— Who knows? There is no certainty. There is only the source. The source of light.

— Are we the source of light?

— No. We are only the eyes that see. The voices that talk.

— Are you saying that without us she cannot exist?

— No. I am not saying that. She can and does. Perhaps without her though it is we who cannot exist. Perhaps she has heard us. Perhaps she has become aware of our presence, here, outside. But only fleetingly. We have become part of the echo, part of the music, the music of light, echoing in the silent room.

— What shall we do then? What shall we do now?

— Who knows? Perhaps when we turn away the echo will stay.

— What must we do for that to happen?

— We must stop talking. We must listen. We must keep still.

— But if we do that won't we forget? Won't we start to think of other things?

— Yes, that too is possible. It is even likely. But it is also possible that the echo will return. As echoes do.

THE WORLD OF YESTERDAY

The German-Jewish 'symbiosis', so-called because of the prominent part played by Jews in the cultural and intellectual life in pre-Hitler Germany, has undoubtedly come to an end, however one looks at this unique phenomenon in modern Jewish history. There are, of course, those who deny that it ever existed, notwithstanding the fact that Jews occupied such a disproportionate place in German literature, the press, the theatre, in music, science, and many other fields. They were German Jews all right, and their contribution, individually and collectively, to German literature and the arts cannot be denied. But the question being asked is: was their contribution, in essence, determined by their 'Jewishness'? Obviously, if it was merely a question of language, the answer would be relatively simple. However, since Jews write in as many languages as the countries in which they happen to live, we naturally look for what they have in common as Jews besides the difference in which they express themselves. So while the Germans may claim, or disclaim, the Jewish contribution to their own culture, we as Jews have every reason to look upon the German-Jewish writers in the various fields as part of the totality of the multi-lingual Jewish literature and culture, irrespective of the time and the place in which they have developed. If this were otherwise we could not speak of Anglo-Jewish, American-Jewish or French-Jewish literature.

The following is a re-assessment of only three among the outstanding German-Jewish writers, each of them occupying a special position, but all three accepting both their 'Jewish affirmation and alienation'.

Heinrich Heine: a Reassessment

HARRY ZOHN

That Heinrich Heine is a figure of endless fascination for Jews and non-Jews alike is evidenced by two recent additions to the enormous scholarly and popular literature on the poet, both published in Germany in 1973. *Heinrich Heine und das Judentum*, originally a Cologne dissertation by Hartmut Kircher, a non-Jew, shows the connection between Heine's attitude toward Judaism and the evolution of his political views; Heine always made a distinction between the Jews' religion and the civil rights to which they were clearly entitled. In his book *Heinrich Heine als Jude*, Ludwig Rosenthal points out once again that despite the poet's shifting attitude toward the Jewish religion, which he criticized as being too austere, his emotionally tinged ethnic attachment to the Jewish people and his intellectual appreciation of the Jewish mind remained constant throughout his life.

Jews have always felt an especial closeness to Heine – not only because of the intrinsic importance and undiminished freshness of this internationally celebrated writer, not just because he is a mirror into which we can look even today, but also because Heine was close to the beginning of the German-Jewish symbiosis, which means that he lived in a maelstrom of religious, political, social, and cultural currents. In him the *Weltschmerz*, the romantic pessimism and sadness over the evils of the world and the precariousness of the human condition, became coupled with a more specific form of that universal woe, the *Judenschmerz*, the age-old insight that it is *'shver tsu zayn a yid'*. Heine's relatively brief life-span of not much more than the first half of the 19th century embraced such crucial and formative events as the rise and fall of Napoleon, the Congress of Vienna, and the Revolutions of 1830 and 1848. In German literature, the currents during his lifetime were Romanticism, Young Germany, and Poetic Realism. Heine described himself as the last of the Romantics and is generally considered the leading and possibly the only poetic rather than merely journalistic member of that group of young revolutionary firebrands, polemicists, and innovators that has been labelled *Jungdeutschland*. But what is of the greatest interest to Jews is the fact that Heine grew up when German Jewry was taking its first, faltering steps 'from the ghetto into Europe', to use Arthur Eloesser's phrase, a step which these Jews had been enabled to take by the work of two great men – Moses Mendelssohn in the cultural sphere and Napoleon in the political and legal arena. The struggle of German Jewry is most strikingly symbolized in this outstanding individual. Heine's creative tension derives from the turbulence of his time, and if Goethe's Faust said of himself that 'two souls, alas, dwell within my breast', there were more than two souls in Heinrich Heine. Sol Liptzin has characterized Heine as follows:

> 'We encounter in him the prophet of a nation at the turning point of its political development – the German nation as it neared the end of its thousand-year struggle for unification; we see in him the embodiment of a most paradoxical age, an age suckled on outworn medievalism and dreaming of liberation through science and industrialism; we behold in him the pioneer of a people at a crisis in its history – the Jewish people as it burst forth from the ghetto confines clamoring for knowledge and joy and power long withheld from it; and finally we discover in him the best personification of the jagged modern soul, torn with unanswered doubts, wrestling with despair, complex beyond analysis, and hypersensitive to the point of morbidity . . . In him East met West, the Orient clashed with the Occident; nay more, in him Jerusalem, Athens, Berlin, and Paris struggled for supremacy.'

Another of Heine's many biographers, Max Brod, sees Heine as 'a Jewish spirit working on alien material', as a Jewish poet whose fate it was to experience his hapless love for the Germans and things German at a time when Western European Jewry found itself at a difficult stage in its assimilation: it was supposed to break out of the ghetto walls and at the same time to countenance continuing political, social, religious, and cultural discrimination. Heine's generation was not up to this challenge of theoretical, external freedom and practical, intellectual bondage. Moses Mendelssohn had lived in the second half of the 18th century, the Age of Enlightenment. German Romanticism, the movement that succeeded Classicism around the turn of the century, impeded rather than promoted the process of emancipation. The early Romanticists rejected the rationalistic philosophy of the Enlightenment; later Romanticism had a strong patriotic, nationalistic orientation, and it is here that we find the roots of modern anti-Semitism (and, according to studies like Peter Viereck's *Metapolitics*, even the seeds of Hitlerism). In sitting in judgment over Romanticism later, Heine said that 'Jew-hatred began with the Romantic School, its delight in the Middle Ages, Catholicism, and the aristocracy, and it was increased by the Teutomaniacs'. Heine witnessed the transition from Romanticism to Young Germany and was himself part of that transition. He harked back to the medieval world with its reactionary tendencies, and also led young rationalists and firebrands, champions of progressive ideas of freedom, democracy and cosmopolitan liberalism, who looked toward the future rather than the past.

Heine's generation was thus a most paradoxical one, one marked by inner discord and strife. The word *Zerrissenheit* – referring to a rift, a lack of wholeness – has often been applied to Heine and indeed to his entire age. In his book *Der Typ des Zerrissenen*, Gerhard Thrum says:

> That inner powerlessness to lend continuity to an idea or a sentiment, to exercise control over one's heart or mind, that constant medley of thoughts and feelings which are at once infinitely delicate and coarsely sensual, longing and mocking, romantically dream-like and crudely realistic – that is the Heine *Zerrissenheit*.

Heine himself expressed that condition in these terms:

> Alas, dear reader, if you would complain about that rift [*Zerrissenheit*], rather lament that the world itself is rent in twain. For since the heart of the poet is the centre of the world, it must indeed have been woefully torn apart in these times. Whoever boasts about his heart that it has remained intact, only admits that he has a prosaic, distantly isolated, provincial heart. But through mine has passed the great world rift ...

Perhaps this will go a long way towards explaining the numerous inconsistencies and contradictions, all the ambivalence and ambiguity, the mercurial, often Mephistophelian quality in Heine's life and work.

The acuity of Heine's historical vision has frequently been noted. In his early, now-forgotten tragedy *Almansor* (1820), which explores the conflicts between Moors and Christians in medieval Spain and may be regarded as a parable of the position of German Jewry in Heine's day, the Moor Hassan's reply to Almansor's horrified remark about the burning of the Koran in the marketplace of Granada contains words of chilling prescience:

> That was only a prelude; where one burns books, one is going to wind up burning people, too.

When Heine gave his birthdate as 1 January 1800 and described himself as 'one of the first men of the 19th century', this was a deliberate (and characteristic) bit of punning obfuscation and need not be taken any more seriously than his parents' attempt to make their first-born two years younger so that he might escape conscription into the army (the records of his birth had been destroyed by fire). Heine was born on 13 December 1797 in the Rhenish city of Düsseldorf as the son of a merchant, Samson Heine, and Betty (or Peira) van Geldern Heine. According to the viciously anti-Semitic German literary historian Adolf Bartels, who wrote a book on Heine in 1906, Heine's name should have been Chaim Bückeburg. The child's name was indeed Chaim, and an ancestor by that name had lived in the town of Bückeburg. The poet was given the name Harry in honour of a British friend with whom his father did business. Heine came to dislike it when his schoolmates teased him by crying 'Haaarrüh', which is what the town's trashman called his donkey. The name Heine also derives from Chaim, via Heymann and Heinemann. The Jewish antecedents of the poet's parents were impressive (both were great-grandchildren of Court Jews), but in Heine's parental home Judaism had been downgraded and was abandoned altogether in the face of financial adversity. The mother seems to have been a stronger influence than the father, and Heine virtually imbibed his love of Napoleon with his mother's milk. The mother dreamed of a military career for her son; later she envisioned him as another Rothschild, and later still she was willing to settle for a great jurist. The child had a spotty and rather dubious Jewish education, but his basic knowledge of Jewish rites and ceremonies, festivals and prayers, and Hebrew and Yiddish words do indicate some measure of orthodox upbringing. It is hard to believe Heine's statement that he had never set foot in a synagogue. In a sort of *cheder* the child did have the ministrations of a *melamed* and acquired a treasury of Bible lore, but one day his parents took him out of the Jewish school and sent him to a lyceum attached to a Franciscan monastery where the teaching was done largely by French priests – an early taste of the French culture and spirit to which Heine was later to become so attached. When Napoleon's armies withdrew from the Rhineland, Düsseldorf became a Prussian town and the old restrictions against the Jews were put in force again. Following a brief sojourn in Frankfurt in 1815, Heine was taken in hand by his millionaire uncle Solomon Heine in Hamburg who not only acquainted him with Jewish tenets and practices but also set him up in business as Harry Heine & Co. Heine promptly fell in love with his cousin Amalie (and a few years later with her sister Therese), but his love was not requited and he later referred to Hamburg as 'lovely cradle of my sorrows' and had a low opinion of Hamburg Jewry. A failure in business and in love, he was nevertheless a published poet by the time he was twenty, his first verses having appeared in an anti-Semitic journal, *Hamburgs Wächter*, under the pseudonym Sy Freudhold Riesenharf, an anagram of Harry Heine Düsseldorf. Then the time came for Heine to further his education, and he did so at the universities of Bonn, Göttingen, and Berlin. His two and a half years in Berlin were especially fruitful, for there he came under the spell of the critic August Wilhelm Schlegel and the philosopher-historian Hegel. In that city, too, Heine, who then affected a Byronic stance, frequented the literary salons maintained by such brilliant Jewish (albeit converted) women as Rahel Varnhagen, Henriette Herz, and Dorothea Mendelssohn Schlegel. In 1822 he joined the *Verein für Kultur und Wissenschaft der Juden*, the Society for the Culture and Scholarship of the Jews. This society had been founded in 1819 for the purpose of continuing Moses Mendelssohn's work of cultural emancipation and applying the new scholarly insights and methods that were an outgrowth of the Romanticists' wide-ranging interests to the investigation of Jewish religion, Jewish history, and Jewish tradition. Such eminent men as Leopold Zunz, Eduard Gans, Moses Moser, and Ludwig Marcus were leaders in both the *Verein* and the scholarly endeavours known as *Wissenschaft des Judentums*. Heine became the secretary of the Society, which had branches in a number of cities, and also taught history and languages in its school. While he admired men like Leopold Zunz, he soon realized that the Society's overly theoretical approach isolated it from the masses of the Jewish people and their needs. Referring to the middle-class Jews of Berlin and Hamburg in programmatic contrast to Polish Jewry, he wrote: 'We no longer have the strength to wear beards, to fast, to hate, and to suffer hatred.' He described the Jews of Hamburg in his inimitably ironic and satirical manner:

> The Jews are, however, divided again
> Into two very different parties:
> The old one goes to the synagogue,
> In the temple the new one's heart is.
> The new party eat the flesh of swine,
> Their manners are somewhat dogmatic;
> They're democrats;
> But the old school
> Is much more aristocratic.

One might have expected Heine to be a leader in the Reform movement which emanated from German Jewry at that time. But while his rational intellectual side hailed this Western movement, emotionally he was on the side of Eastern orthodoxy. In the autumn of 1822 he visited Prussian Poland, and despite their crudity and aloofness from European culture he appreciated the self-assurance and unity of these Jews who, unlike German Jewry, were not prey to heterogenous emotions and resentments. He wrote about his experience:

> I shudder when I remember the first Polish village I saw which was mainly inhabited by Jews ... Despite the barbarian fur cap which covers his head and the even more barbarian ideas that fill it, I prefer the Polish Jew who smells of garlic with his dirty fur coat, his beard, and his queer speech to many a German Jew in all the glory of his gilt-edged government bonds.

To be sure, such Eastern Jews could be found in the West, too. Later, in his prose work *The Baths of Lucca*, Heine glowingly described such a Jew, who lived in the slums of Hamburg amidst filth and poverty.

> But when Moses Lump comes home on Friday evening, he finds the seven-armed candelabrum lit; the table covered with a white cloth; he puts away his bundles and his worries and sits down with his unshapely wife and still more unlovely daughter; he eats with them fish cooked in a pleasant white garlic sauce and sings the most splendid songs of King David; he rejoices from the bottom of his heart at the exodus of the children of Israel from Egypt and is happy that all the tyrants who plotted evil for them have died, that King Pharaoh, Nebukadnezzar, Haman, Antiochus, Titus, and all such folk are deceased, but that he, Lümpchen, still lives and eats fish with wife and child. This man is happy; he does not have to torment himself with an education; he sits, contented with his religion and his green robe like Diogenes in his barrel; he looks clean. And I tell you, though the lights burn somewhat dimly and the Sabbath-woman, who is supposed to clean them, is not available, even if Rothschild the Great were now to enter with all his bankers, brokers, shipping-agents, and department chiefs, with whom he has conquered the world, and were to say: 'Moses Lump, ask for a favour; whatever you wish, shall be granted,' I am certain that Moses Lump would calmly reply: 'Clean the lights for me!' And Rothschild the Great would exclaim in amazement: 'Were I not Rothschild, then I should like to be such a Lümpchen.'

On the other hand, Heine saw a spiritual affinity between Germans and Jews and insisted that the cause of the German Jews was identical with the cause of the German people. 'The Jews must finally realize,' he wrote, 'that they will achieve full emancipation only when the emancipation of the Christians is completely won and secured ... and they should not need to demand as Jews what has long been due them as Germans.' Elsewhere he wrote: 'Is the mission of the Jews fulfilled? I believe it will be when the worldly saviour comes – industry, labour, joy.' In his analysis of Shakespeare's *Merchant of Venice* he wrote in 1838:

> The affinity which prevails between the two ethical peoples, the Jews and the Germans, is indeed remarkable. This elective affinity did not originate in historical facts though the Bible, that great Jewish family chronicle, became the educational manual of the whole Germanic world, and Jews and Germans faced from early times the same implacable enemy, the Romans, and thus were allies. The affinity has a deeper root:

both people are fundamentally so much alike that one might regard ancient Palestine as an oriental Germany, just as one might regard today's Germany as the house of the Holy Word, the mother soil of prophetdom, the citadel of the pure Spirit.

Though this view may be more fanciful than factual, a remarkable blend of the Jewish and the German past may be found in a prose work which Heine wrote in 1824, a book which was intended to glorify medieval Jewish life as Sir Walter Scott had glorified medieval Scottish life and which Heine conceived of as 'an ever-burning lamp in the cathedral of God': *The Rabbi of Bacharach*. The poetic prologue to this story starts with 'Brich aus in lauten Klagen', and the first and last stanzas read as follows in Aaron Kramer's translation:

> Burst forth in loud complaining,
> Oh mournful martyr-song
> That I have been restraining
> Within my soul so long!
> And the tears flow on forever,
> Southward in silent ranks;
> They flow to the Jordan river,
> And overrun the banks.

In Heine's story, Rabbi Abraham of Bacharach and his wife Sara sit at the Seder table on the eve of Passover when two strangers ask to join them and are admitted to the circle of relatives and friends. When Abraham discovers an object under the table which he recognizes to be the corpse of a child, he realizes that there is a ritual-murder plot against him. He and Sara manage to escape unnoticed. A handsome blond youth, encountered on the banks of the Rhine, takes them in his boat on a night-long passage to Frankfurt. There they are admitted to the ghetto and enter the synagogue to attend the Passover morning service. After the service they meet Don Isaac Abarbanel, a friend from Abraham's student days who now poses as a Spanish knight. At this point Heine's story comes to an abrupt end. The German-Jewish novelist Lion Feuchtwanger, who wrote his doctoral dissertation on this work, said that the fragment was a form deliberately cultivated by the Romanticists. According to other sources, Heine did continue and possibly even complete this work, but the succeeding chapters were destroyed by fire. The most plausible explanation, however, is that Heine was hampered by his limited knowledge of Judaism and Jewish life and, furthermore, foresaw that he would not be able to complete this tale before the fateful step which he was then contemplating: his conversion.

Heine converted to Protestantism at Heiligenstadt near Göttingen on 28 June 1825, four weeks before he took his doctorate of laws at Göttingen. The adoption of Lutheranism, the state religion of Prussia, was to have facilitated Heine's law practice – something that he never even attempted; he also thought that it might get him a professorship, but it did not. Heine often expressed himself on this conversion in ironic, cynical, and even self-lacerating terms.

> I am now hated by both Christians and Jews ... I regret that I have been baptized; I don't see that it has helped me very much; on the contrary, it's brought me nothing but misfortune.

Early in 1826 he wrote: 'I have become a true Christian; I now sponge on rich Jews.' In other contexts he wrote:

> I often get up at night and stand before a mirror and call myself all sorts of names.
> I had *shabbes* dinner with Cohen who heaped fiery *kugel* on my head, and penitently I ate the sacred national dish, which has done more to preserve Judaism than all the numbers of Cohen's Journal. Of course, it has enjoyed a much wider circulation.

(Heine was, among other things, a culinary Jew, as witness his paean of praise to *sholet* or *tsholent* in one of his later poems:

> Sholet, lovely spark of heaven,
> Daughter of Elysium!
> Thus would sound the ode of Schiller
> Had he ever tasted sholet.

Louis Untermeyer has pointed out that Heine's ethnic inheritance is expressed in the very flavour of his writings, a flavour which is not 'bittersweet', as it has often been characterized, but 'sweet-sour' – the result of generations of cultural as well as culinary pungency). Shortly before Heine's conversion, Eduard Gans, one of the leaders of the *Verein*, also had himself baptized, and this move promptly gained him the chair of jurisprudence at the University of Berlin. Attributing this step to Gans's reading of Friedrich Schlegel and Karl Ludwig von Haller, both of whom had become Catholics, Heine bitterly wrote:

> With what face would Gans stand before Moses if he were suddenly to appear on earth again? And is not Moses the greatest jurist that ever lived? Indeed, his legislation has lasted unto the present day.

Heine's poignant poem 'Einem Abtrünnigen' (To an Apostate) is obviously addressed to Gans, but surely Heine is also speaking of and to himself when he says: 'And so you crawled to the cross that you despise, to the cross that only a few weeks ago you thought of treading under foot... Yesterday a hero and today already a rascal.' Another widely quoted statement is this one:

> That I became a Christian is entirely the fault of those Saxons who suddenly changed saddles at Leipzig, or of Napoleon, who surely did not have to go to Russia, or of his teacher of geography at Brienne, who did not tell him that Moscow winters are very cold.

(The Saxons' changing of saddles refers to soldiers in Napoleon's army who went over to the Allies and thus sealed Napoleon's doom. Heine always thought that the Jewish problem would have disappeared if Napoleon had definitively vanquished the old monarchies of Europe.) An equally characteristic statement is the one contained in a letter to Moses Moser dated 14 December 1825: 'I assure you that if the laws had permitted the stealing of silver spoons, I would never have undergone baptism.' The farcical nature of Heine's conversion is indicated by his remark that 'no Jew can ever believe in the divinity of any other Jew'. The certificate of baptism that Heine called 'an admission ticket to European culture' turned out to be invalid. His frame of mind both before and after his conversion is revealed in a letter to Moser written in September of 1823.

> From my way of thinking you can deduce that baptism is a matter of indifference to me, that I do not even attach any symbolic importance to it, and that in my situation and in the manner that I might go through with it, no one else need attach any significance to it. The only effect it might have upon me would be that I would dedicate myself all the more to the struggle for the rights of my racial comrades. Nevertheless, I

regard it as beneath my dignity and as a stain on my honour if I had myself baptized in order to accept a position in Prussia. In Prussia, of all places! I really don't know how I am to help myself in my bad situation. In chagrin I may yet become a Catholic and hang myself ... We are living in a sad age; rogues get to be the best people and the best of us must become rogues. I understand well the words of the Psalmist: Lord, give me my daily bread, lest I blaspheme Thy name.

Heine's baptismal name was Christian Johann Heinrich Heine. He may have been ashamed of his new German name, for he commonly used H. Heine as his signature and on his books. There is much to indicate that Heine's Jewish education started in earnest with his conversion, and he particularly studied the Bible, which he called 'an imperishable treasure with which the Jews trudged around throughout the Middle Ages as with a portable fatherland' and the great 'medicine chest of humanity'. In 1830 he wrote:

> I confess that although I am secretly a Hellene, the Book not only entertained me but edified me immensely. Great and wide as the world, rooted in the depth of creation and towering aloft into the blue mysteries of heaven — sunrise and sunset, promise and fulfilment, birth and death, the whole drama of mankind, all is in this book.

Heine's knowledge of Judaism was sometimes faulty; for example, in one of his poems he confused Judah Halevy with Salomo Halevi Alkabez, the author of *Lecha dodi, likrat kallah*, and in a letter dated 1824 the phrase '*Ho lachma anya*', heard near the beginning of the Seder, is transcribed as 'Caholach Manga'.

In the second phase of his life, Heine conceived of Judaism and Christianity as religions of asceticism and of Greek Paganism as a life-affirming religion based on the pleasure principle, and this led him to set up a dichotomy between the fanatical, self-denying Nazarenes and the joyous Hellenes, numbering himself among the latter. This was one explanation for Heine's falling-out with Ludwig Börne, born as Loeb Baruch, another converted German Jew and, like Heine, close to the Young Germany movement; Heine said that he himself was by nature a Hellene and a spiritual descendant of Aristophanes, while Börne was a Nazarene, a stern Hebrew prophet and a descendant of Jesus, the Jew. Heine dreamt of a civilization in which the mind and the senses would be in perfect tune and could flourish freely; he thought that the Judeo-Christian view of life excluded such a harmony.

This, to be sure, indicates a misunderstanding of Judaism. Not until much later did Heine recognize Judaism's affirmation of life – among other things, by reading Michael Sach's book on the religious poetry of the Jews in Spain, which showed him that Judaism and artistry were by no means incompatible. Yet even while he despised positive religions in general and Jewish monotheism in particular, he fought for the civil rights of the Jews and their cultural regeneration. Far from preaching assimilation, he felt that the Jews must be preserved as a distinct religious, cultural, and social entity. Heine thought of himself as a soldier of mankind, a warrior in mankind's struggle for liberation, and he rejected any group identity or any label, be it Jew, Christian, German, or Frenchman. After all, it was the Jewish tradition that had prepared him for a spirit of internationalism, universal brotherhood, conciliation among nations, and – not least – the ever-active spirit of criticism and scepticism. 'Every age has its task,' he wrote. 'And what is the great task of our day? It is emancipation. Freedom is the new religion, the religion of our age.' He fought for 'the emancipation of the whole world, and especially of Europe, which has now come of age and is tearing itself loose from the apron-strings of the privileged classes, the aristocracy.' In later years Heine felt close to Saint-Simonism, an earthly religion that preached emancipation of the flesh, a new church and a new science, and social, industrial, and educational reforms.

In the years following his conversion, Heine published the great works that were to bring him worldwide renown and the stature, variously, of the German Aristophanes, the German Rabelais, the German Byron, the German Voltaire, and the German Swift. In 1826–7 he published the *Reisebilder* (Travel Pictures), beginning with the famous *Harzreise*; in 1827 appeared the *Buch der Lieder*, the Book of Songs, a collection which, like its earlier and later companion volumes, contains poems combining simplicity with sophistication and subtlety, poignance with eloquence, an epigrammatic conciseness with an expansive folk-song quality, in addition to presenting intentional dissonances and vulgarity in the manner of 'romantic irony'. These are the lyrics that inspired musical settings by Schubert and Schumann, Mendelssohn and Brahms, Franz and Wolf, Rubinstein, Liszt and R. Strauss. Heine's works are as much 'fragments of a great confession' as Goethe's are. 'Out of my great pains I make little poems,' he once wrote.

Heine spent the last twenty-five years of his life in exile. Attracted by the July Revolution of 1830, but fully as much because he could not find any suitable employment in Germany, he went to Paris in 1831, and there he was to spend the rest of his life, except for brief and furtive visits to Germany in 1843 and 1844. (One of these gave us his marvellous satirical poetic sequence *Germany, A Winter's Tale*.) Heine's presence in France was widely noted, and except for his last years, he was neither isolated nor lonely. He associated with men like Gérard Nerval, Theophile Gautier, Victor Hugo, Béranger, Baudelaire, Balzac, and Dumas. Heine became a cultural mediator, interpreting his native land to the French and vice versa. For some years he was a correspondent of French and German newspapers, often producing journalistic potboilers and other hack work, but also creating literary genres new to German literature, such as the travel letter and the *feuilleton*, the latter being an elegant, witty, wide-ranging, stylistically notable essay on many aspects of culture. A great blow was the edict of the Prussian government which proscribed his writings along with those of the other members of the Young Germany group and precluded his return to Germany. Until 1848 Heine was supported by a pension from the French government from a fund established for 'all those who by their zeal for the cause of the Revolution have more or less compromised themselves at home or abroad'. There was also an annual allowance from his uncle Solomon which was suspended for some years following the uncle's death in 1844 and a quarrel with Heine's ungrateful cousin Karl. In Paris Heine remained what he had always been: a German Jew. 'I did not become a naturalized Frenchman,' he wrote, 'for fear that I would get to love France less well; just as a man cools toward a mistress the moment he is legally wedded to her. I shall continue to live with France without benefit of clergy.' Despite the fact that he spoke and wrote French fluently, Heine said that 'in France my mind feels as if it were in exile, banished into a foreign tongue.' On the other hand:

> At night I think of Germany,
> And then there is no sleep for me.

For the rest,

> I am a German poet,
> Well known in the German land.
> When the best names in it are reckoned,
> My name amongst them will stand.

In 1834 Heine met a 19-year-old French *grisette* or shopgirl named Crescentia Eugenie Mirat whom he named Mathilde and with whom he fell in love. By all accounts, this girl was a near-illiterate, vain, shrewish, selfish, a terrible housekeeper and the owner of a horrible screeching parrot named Cocotte. Almost uneducable, she never mastered more than four or five German words and had only the faintest notion that her Henri was a distinguished foreign poet, let alone an appreciation of his work. Just as Goethe had loved and eventually married Christiane Vulpius, a similarly earthy and natural creature, Heine married Mathilde – in a Catholic church, to please her – in 1841 after living with her for a stormy seven years. Regarding his infatuation with her, he wrote to a friend: 'Have you read the Song of Songs of King Solomon? Well, read it again and you will find in it all that I could tell you.' Two important prose works date from the 1830s: *History of Religion and Philosophy in Germany* and *The Romantic School*.

Soon after his arrival in Paris, the first symptoms of an illness made themselves felt, a progressive crippling malady that slowly paralysed Heine's body but not his spirit, for his mind remained keen, supple, and scintillating even when his body had wasted away and shrivelled to the dimensions of a child's. *Rückenmarkschwindsucht* is the German word for Heine's malady; it was a consumption of his spinal marrow, a softening of the spinal column that was undiagnosed by Heine's doctors and is often glossed over in the literature. Today we know that Heine was dying, with excruciating slowness, of a syphilitic infection which he had contracted in a period of loose living in Germany. The last time Heine went out was in 1848; he disliked the Revolution of that year, distrusting the masses and fearing a mobocracy. The last eight years of his life he spent in the *Matratzengruft*, his self-styled mattress grave or crypt, in a state of progressive paralysis, but creating until the end. (In his book *Dreamers of the Ghetto*,

Israel Zangwill described the dying Heine in a section called 'From the Mattress Grave'.) Heine had an apocalyptic view of the future. In 1842 he predicted that a world war was inevitable. He foresaw the disintegration of the British Empire and the rise of a brutal dictatorship that would crush European culture. America, which he had once called the land of 'egalitarian boors', now was to him the last refuge of liberty-loving individuals.

Heine's gradual return to Judaism – not to the synagogue, but to the Jewish fold nevertheless – began in 1838. In 1840, for example, he wrote an eloquent essay pleading for the Jews of Damascus who were being made the victims of a blood libel. Having passed through the stages of Saint-Simonism, pantheism and agnosticism and having abandoned his pagan-pantheistic hedonism, he conceived a stronger sympathy for religions that acknowledge a personal and transcendent God. In 1849 he confessed that he was no longer a pleasure-loving Hellene but only a poor, unhappy Jew with a fatal illness. When he returned to God – and he announced this return and recanted some of his earlier writings – it was not necessarily the Old Testament God, to be sure. He told friends late in life:

> I am convinced that the sick and the healthy need two entirely different religions... I am no longer the Great Heathen No. 2, another vine-crowned Dionysus, excelled only by my colleague, No. 1, to whom was given the title Grand Duke Jupiter of Weimar [Goethe]; I am no longer a joyous Hellene sound in body, smiling down gaily on the melancholy Nazarenes. I am now only a poor sick Jew.

In 1850 he said: 'I make no secret of my Judaism, to which I have not returned, because I never left it.' Later still, in 1854, he wrote in his *Confessions*:

> I see now: the Greeks were only beautiful youths, but the Jews have always been men – not just in days of yore, but to this day. In later life I have learned to appreciate them more. And if any pride of birth were not a foolish contradiction in a fighter of the Revolution, this writer might be proud that his ancestors belonged to the noble house of Israel, that he is a descendant of those martyrs who have given the world a god and a morality.

It is revealing that Heine says 'his ancestors belonged', not that *he* belonged. This lends plausibility to Lewis Browne's thesis that

Heine did not belong anywhere. Therein perhaps lies the tragedy of his life, both his individual unhappiness and his communal consolation. And Heine would not have been Heine if he had not continued to be full of conflicts and contradictions. In his valuable book *Judaic Lore in Heine*, Israel Tabak quotes from the memoirs of one of Heine's visitors, Philibert Audebrand:

> To write about the Jews gave him particular pleasure. A glance at his correspondence shows everywhere this remarkable predilection. I say remarkable, for he wrote good things and bad about his coreligionists with equal delight. He raised them to the sky and tore them cruelly down. When one talked with him about it, he showed himself at bottom full of admiration over the wonderful diffusion and indestructibility of the seed of Abraham.

The *Hebräische Melodien*, which forms part of Heine's last poetry collection, the *Romanzero* of 1851 (the title was undoubtedly suggested by Lord Byron's *Hebrew Melodies*), contain such vibrant poems of Jewish content as 'Yehuda Halevi', 'The Golden Calf', 'King David', 'Solomon', and 'Princess Sabbath'. The beginning of the last-named poem indicates the solution found by Heine, the worshipper of beauty *and* the Jew.

> In Arabia's book of fables
> We are shown enchanted princes
> Who may now and then recover
> All their former manly beauty...
>
> But the magic-time runs out,
> And we suddenly discover
> All is high and regal grandeur
> Turning into something monstrous.
>
> Here I sing of such a prince.
> He is known as Israel.
> Words of witchcraft have transformed him,
> Turning him into a dog...
>
> But on every Friday evening,
> At the hour of dusk, the magic
> Suddenly grows weak; the dog
> Once again becomes a person.

But there is also a long and typically Heinesque poem entitled

'Disputation', in which the poet, having listened to the arguments of Rabbi Juda of Navarro and the Franciscan Friar José and using a queen as his mouthpiece, comes to the conclusion of a sardonic 'plague on both your houses', as it were:

> Which is right I hardly know —
> But to tell the truth, I think
> That the rabbi and the friar —
> That they both — forgive me — stink

The *New Poems* of 1844 include one of Heine's most striking creations, a poem about the hospital founded a few years previously by his uncle Solomon, 'The New Israelite Hospital in Hamburg':

> A hospital for sick and needy Jews,
> For the poor sons of sorrow thrice accursed,
> Who groan beneath the heavy, threefold evil
> Of pain, and poverty, and Judaism.
>
> The most malignant of the three the last is:
> That family disease a thousand years old,
> The plague they brought with them from the Nile valley —
> The unregenerate faith of ancient Egypt...

Once more Heine reverted to the relationship between Jews and Gentiles in his poignant poem 'To Edom':

> For a thousand years and longer
> We have lived like faithful brothers;
> You have suffered me to breathe,
> And your raving I have endured.

At times, to be sure, Esau — that is, non-Jews generally — got out of hand and dyed his piously affectionate claws with Jewish blood. Now, however — so the poet points out — the friendship is becoming firmer, 'for I myself have begun to rage, and I am becoming almost like you.' In one of his 'Lazarus' poems Heine concerns himself with the problem of Job:

> Whose is the responsibility?
> Is perhaps our Lord not fully all-powerful?
> Or does He Himself play these mischievous tricks?
> Oh, that would be beastly.

> Thus we ask incessantly
> Until they stuff our mouths
> With a handful of earth.
> But is this an answer?

In his last year Heine experienced a lovely angel of death in the form of a somewhat mysterious girl, a literary adventurer named Eliese Krienitz (or Camille Selden, as she also called herself) whom Heine named La Mouche, the Fly. In a long poem devoted to her, Heine summarizes his past self-division and his present inner conflict, his mixed inheritance, and his attempt to unite the blithe Hellene with the Jew yearning for God. Two of Heine's last utterances bear repeating here. In his last prose work we find this revealing line: 'Goodness is better than beauty'. And to a visitor who asked the old sinner whether he had made his peace with God, Heine replied: 'Dieu me pardonnera; c'est son métier' (God will forgive me; that's his business). Heine was released from his sufferings on 17 February 1856, and was buried in the cemetery of Montmartre – at his own request, without the ministrations of clergy.

Israel Tabak comes to the conclusion that 'through his Hebrew background, which was deeply implanted in the recesses of his soul, and his thorough acquaintance with the thinking of his time, Heine endeavoured, in the final stages of his mental development, to effect a synthesis of Hebrew culture with Western thought.' This synthesis necessarily remained incomplete because, as one of Heine's translators, the American-Jewish poetess Emma Lazarus, put it, Heine was a Jew with the mind and eyes of a Greek, a beauty-loving, myth-creating pagan soul housed in a sombre Hebrew frame. The very titles of some English-language books on Heine are revealing of his afterfame: *Paradox and Poet*, *The Sardonic Smile* (Matthew Arnold had called Heine 'the sardonic smile on the face of the world'), *Poet in Exile*, *A Life Between Love and Hate*, *The Strange Guest*, *That Man Heine*. In his book *The English Legend of Heinrich Heine*, Sol Liptzin points out that the English have viewed Heine in turn as Blackguard and Apostate, Martyr of Montmartre, Continuator of Goethe, Hellenist and Cultural Pessimist, Bard of Democracy, and Citizen of the World. There has been an occasional detractor like Thomas Carlyle, who called Heine 'a dirty blaspheming

Jew... a slimy and greasy Jew, fit only to eat sausages made of toads' – just as one of Heine's German enemies, Wolfgang Menzel, called him 'an ape that uses its own faeces as a missile'. Germany, of course, is a chapter by itself, a story of many decades of neglect and ambivalence highlighted in recent years by the refusal of the University of Düsseldorf to adopt the name of that city's greatest son. In the 1920s the German-Jewish satirist Kurt Tucholsky said that 'in Germany, the number of war memorials is to the number of Heine memorials as force is to the spirit' – that is, many war memorials, no Heine memorial; much force, no spirit. During the Third Reich, Heine was regarded as the typical Jew in literature: rootless, corrosive, and unwholesome. 'Die Loreley' was too well known and too beloved as a folksong to be expunged, so it appeared in schoolbooks and other collections with the notation 'Dichter unbekannt' (author unknown). More than one Nazi writer remarked that the poem's first line, *'Ich weiss nicht, was soll es bedeuten'*, had faulty word order and was thus more Yiddish than German!

'Keine Messe wird man singen', wrote Heine in one of his best-remembered poems.

> There will be no whispered masses,
> There will be no songs nor crying,
> None will rise to say a Kaddish
> On the day that I lie dying...

But again and again during the past century, Jews *have* been moved to say Kaddish for Heinrich Heine, for they have seen in him, despite everything, a great God-seeker and a kindred soul in whom there was a preponderance of affirmation over alienation.

Lion Feuchtwanger: Jewish Novelist of Our Time

LOTHAR KAHN

Several of Lion Feuchtwanger's many novels have passed the test of time. In general, these enduring works direct their light penetratingly into questions of Jewish concern. In some, such as *Power* and the Josephus trilogy, Jews serve as the infinitely complex and internally torn protagonists. In other fiction of lasting quality, *Success* and *Paris Gazette*, he depicts, respectively, the conditions giving rise to an anti-Semitic movement and the problematic conditions of exile. *The Oppermanns*, which sketched the impact of Hitler's seizure of power on a Jewish family, has been called the first novel to alert the world to the more subtle, non-physical tortures inflicted by the Nazis. In *Raquel* or *The Jewess of Toledo*, dealing with the famed legend of the beautiful Jewess who ensnared a King of Castile, he demonstrated that pogroms, flight and resettlement, were a seemingly permanent feature of the Jewish condition. In his final novel, *Jephta*, he turned toward a Biblical subject. In so doing, he finally yielded to his life-long passion for the Bible as history and as an expression of the Jewish soul.

The preoccupation with Bible and Jewish learning was about all that was left of the Jew Feuchtwanger in his late teens. His parents, wealthy Munich manufacturers, imposed their rigid orthodoxy upon nine children, of whom Lion was the oldest (born 1884). But, one by one, the others followed his lead in rebelling against the narrow, ritualistic demands of the home. Yet none revolted against their Jewishness as such and nearly all were to be associated with Jewish cultural or national interests. Lion's own persisting Jewish affinity is reflected in the choice of his doctoral thesis: Heine's fragment *The Rabbi of Bacharach*. Perhaps the children's insurgency was not directed against orthodoxy itself, or the taxing practices it required, but rather against the bourgeois-conventional values that seemed associated with them. Because the home of the highly respected Feuchtwangers was thus internally rent with bickering and dissention, Lion willingly sacrificed parental subsidies to secure his independence and freedom and join the free and exciting life of Munich Bohemia. Here, among editors, writers, stage directors and actors he established his first literary contacts. For a short time he edited a literary journal and became a much feared theatrical critic. His harshness was at least partly a product of the conflicts within, not least of which was his sense of inferiority over physical size and appearance.

His timidity was at least partly helped by his marriage in 1911 to the stunning Marta Loeffler. The marriage led to a two-year honeymoon beginning in Switzerland, continuing with virtual vagrancy in Italy, and ending only in North Africa with the outbreak of World War I. Through the ingenuity of his wife Feuchtwanger succeeded in escaping in dramatic fashion on an Italian steamer, hiding beneath coiled ropes in the hull of the ship. His hair-raising adventures, the result of inflamed anti-German sentiment, converted him for the briefest time into a German patriot. But return to Germany convinced him that divisive, hateful nationalism was no French monopoly and, though forced to serve in the Kaiser's army, he made known his antipathy to war and the economic and nationalist factors which nurtured it. During the conflict, Feuchtwanger adapted several antique dramas which pointed up discreetly the follies of ethnocentrism and war. In preparing for these plays, he became intrigued with Indian philosophy whose do-nothing, want-nothing emphasis preoccupied him for nearly a decade.

It led him to write, among other plays, *Jew Suess*. Feuchtwanger made it plain that in dramatizing both the evil-doings and nobility of the 18th century court-Jew, he was drawn less to the controversial historic figure or even the perennial dilemma of Jew-hate, but to the fact that Suess had let himself fall from power and grace, that he had opted for resignation, that, having known power, he had recognized its ephemeral character. Yet there was conscious design in Feuchtwanger's choice of a Jewish hero to deal with an Indian theme: in the Jew Feuchtwanger envisaged the bridge between Europe (power) and Asia (resignation), between Nietzsche and Buddha, between the 'old and the new covenant'.

At the very time that Indian notions exerted this powerful grip, events in Europe pulled him unobtrusively at first, in an opposing orbit. War was force, not renunciation; its end was likely to come through the triumphant force of the one side over the other, or perhaps one people employing force against its own government. This was indeed happening in his native Munich in 1918. Here, under the leadership of Jewish intellectuals a revolution deposed the ruling Wittelsbach dynasty and helped speed the end of World War I. The Jewish intellectual leaders had several factors in common: they all died a violent death; they were naively idealistic; they were inept in the bloody business of revolution. In *Thomas Wendt*, a 'dramatic novel' was inspired by the Bavarian revolution: contemplation-activism. Thomas Wendt resembles a real-life writer, Ernst Toller, idealistic, well-spoken, an orator of fiery power. Wendt, like Toller, hurls himself headlong into the revolutionary mêlée only to be horrified by the bloodshed it engenders. Ethics recoil before politics as, in the end, the hero withdraws, guilt-ridden, from the blood-drenched political arena. Into the vacuum created by his voluntary retirement steps Herr Schulz, the industrial magnate, who had cynically feigned sympathy for revolutionary goals. Broadly speaking, the political course of the play was to foreshadow that of Germany.

Feuchtwanger's use of the 'dramatic novel' as his literary medium led to two broad results. First, it directed Bertold Brecht, whom Feuchtwanger discovered at this time (and whose early career he masterminded) toward theories of 'epic theatre' and served Feuchtwanger himself as a bridge to the novel. He had become frustrated over the natural restrictions inherent in drama. So many ideas that had needed expression in his play *Jew Suess* had been left dangling that Feuchtwanger in his intense dissatisfaction had 'recalled' the play. In 1921 he started rewriting *Jew Suess* (U.S. version: *Power*) as a novel. While he fretted over the patience needed, he did realize that at last he could say what needed to be said. But how much had happened between 1919 and 1922! His Munich, virtually untainted by anti-Semitism in his youth, had become a hotbed of nationalist fervour, reaction and Jew-hatred. Countless small and often secret societies suddenly sprang up to pose as the superior legatees of the German past and committed to protecting 'German values' from the international Jewish conspiracy and its recently proven subversive influence. Those responsible for the war – industrialists, officers, die-hard nationalists – had found their ideal scapegoats in the highly visible Jewish leadership in the post-war events. When Walther Rathenau, another Jew – though hardly a revolutionary – was designated Foreign Minister in 1922, and concluded with the Soviet Union, another pariah nation at the time, a pact designed to end German isolation, the same Right Wing groups denounced the action as another Jewish betrayal. Rathenau fell victim to three young nationalist assassins. The news had been greeted with the greatest outpouring of grief and revulsion following a political murder since Lincoln's assassination in America sixty years earlier. Feuchtwanger had been so shaken by the cancerous spread of anti-Semitism that he briefly tried to tell the Jew Suess story though Rathenau, an adviser of state like Suess and to whom he bore in many ways a striking resemblance. But the events were too fresh in his mind and Feuchtwanger recognized that the historical setting of a novel provided a magnificent frame for discussing a current issue – lending it distance, perspective, objectivity, detachment from the passions of the moment.

Whereas for the play *Jew Suess* Feuchtwanger had gone to some length to minimize the Jewish aspect, anti-Semitism suddenly rose up to prominence in the novel. But so great was the anti-Semitic hysteria following the lost war and abortive revolution that a publisher who admitted to being spellbound by the book, declined to publish it in the prevailing climate. But he ordered from this new master of historical fiction another novel of the past. The result was *The Ugly Duchess* into which Feuchtwanger inserted Jewish characters who are sympathetic and whose plight is correctly understood by the ruling Duchess, herself oppressed by an accident of birth, a pocket-mouth.

Power was finally published in 1925, became an instant success in Germany and, following Arnold Bennett's almost reverential review in London, in the Anglo-Saxon countries as well. It established his name as that of one of the dynamic writers and perhaps the boldest and most original practitioner of historical fiction in modern times. Yet the novel was assailed from two sides: some Jews were not happy with a less than idealized portrait of a Jew; nationalists, by contrasts, denounced it as a defence of Jews and an assault on Germany and Christianity.

In 1925 Feuchtwanger could no longer bear the harassments to which Right-wingers, now led by one Adolf Hitler, exposed him in Munich. He moved to Berlin which was rapidly becoming the symbol of what was liberal in German life and culture. At first, Feuchtwanger contemplated a series of novels on Flavius Josephus, the Jewish-Roman historian, but events in Bavaria pressed for artistic expression. As a result he wrote *Success*, 'the history of a province (Bavaria) over a three-year span (1920–1923)'. Feuchtwanger displayed the same incisive narrative power which had distinguished *Jew Suess* as he addressed himself to the story of a woman seeking to free her lover, an art critic, charged with having perjured himself. Actually, the art critic had become an embarrassment to the conservative Bavarian government, a victim of politicized justice. It is a Jew, almost blindly devoted to justice, who defends the avant-garde critic, only, like him, to be vanquished by the staunch alliance of army, church and economic potentates. Perhaps more significantly, *Success* was the first anti-Nazi novel in world literature and one of the neglected masterpieces of social fiction in our time. Although Feuchtwanger satirized Hitler in the person of Rudolf Kutzner and thus earned the undying hatred of the Nazis, he no longer laughed in 1930, when the novel was finally published. By that time their movement had spread infectiously from Munich to the rest of Germany. Their cries of hatred upon the publication of *Success* persuaded Feuchtwanger that he would be among the first victims should they ever achieve power. To friends he pronounced Berlin a city of future emigrants. Earlier, when the Nazis had first spread their anti-Semitic venom, Feuchtwanger had this vision of a world controlled by anti-Semites: 'And then the room grew much larger and became a huge square which was filled with smoke and blood. Towers of Hebrew books were burning, and funeral pyres were erected, high up into the clouds, and men were being charred, countless men, and the voices of priests were chanting "Gloria in exelsis Deo". Long lines of men, women, and children were dragging themselves across the square, coming from all sides: they were naked or in rags, and they had nothing with them but bodies charred, dismembered, broken, hanged, nothing but bodies and the scraps from book scrolls, scrolls torn, violated, soiled with excrement.'[1]

Feuchtwanger was on a lecture tour in the U.S. when Hitler was designated Chancellor in January 1933. Since the Nazis had suffered a loss in the last free elections, Feuchtwanger had thought Hitler's strength might be on the wane. He was taken aback when the German ambassador to the U.S., on 30 January, notified him of Hitler's appointment. 'Hitler means war,' he now declared to the American press, but Congressmen whom he met insisted that 'you have to give Hitler a chance.' Feuchtwanger knew that for him there was no returning to Berlin, that he would be deprived of all his property, including his prized possession, his library. In March, he sailed for Europe and, after a brief stay in Austria and Switzerland, settled in Southern France, in the fishing village of Sanary. In this area, where D. H. Lawrence had lived and Aldous Huxley was living now, a whole new congregation of intellectuals was settling, some for the summer, others, like Feuchtwanger who was first, all the year round. The Sanary exiles included Thomas Mann and his brother Heinrich, Bruno Frank, Franz Werfel, other stars of the cultural firmament of the Weimar Republic.

The first Josephus volume, perhaps Feuchtwanger's greatest work, had been published in 1932, the second volume was lost when Storm Troopers invaded his Berlin home, confiscating or destroying all in sight. Now Feuchtwanger had to rewrite it, continuing the narrative of the controversial historian who, like Feuchtwanger, had sought to interpret the history he had experienced. Feuchtwanger's Josephus figure is powerfully drawn to Rome, but events keep casting him back into the Jewish orbit. Whereas in the first volume, Josephus had been a Jewish nationalist attracted to Western, i.e. Roman ways, he is wholly Romanized in the second volume. In the third sequel, completed ten years later under more harrowing circumstances yet, Josephus abandons the striving for world citizenship and returns to his native land and roots. The scenes of Josephus wandering guilt-ridden through the streets of Jerusalem, following the razing of the Temple, and his final return to Judea to die, rank among the most beautiful and touching in the annals of Jewish fiction. While

Feuchtwanger is known chiefly as the author of *Jew Suess*, his reputation should rest more firmly on the monumental trilogy.

During his French exile, Feuchtwanger was horrified by the failures of the democracies to recognize the danger of Hitler. The suspicions, vaguely expressed in *Success*, that nationalist demagogues were being assisted by industrialists as a bulwark against Socialism, became virtual certainty in exile. Increasingly Feuchtwanger turned towards the Soviet Union as the ultimate defence against Nazism. In 1937, he visited Russia, writing a glowing report about the vigour and youth of the socialist experiment. Eager to offset the loss of André Gide from the ranks of Western supporters, the Russians cultivated Feuchtwanger's friendship. Stalin volunteered an interview. When Feuchtwanger depicted the dictator, whom he had previously disliked, in more favourable terms than was common in the West, he was promptly accused of 'sellout' and outright Communism. Indeed, there can be little question that Feuchtwanger's account was in part naïve, especially in his assessment of the purge trials then in progress. But Feuchtwanger's admiration, notwithstanding reservations expressed publicly and in private, was genuine: he was impressed with the determination to establish social justice, to remove ancient iniquities, to shape 'a reasonable and just society'. But Stalin had dropped disquieting hints in their discussion that he might have to seek an accommodation with Hitler who, he was certain, would attack Russia sooner or later. But only Hitler, in the meanwhile, could offer him the time – yes, and the arms – needed for the eventual defence against him.

In the 1930s Feuchtwanger turned publicist as much as novelist. He urged increasing unity – including Communists – among those who would oppose Hitler. His own sympathies were veering ever further towards the extreme Left, although he never became a party member or lost his inner and outer independence. He knew that in his fifties he was too old a man to renounce, for whatever cause, the freedoms he had always cherished. Ideologically, he also knew that while the world could not be explained without Marx, it could not be explained by Marxism alone. In novel after novel Feuchtwanger now combined his attacks on Fascism with the theme of economic exploitation by the few and the need of greater justice for the many. His vivid sympathy for the Russian experiment and his own inability to participate in it are subtly delineated in the conflict between the composer Trautwein and his son in *Paris Gazette*. This novel, published in Europe shortly before the Nazi rout of France in the late spring of 1940, was almost lost in the shuffle. Along with *Success*, it is Feuchtwanger's greatest *Zeitroman*, and one of the important works of exile literature. Exile, Feuchtwanger maintained, made the weak weaker and the strong stronger.

Events were soon to prove that he belonged to the strong. He was twice interned in 1939-1940, beset by serious illness, a potential victim of Clause 19 of the Peace Treaty – whereby the Vichy government obligated itself to deliver to the Nazis all wanted enemies of the regime. Now began a rescue as dramatic as any conceived in fiction. It involved persons ranging from the President of the United States to consular officials, to publishers, to rescue committees, to a veritable staff of known and unknown 'saviours'. It entailed being sneaked out of a camp, dressed as a woman, hiding in the home of a U.S. consul, travelling under a false name, bribery and using a smuggler's route across the Pyrenees. No sooner was Feuchtwanger safely in New York than he set about describing his experiences in *The Devil in France*. He also completed the final *Josephus* which, considering the uncertainty of his flight, was brought to the U.S. via diplomatic pouch. Just before leaving for California, his final residence, Feuchtwanger learned that the Nazis had at last managed to revenge themselves: they had abstracted from his *Jew Suess* novel those elements which lent themselves to making one of the most viciously anti-Semitic films ever produced. Feuchtwanger was impotent in the matter except to write an open letter to the actors, some being former friends. But Feuchtwanger continued the anti-Fascist battle by writing with Brecht *The Visions of Simone Machard*, out of which Feuchtwanger alone later fashioned his novel *Simone*. Simone is a Joan of Arc figure whose experiences point an accusing finger at the French bourgeoisie which had allowed itself to be drawn into betraying the nation for economic gain and security.

Feuchtwanger's three post-war novels, *Proud Destiny* (the link between the French and American Revolutions), *This Is The Hour* (Goya's conversion through experience from a craftsman to an artist) and *T'Is Folly To Be Wise* (dealing with the French Revolution and its aftermath) revealed how much the events of the thirties and forties had propelled him toward political engagement. They disclosed just as unequivocally how much he equated the artist's engagement with the battle for social justice. He who had been a pacifist in World War I and the twenties had now accepted the use of force as a possible means of effecting major changes. Thus, in the struggle for Israel, Feuchtwanger endorsed the *Irgun* as a realistic means of achieving needed ends. Of course, Feuchtwanger was not blind in the post-war world to the shortcomings of the Eastern bloc nations, but they embodied for him, however inadequately, an ideal and potentiality he still clung to. But towards Stalin, whom he had helped make palatable in the West in the years of war-time collaboration, his attitude had changed markedly. After 1951, he became increasingly convinced that Stalin was suffering from paranoia.

But his many reservations and the dictator's shortcomings did not weaken a conviction he expressed through *T'Is Folly To Be Wise*. A revolution is a bloody mess and transition to a new normalcy a frightful strain; the ultimate rewards, however, may be considerable. There is reason to believe that Feuchtwanger's extraordinary popularity in the Eastern nations – who yet consider him no more than a bourgeois liberal – is related to this implied exhortation to wait out patiently the era of transition.

But in *Raquel, The Jewess of Toledo*, Feuchtwanger abandoned the revolutionary themes and returned to another court Jew, an imperfect though idealistic individual, who exerts a constructive influence on the feudal King of Spain. Alas, for his services he was rewarded with a murderous pogrom as the forces of Church and landed gentry recognized in the Jewish Finance Minister the ultimate threat. Resignation, this earliest of Feuchtwanger's motifs, reappears and implies at least a surface weariness with the activist stress of recent years. Feuchtwanger describes warmly the intense cooperation and the meeting of minds between medieval Arabs and Jews and there is at least the inferred hope for a renewal in modern times.

Feuchtwanger was in his seventies when he began work on *Jephta* which was to be his final novel. He had read copiously for this work, as indeed he had for others, but this time his longstanding interest in the Bible threatened to gain control over his material. This final work, ambitious in its aspirations, skilful in execution, failed to achieve the heights of his earlier work.

The author's last twelve years of life were marred by renewed forms of persecution. Like many of his friends, he was harassed as a result of the witchhunting hysteria of the late 1940s and the McCarthy era. His application for U.S. citizenship, kept 'pending' and 'in active status' for over ten years, was neither granted nor refused. Repeated interrogations concerning his religious beliefs, his associations with Thomas Mann (hardly a Communist), an early 'revolutionary poem' (1915) and 'revolutionary play' (*Thomas Wendt*, 1918) etc. ended only one month before the author's death in December 1958. Without a U.S. passport he would never chance travelling to Europe and being denied re-entry to the U.S.

Today Feuchtwanger's reputation in the West is still partly eclipsed by the Communist issue and the continued low standing of the historical novel. Feuchtwanger's historical fiction is intellectual and political in character though it also offers a virtual course in the history of human thought, a thematic illustration of the constants in Jewish life throughout the ages. It depicts the tensions of his own time though transplanting them to an earlier period in the past. Yet Feuchtwanger even in his most socialist period never allowed doctrinaire thoughts or essay-like elements to intrude into the novel, to break the flow of easy, exciting narrative, the building of character, the creation of movement and suspense. A novel was first and foremost a novel – any ideas had to flow from the evolution of the story itself. The thematic ideas are broadly expressed in polar tensions that remain as unresolved in the novel as they were in the author's mind. But the issues of our day are all present, whether they are clothed in the problems of ancient Judea, or Rome, or medieval Spain, revolutionary Spain, or Weimar Germany.

Fuechtwanger's work is that of a predominantly rational mind. Emotion and passion, though eloquently present, seem subservient to the machinations of lucid intelligence. Yet this intelligence is not always triumphant. Feuchtwanger's conception of historical processes encompasses great diversity of motivation and suggests faithfully the complexity of human life.

Jewishly, Feuchtwanger was committed to the message of the prophets – their cry for the good life, the just society. While he rejected ritual for himself, he respected it in others who comprehended its significance and observed it. His Jewish protagonists are far from idealized, are men of flesh and blood, statesmen, thinkers, businessmen. He is a master of sketching the mental convolutions of the Jewish intellectuals he knew so well. He had never rid himself of the Talmudic training he had received in his early years. If Feuchtwanger's Jewish characters often inspired fear in Jews of arousing anti-Semitic sentiment, he himself remained largely unaffected by it: Jews had to shed the last vestiges of a Ghetto psychology. It was perhaps for this reason that, though not an orthodox Zionist, he endorsed vigorously the ideas for a Jewish homeland. For a long time he had held on to the dream of Yohanan ben Zakkai that Jewish peoplehood could continue independently of land and the trappings of nationhood, but the Nazi experience had demonstrated the impossibility of this dream in a contemporary setting. Yet he never ceased to believe that Jews were held together by their history. When a delegation visited him in the immediate post-War II years, seeking to enlist his support for a new territorial rather than Palestinian solution, Feuchtwanger could not give his support. The same delegation visited Thomas Mann and he saw merit in the proposal. The Land of Israel meant something to the Jew Fuechtwanger that it could not mean to the Christian Thomas Mann, though Mann, too, was motivated by the friendliest and most humanitarian motives.

1 'Gespräch mit dem ewigen Juden', 1921, in *Centum Opuscula*, edited by Wolfgang Berndt, Greifenverlag, Rudolstadt, DDR; translation is mine.

Beer-Hofmann: Last of the Great Viennese

ALFRED WERNER

The last major writer of old Austria, Richard Beer-Hofmann, died in the autumn of 1945 in New York, at the age of seventy-nine, shortly after having become an American citizen. He was the only old Austrian writer of importance not only to witness the invasion of his beloved country by the Nazis, but also to live long enough to learn of the Nazis' capitulation. He survived all of his prominent colleagues – Peter Altenberg died in 1919, Hugo von Hofmannsthal in 1929, Arthur Schnitzler in 1931, Hermann Bahr in 1934, Karl Kraus in 1936, and Robert Musil in 1942. All of them, with the exception of Bahr and Musil, were Jews; Hofmannsthal's grandfather was already a convert to Catholicism. The 'Aryan' Musil, married to a Jewish woman, left Greater Germany in disgust, to die in Switzerland. The eminently gifted Josef Weinheber, author of classical verse as well as folk poetry, switched from being a Social Democrat to becoming an ardent Hitler fan, and committed suicide when the Allied troops were approaching Vienna.

The Vienna of the *fin de siècle* has often been compared with the Athens of the fifth century B.C. Yet the arts flourished in the capital of the slowly disintegrating Austro-Hungarian monarchy despite the lack of a Pericles to encourage them. Vienna had at least one advantage over ancient Athens – it had the *Kaffeehaus*, where impecunious writers had unlimited credit, and where, over a *Mokka* or *Kapuziner* some of the finest lyrics and prose poems of the German language were produced. In one of the centres of literature and art, the famous Cafe Griensteidl on the Michaelerplatz, near the old Hofburgtheater, a literary movement was born around 1890 – 'Young Vienna'. Its founder was the versatile Upper Austrian, Hermann Bahr, who was prone to sponsor new persons and trends, and to flirt with almost any new political movement, from the Catholic 'Ultramontanism' to the intellectual architects of National Socialism. A certain E. M. Kafka – not related to Franz – who was editor of the periodical *Moderne Dichtung*, had suggested the forming of the group as a protest against Berlin and the militant naturalism of Arno Holz, Johannes Schlaf and Gerhart Hauptmann.

'The available material,' wrote Bahr, retrospectively, 'consisted of a young physician, Dr Arthur Schnitzler; a person famed about town because of the splendour of his neckties, Dr Richard Beer-Hofmann; and a high school youth, Hugo von Hofmannsthal, who wrote under the name of Loris. I looked them over and took the risk of founding the school.'

These four were joined by a host of lesser writers. Who remembers now, for instance, Leopold von Andrian, who became a follower of Stefan George and ended up by writing a volume in praise of the reactionary *Heimwehr* movement of Prince Starhemberg? Or Felix Doermann, who, after having published some remarkable poetry, turned toward the more lucrative writing of operatta librettos?

In the English-speaking world, Schnitzler's sensitive and psychologically interesting plays and stories have found many admirers: a few Englishmen and Americans realize that the young Hofmannsthal wrote some of the noblest verse since Goethe. Regrettably, however, very few people in London or New York, including students of German literature, can boast of a more than fleeting acquaintance with the works of Beer-Hofmann. This was due, to a degree, to the fact that, as a rule, they have appeared in small editions that were soon out of print. By contrast, many of Schnitzler's stories and plays were translated into English (some of his plays even appeared on the stage, while several of his stories were adapted for the B.B.C.).

Of Beer-Hoffmann's poems, only two or three were translated into English. His major work, *Jaakobs Traum*, was published in the U.S.A. under the title 'Jacob's Dream', in the versified translation of Ida Bension Wynn, but in a very small edition. Those able to read German, had to wait until 1963, when the Frankfurt firm of S. Fischer published his *Gesammelte Werke* (Collected Works). Printed on very thin paper, it contains 900 pages, including a preface by Martin Buber, and a section of explanatory notes. Since this hard-cover edition is rather expensive, one would like the famous firm of Fischer to prepare a less expensive one, in soft-covers, for the benefit of the young. From this popular edition, the scholarly apparatus (at the book's end) could be omitted.

Curiously, Beer-Hofmann was mentioned in the American press long before the American public learned of other modern Austrian writers. In the summer of 1895, a New York paper, the *Commercial Advertiser*, published a brief unsigned item about him:

'A Viennese novelist, a young author who has recently appeared in the field of letters in Vienna, is destined to make a more than ephemeral success. His name is Richard Beer-Hofmann, and he belongs to the coterie of writers in Vienna known as *Jung-Wien*. These writers – novelists, essayists, poets and journalists are included in the flock – are not so flecked with the circumstances of filth as their Paris confrères are wont to dwell upon. This author has written a book of short stories entitled *Das Kind* [actually, this story appeared in one volume with *Camelias*, under the title *Novellen*, in 1893], and his treatment of psychological analysis is strictly in keeping with that followed by the disciples of the latter day school. It is full of stirring episodes, and the vein of gentle pathos running through the entire volume gives it a refinement which is worthy of the pen of a writer of experience. Beer-Hofmann knows his Vienna as thoroughly as Zola his Paris, and his types, with their consistent environment, put one in the very atmosphere of the gay Kaiserstadt.'

(For reasons of his own, the author, in his New York exile, decided that the *Novellen*, somewhat reminiscent of Maupassant, must not be included in any future edition of *Gesammelte Werke*.)

The prophecy of 1895 came true, for Beer-Hofmann did make 'more than an ephemeral success' in German literature. In the U.S.A., he would be mentioned rarely, if at all – until, fifty years after the *Commercial Advertiser* review, the Viennese writer's name suddenly loomed conspicuously in the entire American press. For the National Institute of Arts and Letters, with headquarters in Upper Manhattan, bestowed upon the seventy-nine-year-old refugee the newly created Award for Distinguished

Service, to be given to an exiled artist residing in this country. In the auditorium of the American Academy of Arts and Letters, William Rose Benét hailed the great old man as 'the surviving member of the Vienna school of writers, two of whose foremost representatives were Arthur Schnitzler and Hugo von Hofmannsthal', stressing his 'candour, uncompromising integrity as an artist, and the purity of his moral attitude'. Answering the American poet by reading a prepared English text, Beer-Hofmann, in his unforgettable clear, bell-like voice spoke in praise of American democracy, which had accepted him as a citizen and shown its appreciation of his artistic endeavours: 'I do not know how well I succeeded in what I did. A writer's work can never hope to be complete. Yet it was worth trying – if only to learn this lesson.' This was the first and last time that Beer-Hofmann addressed a large crowd in English; a few months later in September 1945, he died of pneumonia in his home on Cathedral Parkway, opposite the Cathedral of St John the Divine.

He was the son of a well-to-do Viennese-Jewish lawyer, Dr Hermann Beer. The young mother died right after having given birth to Richard. Hence, it was decided that he should grow up in the home of his aunt and her husband, Alois Hofmann, a wealthy factory owner in Bruenn (Brno), an important industrial centre in what is now Czechoslovakia. When Richard was still a teenager, the Hofmanns, who had adopted Richard (hence his double-name), moved with the boy to Vienna, there to settle for good.

Richard's life was what is called 'uneventful' by those who do not consider the creation of a masterwork a great event. From the University of Vienna he got the Doctor of Law degree; he served his compulsory year in the Austro-Hungarian Army. He married Paula Lissy, who bore him three children: Miriam, Naemah and Gabriel (who was to settle in England and to achieve a modicum of success as a novelist under the name of G. S. Marlowe). The family managed to live well in a charming if modest villa in the sylvan part of Vienna. The sole heir of a handsome inheritance, Richard never had had to work for a living, but could, instead, indulge in his favourite pastimes, reading and writing.

Beer-Hofmann never hurried. He was twenty-seven when he broke into print. Thereafter, he slowly surpassed most of his friends, ridden as they were with aesthetic Epicureanism and hopeless scepticism. There is no doubt that Beer-Hofmann's literary style was strongly influenced by his surroundings, and the melody of his verse and prose often reminds us of the revered Austrian poets, Grillparzer and Stifter. His healthy philosophy of life outgrew the degenerate atmosphere of Vienna's *fin de siècle*. Waltzing itself to exhaustion, listening to the *Merry Widow* rather than to the revolutionary young Arnold Schoenberg, adoring Kaiser Franz Joseph as some curious antique, and acting in world politics as though the Austrian Hungarian monarchy were still a first-rate power, the Viennese were a sad lot. Their representative writer, Arthur Schnitzler, expressed their hopelessness, their lack of self-assurance, their debonair scepticism, when he made his Paracelsus say:

'Dream and awakening, truth and lie, merge into one another; there is no security anywhere. We know nothing about other people, nor about ourselves: we are always playing. He who recognizes that is wise.'

Beer-Hofmann could have become Vienna's Maupassant, if one may judge by his first novelette, *Camelias*. Its hero is a Viennese dandy who fluctuates between two women. But the writer stepped out of Schnitzler's narrow world of '*suesse Maedel*' and melancholy lieutenants, and his strength also outlived Hofmannsthal's somewhat eclectic aestheticism.

The second story, *Das Kind*, clearly indicated that he was seeking new paths, and avoiding the vicious circle of egocentric self-pity that trapped some of his associates. The novelist's hero, a light-hearted university student, is awakened to a feeling of guilt and responsibility upon finding the grave of his child born out of wedlock; he decides henceforth to face human relations and problems more seriously, for 'all things had not merely form and colour, but were irradiated by a secret sense; they no longer stood as strangers near each other, but were bound together by a single, common thought'.

There has rarely been a more felicitous cultural blending than that of the best Austrian and German literary traditions with the spiritual heritage in Beer-Hofmann, as manifest in his *Schlaflied fuer Mirjam*.

There is a distinctly Jewish element in this beautiful German poem, not only on account of certain phrases, such as *Mirjam*, *mein Leben*, reminiscent of Yiddish expressions of fondness, but also because of its comforting philosophy that everyone is at least a link in an unbroken chain of generations destined to the same fate. And while the individual must perish, the tribe survives, or, as Isaiah put it, 'As a tall tree, and as an oak, whose substance is in them, when they cast their leaves: so the holy seed shall be the substance thereof.' At the same time, the poem, with its evocation of the dim origin of life and its dark unfathomable end, somewhat reminds us of the lofty and philosophical poetry created in the German lands after the Thirty Years' War.

Further development is apparent in Beer-Hofmann's only novel, *Der Tod Georgs* ('The Death of George', 1900). Basically it belongs in the tradition of the German *Bildungsroman*, being the study of the triumph of an individual over the forces of life. Here both the stress upon his Jewish ancestry and the urgency of social action are clearly noticeable. The hero, Paul, is transformed by the sudden death of his beloved friend, George, from a passive sceptic into a man fully aware that nobody stands alone in this world (see *Schlaflied*), and that he, as a Jew, must recognize the mission of his people to teach divine justice to all nations:

> 'Over the life of those whose blood flowed in him, justice was ever present like a sun whose rays never warmed them, whose light never shone for them, and yet before whose dazzling splendour they reverently shielded their pain-covered foreheads with trembling hands ... A people which did not beg for grace but wrestled fiercely for the blessing of its Deity, a people wandering through seas, unhindered by deserts, always as aware of a God of justice as of the blood of its veins, calling its victory God's victory, its defeat God's judgment, selecting for itself the role of witness to God's power, a people of saviours, anointed for thorns and chosen for pains. And slowly releasing their God from sacrifices and burnt-offerings, these ancestors raised Him high above their heads until He stood beyond all transitory suns and worlds, no longer a warrior God of herdsmen, but a guardian of all right, invisible, irradiating all. And of their blood was he.'
> (*translation by the Beer-Hofmann biographer, Sol Liptzin*)

Beer-Hofmann's philosophy was deterministic, but not fatalistic. He did not believe that man's actions and attitudes are governed by a fate that cannot be affected by any human effort. He would rather have agreed with the dictum of the medieval Jewish philosopher, Bakhya ibn Pakuda: 'To what extent man is free no one knows; but he should act as if he were free.' In a conversation I had with Beer-Hofmann shortly before his death, he said to me: 'One cannot change one's fate; the road is predestined for each of us. But the way we walk it, the attitude with which we bear our fate, can be of great influence over events.'

In his drama *Der Graf von Charolais* (1905), which was inspired by the Elizabethan play, *The Fatal Dowry* by Philipp Massinger and Nathanael Field, the disruption of a marriage and the murder of the wife by her jealous husband are precipitated by the fact that the people involved merely followed their instincts, and failed to act as if they were free. The battle between Determinism and Free Will is again the central theme of his great Biblical dramas, *Jaakobs Traum* and *Der junge David*, published in 1918 and 1933 respectively, as parts of a tetralogy he planned to write.

Jaakobs Traum is based on two Biblical episodes: the conflict between the brothers Jacob and Esau, caused by Jacob's theft of the parental blessing, and Jacob's vision during the miraculous night at Beth El, when Eternity was promised to him and his tribe. In *Der junge David*, the struggle is in the hearts of two other men, the aging tyrant Saul and the youthful David. Among many other things, these plays are powerful attacks upon chauvinism and imperialistic greed. Jacob rejects the Archangel's offer of dominion over the earth, of secular riches:

> 'Finds He no use for us but to be kings?
> I will not rule! Does He not know?
> Mizraim, Babel, and the sea-land's Prince —
> Can He believe I envy them their gain?
> *Naught* do I envy — not your bliss, nor you ...
> Could I rejoice when all things suffer pain?
> All come to me, by day, by night, in dreams,
> Green herbage of the earth, man, beast and stone
> Plead for an answer with dumb eyes complaining,
> Asking me — yet all answer is His own!'
> (*translated by the Beer-Hofmann biographer, Sol Liptzin*)

Throughout his life Beer-Hofmann was fortunate — until the Nazis drove him and his family, like thousands of other Viennese Jews, into exile. Mrs Beer-Hofmann died in Switzerland. Accompanied by his daughter Naemah, by Miriam, and Miriam's husband, the 73-year-old poet arrived in New York City, to live out his life in near-obscurity. He had neither the strength nor the peace to complete his Biblical tetralogy (he had intended to write *Koenig David* and *David's Tod*, but only a few scenes were composed). In New York I met the poet again – I had last seen him in 1936, when I presented him with the first copy of my monograph, *Richard Beer-Hofmann, Sinn und Gestalt*. His eyes were still kind and friendly, but they looked very, very tired. Yet his writing career was not completely over, even though *Paula* was fated to remain unfinished. This was, of course, his wife's biography which, inevitably became his own as well. Like Stefan Zweig's memoirs, it constructs *The World of Yesterday*. One reads the story of an assimilated rich Jewish family in Brno; one sees the gay Vienna of the nineties through the clear and happy eyes of Richard Beer-Hofmann, poet as well as doctor of law. The memoirs end about the time Paula turns up, that fascinating and kindly woman whom Fate allowed to become the wife and friend of a truly great poet.

(Before this article went to press, we learned that a Hebrew translation of Der junge David *is being prepared in Israel.)*

RICHARD BEER-HOFMANN

Lullaby for Miriam

Sleep, my child, sleep, it is time now for you.
See there the sun, how it goes to rest, too.
Over the hilltops the evening's aglow.
Neither of sun nor of death do you know,
turning your eyes to the light and the shine –
so many suns, yet in store, will be thine!
Sleep, my child, – my child, go to sleep.

Sleep, my child, sleep. Hear the wind in the trees.
Where does it come from and where does it cease?
Dark are the roads here and hidden from view.
No one can see them, not I and not you.
Blindly we walk – and alone – alongside,
no one's companion and nobody's guide.
Sleep, my child, – my child, go to sleep.

Sleep, my child, sleep. Do not listen to me.
Meaningful only to me can it be –
sound but to you of wind and of rain,
words – though perhaps a lifetime's only gain!
Buried with me will be that which I won.
None to be heir to us, we heirs to none.
Sleep, my child, – my child, go to sleep.

Sleeping, Miriam? Hear me in your dream —
We are but shores of an unending stream.
Deep within us runs our forefathers' blood.
On to the future it rolls like a flood.
All are within us. Who says he's alone?
You are their life from which your life has grown.
Miriam, my life, my child, sleep, my life's own.

Translated from the German, 1956

Two Poems by

NELLY SACHS

Chorus of the Dead

We, hollowed like sieves
by the black sun of fear —
Run-offs of the sweat of the minute of dying we are.
Withered on our bodies are the deaths
done to us,
like field-flowers withered on a sandhill.
O you, who still greet the sand as a friend,
who, sand speaking to sand, can say:
I love you.

We, we tell you:
Torn are the cloaks of the secrets of dust.
The air which was choked within us,
the fires in which we were burned,
the earth into which they threw our remains,
the water pearling away with the sweat of fear,
burst forth within us, in a flash.
We, Israel's dead, we tell you:
By now we are one star ahead,
reaching beyond and into our hidden God.

Chorus of the Orphans

We lament to the world:
They hewed down our branch
And they threw it in the fire –
Firewood they made of our protectors –
We orphans lie in the fields of loneliness.
We orphans lament to the world:
At night our parents play hide-and-seek with us –
From behind the black folds of the night,
Their faces gaze at us
And their open mouths speak:
Drywood we've become in a woodcutter's hand –
But our eyes are the eyes of angels,
Looking at you,
Penetrating the black folds of the night –
We orphans,
We lament to the world:
Our toys became stones,
Stones have faces, of fathers and mothers,
They don't fade like flowers, they don't bite like beasts –
And they don't burn like drywood, when thrown into the oven.
We orphans lament to the world:
O world, why have you taken from us our tender mothers,
And our fathers who say: my child, you are my likeness.
We orphans are like no one in the world any more.
O world,
We accuse you!

Translated from the German, 1966

RESISTANCE AND SURVIVAL

The Warsaw Ghetto... Auschwitz... Treblinka... Bergen-Belsen... There is a danger that these names will be reduced to historical abstractions, relegated to a distant past, faintly recalled, hardly remembered. The recent 'Holocaust' film once again established the bare and brutal facts. In all their horrors, they are only part of the tragic story. That, in the shadow of death, the victims tried to maintain their dignity and humanity, is still little known, if at all. Yet we have literary documents, which miraculously survived, testifying to man's capacity to withstand inhumanity, to resist the onslaught of the deadly enemy, even if that resistance was confined to the few, to individuals and isolated groups. We will never know how much of such documents have been lost, but those which were unearthed from the underground 'Ringelblum Archives' and elsewhere must be cherished and treasured. Can there be anything more moving than the notes by an anonymous lecturer on a literary theme, which he prepared amidst 'crushing walls', showing the strength of his belief in a better future, even though he himself and his audience may not live to see it?

'... as a Hidden Spring Underground...'

ANONYMOUS

The following note (the gist of a lecture given at one of the 'cultural evenings' in the Ghetto) was found in the Ringelblum Archives, so named after their founder and director, Dr Emanuel Ringelblum, who had established a centre for collecting documentary material about life in the Warsaw Ghetto. After the war the Archives were discovered in two parts, the organizers having taken great care in preserving them for posterity. This note is included in a collection of prose pieces by Jewish writers who perished in the Ghetto, first published by the publishing house 'Yiddish Bukh' under the title 'Tsvishn lebn un toit' ('Between Life and Death'), Warsaw, 1955.

We live in a prison. We have been brought down to the level of homeless and neglected animals. Looking at the half-naked Jews lying in the streets, their bodies swollen from hunger, we have a feeling of being sub-human. These Jewish faces, skeleton-like, half-dead, particularly of small, dying children, invoke in us terror and recall pictures we have seen in films showing isolation centres for lepers in India and elsewhere. The reality surpasses the phantasy. There is only one thing which could surprise us: if mass murder were to replace this slow systematic destruction and extermination. Painful as it is to admit, we must say that for those who are starving to death, a quick, violent death would be a relief from their long sufferings and prolonged agonies.

The relationship between life and death has undergone a radical change. Once life came first and was followed by death, incidentally as it were, as its *finale*. Today death reigns majestically, while life flickers as if under a thick heap of ashes. Even that flickering life is weak, mean and poor, without a breath, movement or spiritual content. The soul, both of the individual and of the community, is as if dead and dumb. The body carrying out its organic functions leads only a purely physiological life.

Such is our position in the Jewish quarter of Warsaw and elsewhere. Yet we have not forgotten that we are human beings, not some primitive low creatures. We still remember that not so long ago, only some two years back, we were free men. We formed a living organic society which, notwithstanding its bad and bleak features, had still a human side. We educated ourselves, were striving to be creative in every field and to enrich our lives. We longed for art as the highest expression of human existence and we cultivated the arts as well as we could. We had also an understanding of, and an urge for, science. In a word: we were human beings and everything human attracted our attention. And today? How humiliated we are, how unfortunate, how scorned and spat upon!

Yet, we want to continue living and remain free and creative people. Thereby we shall stand the test of life. If our lives will not be extinguished under the thick layers of ashes – it will be the triumph of humanity over inhumanity; it will be proof that our life-force is stronger than the will of destruction, and that we are capable of overcoming the evil forces which are out to destroy us.

These cultural evenings, of which this is the first, should prove our strong will to survive. They should remind us of our past and urge us on to a better future. They will remind us that we stood at a higher level than some wild tribe in America. They will evoke in us the urge to new creative work and prevent us from succumbing to an eternal sleep. I believe that our youth, which is so tragically affected by the war, being deprived of enjoying the fruits of life, or enjoying school, science, literature, theatre and all the other spiritual and moral achievements, not to speak of their physical sufferings from starvation – our youth will welcome our initiative and will find here new strength for retaining their human appearance.

This first evening is devoted to the late Weissenberg, the writer.

Perhaps the choice was accidental, but it is also of some symbolic significance. Weissenberg was one of those creative writers who are like flowers which bloom in a bare and uncultivated field. In this sense he reminds us of Gorki, the great Russian writer, who grew up in an environment that lacked appreciation of culture and literature. Such writers are evidence of the life-force in man, of his eternal striving for light and progress, of the inner creative strength that breaks through, unexpectedly, like a hidden spring underground. May the memory of Weissenberg be a symbol of our living strength which will continue to flow secretly, despite all fences and obstacles, until it will reach the free world and flow freely, overflowing with joy and jubilation the fields of our life.

Jewish youth! It may be that among you are hidden potential Weissenbergs. Be strong and gather strength to survive until the day will come when the sun will rise for all the children of this earth, without exception. Then there will emerge the new Weissenbergs; then we shall celebrate not only the writers who are dead; then we shall celebrate and honour the living creative Jewish artists in all fields of culture and civilization.

From the Yiddish, 1956

I'll Speak to You Frankly, my Child...

JOSEPH KIRMAN

The author, born in 1896, perished in a Nazi labour camp, near Lublin, 1943.

... My child, on a cold and frosty day, with an evil wind blowing and shaking man and earth, your father dragged himself along, tired, in search of himself. He wandered through the streets, past buildings and people.

Instead of himself, he found wires – barbed wires that cut through the street and cut it to pieces. On both sides of the wire people walked up and down. Poverty and hunger drove them towards the fence through which one could see what went on on the other side. Jews, the badge of shame on their arms, walked on one side and Christian boys and girls on the other. When from the other side a loaf of bread was thrown over the fence, boys on this side tried to catch it. Police in jack-boots, armed with rubber truncheons, beat up a child. The child cried and German soldiers, looking on, shook with laughter. When a Jewish girl sang a song, begging, pleading – 'I am hungry and cold' – policemen drove her away, and the soldiers smiled, when they saw the loaf of bread, rolling on the ground.

People walked up and down. And your father stood there and looked over the fence. Suddenly a flight of doves came down, driven from somewhere out of the blue. Silently they settled on the wires and began quietly to coo. I felt the pain of their sadness and sorrow. I listened to their weeping hearts and understood the anguish of the freezing doves.

And yet, my child, how greedy man is! With his heart he feels sympathy, while his eyes are filled with envy. The doves have wings, and if they want to, they can fly, on to wires or up to roof-tops, off and away!

Your father stood there, dreaming. And a policeman came and knocked him on the head. Ashamed he began to move on, but he wanted to look once more at the doves. And, then, my child, your father saw something terrible:

The doves were still there, on the barbed wires, but ... they were eating the crumbs, out of the hands of the soldiers! ...

My child, your father grew very sad, and sad he still is: not about the doves on freezing wires, and not because they have wings and he has not, but because now he hates the doves, too, and he warns you: keep away from them, as long as the innocence allows itself to be fed by murderous hands ...

My child, when the steel birds hailed down death we all fled to the woods. You remember how terrified we were when the woods along our tracks caught fire and we went on in our flight without hope and without thought that we would ever reach our goal?

Now it is different ... Come, come out into the street. Though a biting frost cuts the ears and it is late in the evening. My dear, beloved son, come, I will show you a fire that lights up the skies over Warsaw. I don't know where it came from and what it is for. Maybe they are fliers from Russian fields or maybe the birds came from the other side of the Channel; or maybe it is the work of hidden hands at home; perhaps this, perhaps that ... But look, how the sky grows red. How beautiful the red is over the snow-covered town; it is evening and it's light and there where the Vistula is frozen to ice, rise up higher, and higher, and almost as high as the sky: giant tongues of fire and of smoke. Wherever we turn we see wide-open spaces lit up by the flames. It smells of sulphur, of white heat, though the frost is grim and the snow lies dense on roofs and walls.

How beautiful is this wintry evening! Something great and unexpected is coming from over there, from the Vistula, where the fires are burning.

My child, you regret that you cannot put out the fire, that you are not a Polish fireman with a little trumpet: *tu-tu-tu!* ...

Don't be a silly child! You'll be a fireman one day. But not yet, not yet. It's too early yet to extinguish the fires. Let them burn, let them burn, my child!

Come children, let's form a ring and dance and clap our hands: *tra-la, tra-la-la!*

A pity the fires grows smaller... Someone asks me:

– What was one fire, Mister Jew, perhaps you know? What was it?

– The wickedness of the world was one fire, I thought...

– Really? – The woman who asked nods knowingly.

My son! You should not regret it that you have been with me in the locked-up streets of the Ghetto – Dzika, Stavki and Mila.

My son, you should not regret your crying today. It does not matter that, when you look up to the sun, tears come into your eyes.

For you will see, my child, you will see: where today there is wailing and sadness hovers in homes; and the Angel of Death reigns supreme like a drunken madman; and people in rags, heaps of shattered hopes, cower along old, dark and smoky walls; and bodies of old men rot away in doorways or on bare floors, covered with newspapers or pieces of stone; and children shiver and whisper: 'We are starving' and like rats stir in piles of refuse; and worn-out women hold up their hands, thin as ribbons, in their last barren consumptive prayers; and frost and disease close in on dying eyes that, in their last agony crave for a crust of bread –

> There, my dear, my sunny child,
> there will yet come
> that great,
> that greatest of days,
> that last, the very last day –
> and it will be as in our dream...

Warsaw, Ghetto, February–March 1942

Translated from the Yiddish, 1960

JACOB GORDON

Autumn

The author perished in the Bialystock Ghetto.

>The sky is lit
>with a pale-blue hue
>and silver clouds
>of sheep.
>The sun smiles
>his last sad smile
>before going to sleep.
>
>The trees stand there
>lonely and ill,
>with black dead hands.
>Great and bare,
>they dream
>their final dream.
>
>Last night the winds knocked off
>their last strand of beauty,
>their last hour of being,
>howling with laughter.
>Now they're asleep.

Filled with passion
and satisfied,
they hide
in a shrub, under leaves,
knee-deep.

Translated from the Yiddish

YITZHAK KATZENELSON

To the Heavens

Yitzhak Katzenelson was born in 1886 in Karltiz, near Minsk, and perished in the gas chambers of Auschwitz in April 1944. He was a prolific writer in Hebrew and Yiddish and lived in the Warsaw Ghetto up to the time of its destruction, in April 1943. The following month he was deported with a group of holders of South American passports to Vittel, a German concentration camp for foreigners in France. With him was his eldest son (his wife and two younger sons had earlier been sent to the death camp of Treblinka). In Vittel his stay lasted for about ten months; after that the Gestapo removed all Jews from the camp and sent them back to Poland. Katzenelson and his son were among a group who reached Auschwitz on 30 April, and were killed the same day.

While in the Ghetto, the poet was not only busy writing but also took an active part in literary and educational activities, besides being a member of an Underground Fighting Unit associated with the Zionist pioneering movement, *Hechalutz*. *The Song of the Murdered Jewish People*, written in Vittel between 3 October 1943 and 18 January 1944, consists of 18 chapters, each comprising 15 stanzas of four long, uneven lines. Often archaic in style and construction, it is both a chronicle of events and an outcry of anger and grief. This 'Book of Lamentation' of our own time will remain a unique literary document for all time. 'To the Heavens' forms chapter nine of the book.

And thus it came to pass, and this was the beginning ... Heavens tell me, why?
Tell me, why this, O why? What have we done to merit such disgrace?
The earth is dumb and deaf, she closed her eyes. But you, heavens on high,
you saw it happen and looked on, from high, and did not turn your face.

You did not cloud your cheap-blue colours, glittering in their false light.
The sun, a brutal, red-faced hangman, rolled across the skies;
the moon, the old and sinful harlot, walked along her beat at night;
and stars sent down their dirty twinkle, with the eyes of mice.

Away! I do not want to look at you, to see you any more.
False and cheating heavens, low heavens up on high, O how you hurt!
Once I believed in you, sharing my joy with you, my smile, my tear –
who are not different from the ugly earth, that heap of dirt!

I did believe in you and sang your praises in each song of mine.
I loved you as one loves a woman, though she left and went.
The flaming sun at dusk, its glowing shine,
I likened to my hopes: 'And thus my hope goes down, my dream is spent.'

Away! Away! You have deceived us both, my people and my race.
You cheated us – eternally. My ancestors, my prophets, too, you have deceived.
To you, foremost, they lifted up their eyes, and you inspired their faith.
And full of faith they turned to you, when jubilant or grieved.

To you they first addressed themselves: *Hearken, O Heavens,
   you* –
and only afterwards they called the earth, praising your name.
So Moses. So Isaiah – mine, my own. *Hear, O hear,* cried
   Jeremiah, too.
O heavens open wide, O heavens full of light, you are as Earth,
   you are the same.

Have we so changed that you don't recognize us, as of old?
Not why, we are the same – the same Jews that we were, not
   different.
Not I . . . Not I will to the prophets be compared, lo and behold!
It's they, the millions of my murdered ones, those murdered out
   of hand –
it's they . . . They suffered more and greater pains, each one.
The little, simple, ordinary Jew from Poland of today –
compared with him, what are the great men of a past bygone?
A wailing Jeremiah, Job afflicted, Kings despairing, all in one –
   it's they!

You do not recognize us any more as if we hid behind a mask?
But why, we are the same, the same Jews that we were, and to
   ourselves we're true.
We're still resigned to others' happiness. Saving the world we still
   see as our task.
O why are you so beautiful, you skies, while we are being
   murdered, why are you so blue?

Like Saul, my king, I will go to the goddess Or, bearing my pain.
In dark despair I'll find the way, the dark road to Ein Dor; I shall
from under ground awaken all the prophets there – *Look ye again,
look up to your bright heavens, spit at them and tell them: Go to
   Hell!*

You heavens, high above, looked on when, day and night,
my people's little children were sent off to death, on foot, by train.
Millions of them raised high their hands to you before they died.
Their noble mothers could not shake your blue-skinned crust –
   they cried in vain.

You saw the little Yomas, the eleven-year-olds, joyous, pure and good;
the little Bennys, young enquiring minds, life's remedy and prize.
You saw the Hannas who had borne them and had taught them to serve God.
And you looked on ... You have no God above you. Nought and void – you skies!

You have no God in you! Open the doors, you heavens, fling them open wide,
and let the children of my murdered people enter in a stream.
Open the doors up for the great procession of the crucified,
the children of my people, all of them, each one a god – make room!

O heavens, empty and deserted, vast and empty desert, you –
My only God I lost in you, and they have not enough with three:
the Jewish God, the Holy Ghost, the Jew from Galilee – they killed him, too.
And then, not satisfied, sent all of us to heaven, these worshippers of cruelty.

Rejoice, you heavens, at your riches, at your fortune great!
Such blessed harvest at one stroke – a people gathered in entire.
Rejoice on high, as here below the Germans do, rejoice and jubilate!
And may a fire rise up to you from earth, and from you strike, earthwards, devouring fire!

Translated from the Yiddish

SELMA MEERBAUM-EISINGER (1924–1941)

I Want to Live

Selma Meerbaum-Eisinger was 17 years old when she died of typhus in the notorious concentration camp of Michalowka, in Transnistria, where thousands of Jews were herded together after the German occupation of her native Czernowitz, Bukovina, in 1941. She wrote German poetry and translated French, Rumanian, and Yiddish poetry into German. A small collection of 58 poems miraculously survived and was published in the original in Israel. The following poem is taken from this collection.

> I want to live.
> I want to laugh and lift a heavy weight,
> I want to fight, to love, to hate.
> I want to grasp the heavens with my hands,
> and to be free, to breathe, to cry.
>
> I don't want to die.
> No.
> Life is red.
> The life is mine
> mine and yours.
> Mine.
>
> Why do the cannons roar?
> Why is life made to die for glittering crowns?
> There is the moon.
> It is here.

Near.
Very near.
I must wait.
For what?
Heap upon heap
they die.
They will never get up.

I will live.
And you, my brother, too.
A breath of air comes from my lips and yours.

Life is full of colours.
You want to kill me?
What for?
From a thousand flutes
weep the woods.

The moon is silvery blue.
The poplars are grey.
And the wind rushes at me.
The roads are bright
Then . . .
And then they come
to choke me.
Me and you.
Death.
The life is red.
It raves and laughs.
And overnight
I am
dead.

A shadow of a tree
ghosts over the moon.
One can hardly see
the tree.
Life can throw
a shadow onto the moon.

And soon
heap upon heap
they die.
They will never get up.
Never.

Translated from the German, 1977

PAVEL FRIEDMANN

The Butterfly

Born 7 January 1921 in Prague, deported to Terezin on 26 April 1942, killed in Auschwitz on 29 September 1944.

The last one it was, the very last
a richly glaring, bitterly blending butterfly
as when a sun-tear explodes on a white-hot stone
such was its yellow

and it carried itself suspended on high
and rising it kissed my last world good-bye

For seven long weeks I've been here already ghettofied
here my own people have found me
the dandelion winks at me
and also in the yard the white twigs of the chestnut tree

but never again have I seen a butterfly
that one was surely the last
for butterflies do not live
               in the Ghetto.

Translated from the German

DAVID SFARD

Farewell

The author, a prominent literary figure in pre-war Poland, spent the war years in the Soviet Union. Upon his return to Poland after the war, he played a leading role in the reconstruction of Jewish cultural life as the editor of a distinguished literary monthly, *Yiddishe Shriftn*, but, with others, became the victim of the anti-Jewish measures by the Polish government, following the Six-Day War of 1967. He was dismissed from his position and the paper itself was closed down. He now lives in Israel.

> It's hard to bid good-bye to Polish autumns,
> when trees are topped with golden crowns
> and fields lie tired and satiated,
> stretching on feather-bed of sun,
> radiant with an airy mildness,
> as women, hours after they have given birth.
>
> To whom will *Elul*[1] winds autumnal
> whisper now in *Mamme-loshn*[2]
> of cemeteries untended,
> to whom will Polish forests
> and shiny, moon-blue rivers
> speak now in Yiddish?
>
> Multitudes of Jews,
> like hunted birds in uproar,
> tear through the night
> as lightning in a storm,
> and I can't turn their flight
> and guide them on the road.

I walk alone,
lost in the fog of days,
and like an open wound
my heart bleeds,
bloodying my ways.

O land where I was born,
may your beautiful autumns shine no longer
upon the mourning thresholds
of my desolated house.
As for me, though, I am destined
to tread, a shadow of myself, barefooted
on your sacred, desecrated soil,
all through the ages,
eternally uprooted.

Translated from the Yiddish, 1969

1 *Elul* — the last month in the Hebrew calendar associated with autumn and seasonal reflections; also a time of visiting the graves of relatives.
2 *Mamme-loshn* — mother tongue, stands for Yiddish.

ANTONI SLONIMSKI

Elegy

A poem written in honour of the Warsaw Ghetto Uprising, 19 April 1943.

They are no more, no more
The Jewish villages.
In Karczew, Hrubieszow,
Brody, Falenica;

Now you will look in vain
For the candle-lit windowpane
And vainly listen for
The old intoned refrain
From the wooden house of prayer,

The dregs of their life are drained,
Their rags swept out of time;
Into the thirsty sand
The blood has soaked away;
And the walls are newly washed
White with cleansing lime
As if a plague has passed
Or a great holiday.

One cold and alien moon
Alone looks wanly down.
No more, my Jewish kin,
You of poetical mind,
No longer will you find
Chagall's two moons of gold
In the night's glittering
Lighting the high road
Beyond the glowing town.

Those moons revolve around
Another planet now,
Like frightened doves are flown
From the stark silence here:
Where is no more to be found
That village artistry,
The cobbler-poet or
The barber-troubadour.

No more, no more the wind
Weaves in a single skein
The old Hebraic theme
With Poland's country airs
And all the Slavonic pain:

Where in those villages
Dappled by orchard-trees
The old Jews still bemoaned
Holy Jerusalem.

There is no more to be seen
Of the Jewish villages,
Passed like a shadow of cloud:
That shadow will lie between
Our speech and thought, until
Our peoples' divided will
For centuries trampled down
Emerge into brotherhood
Welded anew as One.

Translated by Randall Swingler, 1973

THE 'BLACK YEARS' OF THE STALINIST TERROR

The 'Golden Age' of Soviet-Yiddish Literature that was Brutally Destroyed

C. ABRAMSKY

An extraordinary rich anthology comprising a selection from the works of twelve Soviet-Yiddish writers, all of whom became the victims of the Stalin terror, has recently been published in Israel.

The book, *A Shpigl oif a shteyn*,[2] which runs to over 840 pages, has been edited by Dr H. Shmeruck, of the Hebrew University in Jerusalem. In an excellent introduction he presents in a nutshell the history of Yiddish literature in the Soviet Union. In the best scholarly manner there are biographical details about each of the writers represented in the Anthology and a scholarly apparatus regarding each item included in it (sources, dates of first publication, explanatory notes indicating variations in style and text, etc.). Both from a literary and historical point of view the book is of the greatest value; typographically, too, it is a model of representation.

The twelve writers are: Bergelson (1884–1952); Der Nister (1884–1950); Hofshteyn (1889–1952); Persov (1890–1952); Kushnirov (1890–1949); Kvitko (1890–1952); Markish (1895–

1952); Kulbak (1896–1940); Halkin (1897–1960); Kharik (1898–1937); Fefer (1900–1955); Akselrod (1904–1941).

The October Revolution of 1917 continued a process of emancipation of the Jews in Russia, which started with the February Revolution of the same year. All legislation of a discriminatory character was abolished and all restrictions on Jews lifted. For the first time in the history of Russia, the Jews really felt equal with all other citizens. A great wave of enthusiasm swept over the millions of Jews living in that country; they welcomed the Revolution wholeheartedly. Jewish youths flocked in their thousands to join the revolutionary ranks to defend the Revolution against the attacks by the Whites from within, and against the interventionist armies of fourteen states, aiming at its destruction.

Jews became very prominent in every facet of political, economic and cultural activity in Russia, and were to be found in the Communist Party's leadership and administration, in the Red Army, and in other positions of influence. It felt like being released from prison where they had been locked up for centuries.

Very soon, this new experience found its reflection in the new Yiddish literature and culture. It seems that the outburst of revolutionary activity and energy in Russia also led to a unique manifestation of exceptional literary and artistic talents among Russian Jews. This was particularly felt in the Ukraine, where a whole galaxy of extraordinarily gifted writers of both poetry and prose appeared on the scene. This renaissance of Yiddish culture manifested itself also in literary criticisms, in art, and in the theatre in Moscow, Kiev and Minsk. This period between 1917 and 1928 is unique in Yiddish literature and without parallel in the history of Jewish literature except perhaps in the 'golden age' of Spain.

This group of brilliant young writers such as Dovid Hofshteyn, Peretz Markish, Lieb Kvitko, Arn Kushnirov, Der Nister, Dovid Bergelson, Moishe Teyf, I. Kipnis, and many others, breathed new life and vitality into Yiddish literature. Their impact was profound. The rebellious poet Markish, who has often been compared with Byron, welcomed the Revolution with his famous lines, 'I have put the top hat on my feet, and my boots on my head.' Hofshteyn, in more lyrical tones, greeted the

Revolution as a great act of liberation and emancipation of the Jews. In one of the most memorable poems ever written in Yiddish, superb in style and with great economy of words, he gave a gripping survey of the sufferings of the Jews throughout the ages, and with a remark of utmost contempt dealt with the Christian attitudes to the Jews. *The Song of My Indifference*, first published in 1921, is the most powerful, and at the same time most lyrical condemnation of anti-semitism, and a militant manifesto for Jewish equality. It is a poem without sentimentality, bold in its imagery, and yet highly lyrical.

Both Markish and Hofshteyn represented a completely new departure in Yiddish poetry. There is a remarkable affinity between Hofshteyn's poetry of the early 20s and that of Blok, particularly with the latter's famous poem, *Twelve*. To the present writer, *The Song of My Indifference* is even more striking than *Twelve*. Hofshteyn's mastery of rhythm and richness of associations has no equal in Yiddish poetry. He, more than any one of his contemporaries, also showed a remarkable range of European culture and, at the same time, was deeply steeped in Hebrew literature and medieval Hebrew poetry.

Both these poets represented a new type of Yiddish writer – one who was deeply loyal to the October Revolution, while at the same time retaining strong layers of Jewish national consciousness. This led often to contradictions, clashes, and conflicts within themselves. After the Civil War had subsided, both these writers became restless, and left Russia. They spent some time in France, Germany and Poland; they also visited Palestine. Disappointed with the conditions they found there, they returned in 1929 to the Soviet Union. But a certain duality remained with them to the end of their days.

Together with the great upsurge of outstanding poetry, new fields opened up for prose writing as well. Two great writers of prose, who began their literary careers before the Revolution, found new outlets for their talents. They were Dovid Bergelson and Der Nister. They had already made their mark before 1917, and were hailed as outstanding talents by the greatest Yiddish writer of the time, Y. L. Peretz. In their short stories, novels and plays they showed exceptional depth and power of portrayal, presenting a vivid picture of the experiences felt by Jews during and after the October Revolution.

In his play, *Der Toiber* ('The Deaf') Bergelson portrays with great sensitivity the sufferings of an exploited man, and in his great epic, *Baim Dnieper* ('At the Dnieper'), he presents a vast panoramic picture of the life of the Jews in a small town in the Ukraine before the Revolution and immediately after.

Der Nister was a talent of a different calibre. Influenced by mysticism and symbolism, he became the only great Jewish symbolist writer. His short stories are deeply lyrical and have a great affinity with the writings of Bely, the famous Russian symbolist writer. He also drew heavily on early Hassidic lore. His great novel, *The Family Mashber*, stands unrivalled for its unusual style and deep humanistic feelings.

The flourishing period of Russian Jewish literature lasted till the middle 30s. By then the *Yevsektsia*, the Jewish section of the Bolshevik Party, was closed down, and Jewish cultural activities became restricted. A number of Yiddish writers and cultural workers fell victims to the purges which began late in 1934. The following writers, poets, novelists and literary critics were executed between 1936 and 1940: Isi Kharik, an exceptionally gifted poet from Minsk; Moishe Kulbak, a distinguished and highly talented poet, playwright and novelist, who settled in Russia after leaving Poland in 1926; Moishe Litvakov, an eminent literary critic and the all-powerful editor of *Der Emes*, a Yiddish daily in Moscow; Alexander Khashin, who began his career as a prominent polemicist of the Poale Zion and as a literary critic of distinction; and finally, Yasha Bronstein, who fled from persecution in Poland and became the youngest, and in many respects the most brilliant literary critic amongst Yiddish writers in Russia.

Yet in spite of growing restrictions Yiddish writers continued to produce important works. The Second World War led again to a resurgence of Yiddish literary activity. All the Yiddish writers threw themselves wholeheartedly into the fight against Fascism, as active members of the Jewish Anti-Fascist Committee, set up in Moscow under the chairmanship of Solomon Mikhoels, the eminent Yiddish actor and director of the Moscow State Jewish Theatre. He and the poet Fefer toured America and Britain in 1943, mobilizing material and financial support for the Soviet Union in the war against Hitler Germany.

Outstanding among the works produced during the war is the

great epic poem, *Milkhome* ('The War') by Peretz Markish, which gives profound expression to the sufferings of the Jews and of mankind in the life-and-death struggle against the Nazis. This very long poem is full of passion and vigour, and is the greatest expressionist poem in the Yiddish language.

The end of the war created new problems for the Jews in the Soviet Union. In spite of the fact that the Soviet representative at the United Nations, Mr Gromyko, in November 1947 supported the creation of a Jewish State, and the Soviet Union was one of the first states to recognize Israel, when it was established in May 1948, the Soviet Government took strong measures to combat any desire on the part of Russian Jews to have any connections with the new State of Israel. In November 1948 all Jewish cultural institutions and all Yiddish publications were closed down and the leading Yiddish writers and cultural workers arrested. These arrests followed the death of Mikhoels in February of that year. At the time it was stated that he was killed in a car accident, but it has since been admitted that he was murdered in cold blood in Minsk by government secret agents. The arrested writers, after years of imprisonment without trial, were executed on 12 August 1952. This was revealed years later by the Polish Communist Party in April 1956.

After Stalin's death all the Yiddish writers were posthumously rehabilitated and their works have since re-appeared in Russian translations, but not in Yiddish.

The anthology entitled, *A Shpigl Oif a Shteyn* ('A Mirror on a Stone'), taken from a line of a very significant poem by Markish, is a worthy monument to the memory of the martyred writers. But it is more than that. Dr Shmeruck has rendered a great service to literature in general, and to Yiddish literature in particular, by bringing together in one volume a representative collection from the works of twelve outstanding writers whose achievements merit the widest attention beyond the limited circles of Yiddish readers. Let us hope that these remarkable writings, especially the beautiful prose of Bergelson and Der Nister, and the poetry of Hofshteyn, will one day be translated into English, and that an enterprising publisher will be found to make them accessible to a wider public unable to read Yiddish or Russian. They are excellent examples of a great literature that was deliberately destroyed; it would be sad and tragic if it were allowed to be lost and forgotten.

1 The author is Goldsmith Professor of Hebrew and Jewish Studies, University College, London.
2 Y. L. Peretz Library, Tel Aviv, $12.00.

1965

Jewish Culture in Historical Perspective

CH. SHMERUK (Jerusalem)

There is general agreement about the pluralistic and multilingual nature of contemporary Jewish culture as embracing the totality of social, spiritual, aesthetic and artistic values possessing Jewish elements and affinities. This totality extends to both the religious and secular spheres in all their manifestations, be it creativity in the Hebrew language or in any other language spoken or written by Jews, or creativity in any language, even non-Jewish, or in any other medium of communication by Jews and for Jews. The existence and strengthening of Jewish culture in all its various manifestations is our common concern, and this despite the different approaches and trends which prefer one sphere or one medium over another within the sum total of its components. In addition it can be said that the pre-occupation with this or that area within the broad orbit, as indicated, makes it possible now to view Jewish culture in all its manifold aspects, with an eye to the development of each of its constituents as a value in itself.

All this applies, of course, not only to the Jewish culture in the Soviet Union alone, but wherever Jews happen to live. Basically it cannot be supposed that there exists any fundamental difference as regards the aspirations in the sphere of Jewish culture in any of the Jewish centres in the world. There may be differences in emphasis and outlook here and there, which must be seen as developing on two principal levels:

(a) the greater emphasis on the one or the other aspect of Jewish culture in preference to another;

(b) the assessments of the prospects for the existence, development and well-being of Jewish culture in a given country, taking into account political limitations and the coercive authority of the state.

With regard to the differences of outlook existing on the first level, it is only proper to state that they are not specific to the problems of Jewish culture in the Soviet Union. These differences are a natural function of the pluralistic and multilingual character of contemporary Jewish culture. It is thus only natural that there are those who see its essence in the religious sphere, as opposed to those who uphold the concept of a secular Jewish culture, be it in Hebrew, in Yiddish, or any other language. These are legitimate differences of outlook and can, and do, arise wherever Jews live.

However, when we attempt to deal with the differences of outlook on the second level, the very specific problem of Jewish culture in the Soviet Union stands out in all its sharpness. Here the two levels become entangled in a knot, made even more complex by political considerations.

In the 19th century the gaps within the widening monolithic Jewish culture of the time were becoming signally obvious. On the face of it this culture was strongly based on a religious and traditional *weltanschauung*. With all the ravages of time its foundations in Eastern Europe were quite firm. The vast majority of the Jewish people in Tsarist Russia lived, until the Revolution of 1917, in the religious traditional framework, seeing in it the foundation of its existence and holding on to it in the face of the serious crises which followed in the wake of the destructive modern changes. The gaps caused in Jewish society by the social changes of the 19th and 20th centuries were filled with new social ideologies out of which arose a new Jewish culture, secular, or partly secular, in character. It was in Tsarist Russia that the pluralistic and essentially tri-lingual nature of Jewish culture began to crystallize, a culture whose heritage sustains us to this very day.

However, this new Jewish culture, possessing various hues and striving in different directions, was accepted as a natural phenomenon by only a few. A not inconsiderate sector of the Jewish intelligentsia, while working for the development of this culture and contributing its share towards it, found itself in a maelstrom of bitter struggles and debates around the question to determine the hegemony of one sphere or another of Jewish culture, intolerantly excluding any other but their own. Very few indeed were prepared to make their peace with the manifold character of modern Jewish culture and to recognize the legitimacy of the different forms in which it manifested itself. This fateful dichotomy widened still further with the flaring up of the dispute between 'Hebraists' and 'Yiddishists', following upon the First Conference on Yiddish in Czernowitz (1908) which proclaimed Yiddish 'a national language of Jews'.

Despite the sorry divisions, becoming even more pronounced in the sharp debates and clashes of social ideologies, the achievements of modern Jewish culture in Eastern Europe in the pre-revolutionary period have been considerable, adding a vital and glorious chapter to our heritage. The names of Mendele Mokher Seforim, Peretz, Sholem Aleichem, Frug and Bialik, of Ahad Haam and Dubnow, of Borochov and Jabotinsky, are but a select few of those who contributed to these achievements, and an indication of the broad range of this heritage. To this day they bear faithful testimony to the vibrant spiritual forces of Eastern European Jewry.

The political and ideological doctrine of the Bolsheviks did not recognize the existence of the Jewish people as self-evident, and cast doubt on the existence of a specific Jewish culture. The very concept of a pluralistic culture finding expression in different views and approaches in areas of the human spirit, was foreign and basically opposed to the architects of the new regime in the Soviet Union. This regime, whose ideological relationship to our existence as a people and to our cultural needs was in any case ambivalent, to say the least, nevertheless knew full well how to exploit for its own purposes our own internal divisions regarding the special problems of Jewish culture. Stage by stage it reduced the various spheres of Jewish culture inherited from the pre-revolutionary period, denying the very awareness of its existence, at times both in theory and in practice, at other times in practice only.

From the outset religious Jewish culture was outlawed and suppressed. Together with secular Hebrew culture in all its manifestations, the Jewish religion, to all intents and purposes, was driven underground. Religious Jews and Hebrew writers had to keep themselves in great secrecy, at the price of stubborn self-sacrifice and bravery. Gradually all manifestations of an autonomous Jewish culture became more and more limited so that towards the end of the 30s nothing was left of it. By the end of the 40s the remnants of Jewish culture in Yiddish, which alone received the imprimatur of legitimacy after the Revolution, were liquidated too. Thus the dictatorial regime destroyed with its own hands that which it had itself established and encouraged out of pragmatic considerations over a period of thirty years. From the 30s onwards until 12 August 1952, many of the most faithful adherents of the regime, who helped in carrying out its aims in the field of Yiddish culture, were imprisoned, executed or had died in the concentration camps.

After the death of Stalin the brutal discrimination against the Jews in the Soviet Union continued, in sharp contrast to other nationalities in the state. Thus the survivors among the bearers of Jewish culture in its various forms known to us from Tsarist Russia and the early days of the new regime were at first not granted the right to renew their activities and creative work. It was only after persistent demands and pressures from abroad (particularly from circles friendly to the Soviet Union) that a tentative and limited renewal of Yiddish culture was brought about. The outward manifestations of it can be seen in the literary monthly in Yiddish, *Sovietish Heymland*, the regional paper *Birobidjaner Shtern*, itself very limited in scope and circulation, in the publication of about forty works of prose and verse since 1959, and in the presentations of Yiddish song recitals and theatrical performances.

Simultaneously with the demands for the restoration of Yiddish culture a struggle was carried on for freedom of religious ritual for the Jews, in accordance with the provisions of the Soviet constitution guaranteeing religious freedom to all citizens. Here, too, resulting from pressure abroad, small concessions were granted to religious Jews in the Soviet Union. The printing of a prayer book and a calendar was permitted, the attempt to establish a *Yeshiva* (religious seminary) was sanctioned, as was the baking of matzot. All this proved that there still existed a religious Jewish culture among Askenazic (European) Jews and even more among non-Askenazic (Asian and Oriental) Jews, in spite of the atheistic trend in Soviet education for over fifty years.

In evaluating the significance of these concessions to Jewish culture from an historical perspective we must take into account the changes which occurred within Soviet Jewry since the Revolution. That which exists today, for instance, in the area of Jewish religious culture bears no comparison to that which existed immediately after the Revolution. If we may ignore the non-Askenazic Jews in Central Asia, what remains today of the once flourishing Jewish religious life is but a faint shadow of the past. The same holds good with regard to Yiddish culture. Not only have the Jews been denied equality of rights to develop their Yiddish culture in comparison to other Soviet nationalities, not excluding the German citizens equally lacking territorial concentration and national self-government, but not even those cultural and educational institutions in Yiddish which had existed throughout the twenties and thirties, and whose remnants were liquidated during the forties, even these were not rehabilitated. That which exists today in this field at present is but faintly reminiscent of the past; it is limited in essence and extent in spite of the propagandist efforts to prove the contrary as evidenced in *Sovietish Heymland* with its circulation of some 20,000 copies and the number of Yiddish books published. No concessions whatever were made in two most important linguistic areas of Jewish culture, namely in Hebrew and Russian, not even in the restricted form permitted at the time. Strange as it may seem, there is today not a single Jewish journal in Russian in the Soviet Union, at a time when Jewish underground publications do appear periodically – not in Yiddish nor in Hebrew, but in Russian.

The tactics applied by the Soviet authorities in this respect appear to be quite shrewd. They have clearly taken into account the changes which have occurred among Jews not only in the Soviet Union but also abroad. The concessions granted extended to spheres that in any case are in full retreat as regards their scope, weight and influence; neither religion nor Yiddish embrace a majority of Jews. As regards religion, it is almost exclusively the elderly among the Ashkenazic Jews who require the services of the synagogue or other religious facilities. As regards the Yiddish language, the number of Jews who declare Yiddish as their mother tongue, it shows a constant downward trend. Their number according to the population census of 1959 was 408,000, which represented 21·5% of the total Jewish population in the Soviet Union. Their number in the census dropped to 387,000, i.e.

17·1% of those registered as Jews. With all the reservations surrounding these census figures there is no reason to doubt the accuracy of the relative statistics. It should further be noted that this latest regression occurred precisely at the time of an unusual upsurge of Jewish awareness among Soviet Jews in the wake of the Six-Day War. It has to be accepted as a fact that Yiddish is no longer the mother tongue of a majority of the Jews either inside or outside the Soviet Union. Hebrew has now a greater attraction as one element in the spiritual affinity which Russian Jews have shown towards the State of Israel while Russian is in effect known to all of them including those who claim Yiddish as their mother tongue. In those two vital linguistic spheres the Russian authorities have made no concessions whatever; those that were made relate to branches judged by them less important, and do not answer the real needs.

Even so, marginal as the concessions may seem, they should not be underestimated. We know of the emotional gatherings of Jewish youth outside the synagogues of Moscow and Leningrad on holidays and Jewish festivals. These young people do not come to pray and do not declare themselves observant Jews. In the absence of other Jewish meeting places, the synagogue serves as a focal point and the gatherings turn into demonstrations of identification.

In their search for means by which Russian Jews could legitimately or quasi-legitimately express their national and cultural identity, they flock to the occasional public performances in Yiddish of song and drama. Such performances always have full houses though the audiences consist partly of people who no longer understand the language. It can be assumed that to a certain number of Jews who declared Yiddish as their mother tongue, the Yiddish monthly, *Sovietish Heymland*, serves a similar purpose of self-identification and as a source of information on Jewish cultural matters. However much some of the material published there may not be to our liking, and however much the information may be limited and at times even distorted, no other material of Jewish significance appears anywhere else in print in the Soviet Union, nor in any other language.

This is not the place to enlarge on this point, but it should be noted that even *Sovietish Heymland* is aware of the pluralistic nature of Jewish culture. Thus this journal has found it necessary to publish translations from contemporary Hebrew literature, and has attracted to it Jewish writers who write in Russian and whose writings on Jewish topics are presented in Yiddish translations because they cannot be printed anywhere else in the Soviet Union. And whatever the propagandist intentions of the editors may be, Russian Jews have grown accustomed to read between the lines, and give their own interpretations to the things presented to them.

Notwithstanding the visible decline of Yiddish as compared with the past, there are to this day creative forces at work whose vitality is revealed in the writings reaching us from the Soviet Union and which did not find their way into print. The book of poems by Yosef Kerler, *Dos Gezang tsvishn Tesyn* ('The Song Between Teeth') published in Israel but written in the Soviet Union, is proof of this. And this is not the only book of its kind.

This author and his writer friends, some of whom were associated with *Sovietish Heymland*, and who recently arrived in Israel, are additional proof that the great heritage of Mikhoels, Bergelson, Der Nister, Markish and Hofshteyn, created under conditions of a hostile regime, has not been lost. It still awaits proper evaluation beyond the passing pronouncements by the Soviet cultural commissars and their helpers. Nor has it been properly assessed at the time by many well-intentioned people even among those who were greatly concerned with Soviet Jewry. Who can reveal the hidden thoughts of those who still remain in the Soviet Union and are now obliged to serve Vergelis and his masters?

To sum up: there is indeed a positive side to the few concessions made after Stalin's death, little as they can be said to satisfy all the cultural needs of Soviet Jewry. For one thing, the wall of proscriptions against the Jews has been effectively breached of late by permitting emigration on a large scale.

No one disputes the need to continue with the demands to allow every Jew who desires to emigrate to Israel to do so as a means of solving the problem of Jewish national culture for those who do in fact emigrate. On the other hand, is this not also the right time to fuse this basic demand with increased pressure to recognize the cultural needs of Soviet Jews in all areas, including Hebrew and Russian, as the areas with the greatest potential.

We live in an age of great developments in the mass media which easily penetrate iron curtains serving as a corrective to official Soviet culture, as do the underground publications, the *samizdat*, both of Jews and non-Jews. All these place the Establishment in a posture of self-defence. The influence and mutual interaction between what enters Russia from without, on the air, in print and in writing, and by personal contacts through visits from abroad, have generated new relationships and great creative tensions in all cultural spheres. During all the years of the existence of the regime there has never been such an upsurge of intellectual forces as that which we are witnessing today in the Soviet Union. In practice the Soviet authorities are powerless to reverse the situation because they cannot turn back the wheel towards total terror.

From the Jewish point of view, too, we are witnessing a change of great significance. What characterized the period between the death of Stalin and the Six-Day War was that in the struggle on behalf of Soviet Jewry external pressure was the main factor, while Soviet Jewry itself was, in effect, a passive element, so much so that it was termed 'the Jews of Silence'. After the Six-Day War, which released the traumatic substratum resulting from the Holocaust of the Second World War, Soviet Jewry has developed into a distinctly active element, which knows how to exploit the weaknesses of the regime and all the gaps which have appeared with the loosening of its reins. It would seem, then, that there is a real possibility under these conditions for the expansion of Jewish culture going far beyond what has hitherto been allowed in the Soviet Union.

There are those among us who tend to deny any other claim regarding Soviet Jewry save to the right of emigration to Israel. They see in this the exclusive goal and are willing to forego explicit secular demands, which are just and legitimate, for the existence and development of Jewish culture inside the Soviet Union. It is difficult to make one's peace with the holders of this view, even if it finds expression among recent Russian immigrants to Israel. Behind this tendency there seeps through an astonishing stance of finality, which abrogates to itself the right and authority to take decisions about the spiritual and cultural life of those Jews who will remain in the Soviet Union even if the wave of emigration should continue, and indeed every Jew who wishes to emigrate would be given the right to do so. According to the most optimistic estimates there will be millions of Jews who will stay behind. From whence the authority to pass judgement on those millions remaining in the Soviet Union, and to take decisions for them and in their name? Are we to give them up and abandon them to total assimilation, leaving them with nothing to fall back to in terms of real, day-to-day, national culture? And are we in this way to ease up on the Soviet authorities and repeat the mistakes of the past?

No one has yet suggested a similar attitude towards the Jews in the West, who will not emigrate though they are under no restrictions to leave their countries. There is no justification whatsoever for the discrimination of Soviet Jews in so fundamental a matter, by giving in to the slogans of the activists and maximalists providing neither an answer nor a solution for anybody.

[1] The author is the head of the Yiddish Department, Hebrew University, Jerusalem.

Translated from the Hebrew by David Soskes, 1972

SOVIET-YIDDISH POETRY

It is, of course, impossible within the limits of a few pages to represent the rich variety (in volume and quality) of Soviet-Yiddish poetry published over a period of over sixty years. The following few excerpts from the works of only three from among the most important poets convey no more than glimpses of their art and pre-occupations; all three were prolific writers (Markish, moreover, also wrote novels and Halkin plays). Regrettably, very little of their work is available in English translations.

Translations from the Yiddish

PERETZ MARKISH (1890-1952)

* * *

My name is: 'NOW'
When I stretch out my hands
they reach out to the world's far ends.
When I raise my eyes
they drink in the world above and below.

Thus, with open eyes, my shirt unbuttoned
and my arms outstretched,
I do not know whether I am at home here
or in alien land,
whether I am a beginning
or an end.

* * *

I bid you farewell,
passing time,
I don't know you, time past,
neither belong to me –
really,
you merely dreamt of me.

And what about my future,
with its growth of grey hair?
It is nowhere,
except in my dreams.

There's only the present, the 'flimsy now',
unseen, blind!
And we are both of one kind,
together we die,
and are born the same way!

*   *   *

So I don't know whether
I am at home
or in alien land –
I am on the run!...
I feel lost and abandoned,
I am no one's in a no-man's land,
without a beginning, without an end...

*   *   *

Black crows spinning in the air,
stitching and weaving in waves.
Oh yes, with my voice at night
I betrayed my God.
Now, in the valley of lust,
let me feed your day with my hands.
I'll strike the stones of my heart
to beat out a drink for him.

High above, the sails unfold,
giving another hue to the doe-skinned East.
It'll be an eternity till the bee settles down on the bloom
– day in one eye and smoke in another.
Oh yes, I was once the summit of Mount Sinai.

A Mirror on a Stone

Now that my sight comes back to me again
I see, and feel it with my body's every part,
that, like a mirror on a stone breaks up to bits,
so, breaking with a bang, did break my heart.

Each of the pieces surely does not cease
to be a witness to my being till I'm gone.
 – Don't trample on me yet in judgment, Time,
until I have picked up the splinters, one by one.

I'll pick them up and piece them, bit by bit,
together till my blood-stained fingers hurt.
However I may try my art to make them fit,
they will show up my face forever blurred.

Now only, in my sadness, as I comprehend
the painful process, I begin to feel the pain
of wanting once to see myself reflected whole in these,
the scattered splinters cast upon the seven seas . . .

In Memory of Solomon Mikhoels
(Extract)

. . . Wave after wave, a stream of people follows
each other, paying homage in procession:
Six million will rise up to honour you,
the tortured, murdered millions, dead and silent.

As you have honoured them when you fell down,
alone at midnight, aching from your wounds,
amidst the wastes of Minsk, covered with snow,
in the darkness of a raging whirling storm.

As if, through dying, you were trying still to ease
their pain, set them at rest and save their honour –
a stark reproach against the world at large –
now lying broken, frozen on the ground.

And the sadness flows, a silent warning,
your downfall struck at your people's very heart.
In their graves six million dead will rise to honour you,
who fell, a victim, while you honoured them.

*   *   *

Somewhere in Heaven, amidst blending light,
a star assumes your shining name.
Don't be ashamed for being slandered in your plight –
Eternity's is the eternal shame!

Mikhoels, the world famous actor and director of the Moscow State Jewish Theatre, and chairman of the Jewish Anti-Fascist Committee during the war, was murdered by the agents of the KGB in January of 1948, which was the signal for the subsequent arrests or executions of the most important Soviet-Yiddish writers and intellectuals later that year.

The Last Toast

We reached out far, we reached out high,
Higher than the birds can fly.
The highest mountains we climbed up.
So let us freely fill the cup –
That all the things we want to do,
All we desire may yet come true!

Deeper than the ground at sea
We descended joyfully.
And with a song our thirst we stilled.
Let the cup be freely filled –
That the people's wells shall flow
And not a drop is lost below!

The summer quickly bloomed away,
The autumn's here, early and grey,
And winter waits its turn somewhere.
Let the cup be filled once more –
To the near ones, those to come,
To take our place when we are gone!

We don't regret our growing grey,
For we lived joyfully and gay,
With our people, with our land.
Fill up the cup, show your free hand –
That enviously the future shall,
Remembering us, speak of us well!

How much longer are we spared
To live our lives the way we dared,
Until we reach the saddening brink?
Fill freely up and let us drink –
To the stars and skies above,
To our last longing, to our last love!

This is probably the last poem by the leading Soviet-Yiddish poet, a toast to the New Year 1949. Shortly afterwards he was arrested, kept in prison for the next three and a half years until 12 August 1952, when he together with a number of other Soviet-Yiddish writers and intellectuals was executed after a secret trial.

1956

SHMUEL HALKIN (1897-1960)

A Drop of Dew

You look at me,
as looks a drop of dew down from a tree
Which does not know whether or not to drop.
For on its branch it feels roundly on top,
For on its branch it's pure and clear,
And full of sunshine and of air.
And full of grace apparent:
Filled with itself and yet transparent.

Deep-set Ditches, Reddish Loam

Deep-set ditches, reddish loam –
once upon a time my home.

Orchards blossomed here in May,
autumn birds flew on their way,
and in winter there fell snow.
Woe and sorrow there now.

Stark disaster struck my town.
Doors of houses, nooks and pillars –
open, empty, broken down
by the hands of brutal killers,
murdering babies, sparing none.
Old folk, women, all are gone.

Deep-set ditches, reddish loam –
once upon a time my home.

Years have passed since those black days.
All those ditches turned to graves.
Redder still the red loam grew.
There I set up house anew.
Beneath this earth my brothers lie,
driven from their homes to die,
broken-limbed and maimed and shot
and thrown into the pits to rot.

Deep-set ditches, reddish loam –
once upon a time my home.

Better times will come again.
They will soothe my grief, my pain
and will change my fortune, too.
Once again children will grow
who will sing and play and leap
where the pits stretch, full and deep,
where my holy martyrs lie.
Maybe my sorrow, too, will die.

Deep-set ditches, reddish loam –
once upon a time my home.

Blessed be the Word

(From the poet's literary estate, published posthumously)

Not even youthful courage nor the blood
shed in battle in the desert dust
have attracted me
to the distant eastern land –
none of that.

But then – what marvel! – a song I heard
which tells of sands and caravans,
of sun-drenched earth and fields and groves,
has brought the country nearer to my heart.

And made me feel the wind blow in my face,
wave after wave, so close and hot;
and kinship, dormant through the ages,
re-awakened by whirl-wind and camel's trot.

And though I've been so long away from there,
child of the West, indigenous, at home here,
I feel again a desert warrior,
with sword in hand that cuts through fine hair.

The heat that follows rainy days is mine,
almonds and pomegranates, too.

My thirst I still with juicy grapes and vine,
and there is the Dead Sea, blending blue.

Blessed be the word that, magic wonder,
links again what time and space had torn asunder.

DAVID HOFSHTEYN (1889-1952)

In Russian Fields at Dusk

In Russian fields at dusk, in wintry frost —
where can one feel lonelier, more lonely, more lost?

A squeaking sledge, drawn by an old horse,
slides along the snow-covered course.

Below, in a corner, dimming and pale,
a path fades sadly away down the dale.

In front there stretches the white desert of snow,
in the distance a sprinkle of huts down below,
and behind me my hamlet dreamily dozes.

Narrow lanes lead to one of the houses,
a house like the others but its windows are bigger.
I am the oldest of the children who live there.

My world is narrow, enclosed in my own.
Once only a fortnight I travel to town,

silently longing for the wide-open road,
for fields that are buried beneath the white shroud.

And hidden within me are the pangs of growing,
waiting and waiting for ploughing and sowing.

In Russian fields, at dusk, in wintry frost —
where can one feel lonelier, more lonely, more lost?

1919

Such Moments as These...

(Extract from the poem, '1944')

...Such moments are now
my sole consolation.
At such moments as these
I can reach for my pen
and write once again
in the style of my own.
My memory is awake –
though much I've forgotten –
spinning the threads
of those radiant days
when a whole generation
kept on repeating
the two lines I wrote then.
It was not a question
not a complaint.
The simple statement I made by the way
is still remembered to this very day:
'In Russian fields, at dusk, in wintry frost –
where can one feel lonelier, more lonely, more lost?'

CONTEXT AND CONTINUITY

The Golden Chain

(Extract from a play)

Y. L. PERETZ

Peretz calls his dramatic poem – 'drama of a chassidic family'. The family: SHLOIME, the chassidic Rabbi and living link in the 'golden chain' connecting his own generation with the Baal Shem-Tov, the founder of the chassidic sect; PINCHAS, Rabbi Shloime's son and heir, who takes his place when his father insists on 'holding on' to the Sabbath, symbol of the messianic age. 'My black son!', his father calls him for giving in to the clamour of the masses by 'ending the Sabbath', thus reconciling the existing order with the uncompromising and unquestioning belief in God. But the hope for final release and redemption remains and is renewed with each succeeding generation. Pinchas's successor, MOISHE, rises for a short moment once more to the glory of his grandfather in his vision of world redemption but he, too, is too weak to stand the strain. Yet the 'link' is maintained; JONATHAN, the son of Moishe, steps in, following in the path of his predecessors. It should be noted that the Rabbis, in each successive generation, don't present themselves as the 'redeemers'; they are merely the spokesmen of the desires and dreams of their followers, voicing their pains, and 'storming the heavens' to avert the disaster of doom and destruction. In this sense 'the golden chain' links the past with the present and the future. The idea of the 'Sabbath' here is not just that of a day of rest to soothe the pain and to halt the drabness and hardships of everydayness, but of a new order of things which is to put an end to pain and misery and open up an era of joy and contentment; in other words it is the vision of the messianic age.

'*We, the Sabbath-inspired and festive Jews*' – Rabbi Shloime's great call to his bewildered followers – assumed the significance of a battle-cry for the younger generation which followed in Peretz's footsteps, looking upon him as their teacher and mentor. It gave birth to what was later termed 'Peretzism' not only in literature but also in the arts. For a time it developed into a new movement in search of beauty and new ideas, a kind of Neo-Chassidism which reconciled the old with the new, freeing the former of its mysticism and linking the latter with the concept of continuity and change.

The following short extract from the First Act of *The Golden Chain* leads up to the vision of Rabbi Shloime and ends with his sad and resigned utterance: 'So it was not to be!' Although this poetic drama is generally considered Peretz's greatest artistic achievement (besides his Stories and Sketches), there is, as far as we could ascertain, no English translation of it available.

The Rabbi's house. It is late evening following Sabbath Day. Dim light reflects a strip of pale moonshine and snow from outside, swallowed up by growing darkness until, later, towards the end of the Act, a snow storm lends a ghostly grey colour to the scene. The room looks disorderly and deserted as if it had just witnessed disaster. Outcries and murmurings penetrate, whenever a door opens.

ABRAHAM, LEMACH and BEINISH – three Elders among the Chassidim, who are closest to the Rabbi.

ABRAHAM: Sabbath!... Sabbath!
   It's Sabbath still
   as long as *Havdolah*[1] is not pronounced...
LEMACH: A strange beginning of a week...
BEINISH: What a week this one will be...
   May God Almighty save us!
LEMACH: Yet my heart foretold it,
   I felt I had to come here...

BEINISH: And I was drawn as if by magnets.
LEMACH: Just then my son-in-law decided
on divorce ...
BEINISH: And I was held up by the river;
no bridge, no barge to cross it;
big waves followed by bigger still!
ABRAHAM: So you envy my earlier arrival here?
LEMACH: Pray, tell us what has happened!
BEINISH: You drag our souls out with your silence!
ABRAHAM: What has happened?... Nothing!
Almost nothing ...
He spoke of visions,
of visions he had seen ...
LEMACH: Did someone gather, guess their hidden meaning?
ABRAHAM: Miryam ...
LEMACH and BEINISH: Miryam ... Miryam ...
OTHER CHASSIDIM (*enter silently, remaining in respectful distance from the Elders*).
ONE: Merchants are in a hurry for home,
afraid to stay, afraid to go ...
ANOTHER: A woman in the gallery
is fainting ...
A THIRD: She cannot come to ...
The prayer-house, in darkness, clamours ...
SECOND: Like a rushing river ...
FIRST: Like a rustling forest ...
ABRAHAM (*as if in a trance*): He fell asleep ...
Exhausted ...
And then, shaken from within,
he opened his eyes,
horrified ...
'A world in red!' – he said –
'A world in red!' –
and trembled.
Miryam stood nearby ...
Said she, turning to us:
'Blood will flow,
Jewish blood will flow like water ...'
ANOTHER CHASSID (*entering*): In groups they stand around in the street,

        stricken with fear and speaking in whispers.
        And the darkness grows...
        The shops stay closed,
        the lights un-lit...
ABRAHAM: ...And again he fell asleep...
        And then, shaken once more, he awoke,
        his white beard trembling
        and swaying his head.
        'Flames' – he said –
        'flames are flying through the air!'
        And Miryam spoke:
        'Cities and towns
        will go up in smoke...'
        And then, later, he has seen a forest,
        stretching without end...
        The trees close together,
        the crowns interlocked,
        the branches interveined,
        the naked roots turned upwards,
        twisted, crowded, tight...
        And when the time had arrived
        for a tree to die...
        the tree, torn up from its soil,
        suspended in mid-air remained,
        with no room to lay down
        to its final rest...
        ...And on the ground below, around the trunks,
        there moved, in circles, mysterious things,
        like beasts,
        like beasts of prey,
        with flashing and hungry eyes,
        running and tearing themselves away,
        out of the woods... (*Pause*)
        Said Miryam upon these:
        'Evil decrees,
        deaths and disease...'
LEMACH: Deaths and disease...
BEINISH: ...and evil decrees...
ABRAHAM: ...And high up there,
        among the twisted twigs,

where death and life unite and mix,
there, he said, nest heavy birds,
big and heavy birds – they hop
and jump from branch to branch,
from tree to tree
laughing . . .
mocking . . .
Yea, Yea. They laugh and mock . . .
And Miryam, listening, explained:
'A laughing-stock
and a mockery
we will be . . .'

MOISHE (*entering from the Rabbi's Room, sad and pale*):
Stop . . . stop . . .
Stop it, venerable men, old Jews!
Is there not enough of sadness?
We are sunk in sadness,
soaked with sadness . . .

RABBI SHLOIME (*tall, grey-haired, pale; excepting his pointed black cap, he is clad in pure white. Enters, walking up into the centre of the room, reluctantly followed by* YISROEL, *his First Secretary, and others*).

VOICES: The Rabbi!
Long live the Rabbi!
The Rabbi!

RABBI (*turning to Yisroel and to others behind him*):
In vain all your talk!
Your prayers in vain!
I refuse! I refrain!
I shall not make the *Havdolah*!

YISROEL (*pointing backwards*):
But, Rabbi, the public demands . . .

OTHERS: The public implores . . .
   – People are hunted with fear . . .
   – Have mercy, Rabbi, with the people!

RABBI: The people . . .
The public . . .
One . . . three . . . four . . .
five small congregations . . .
Little poor Jews . . .

    Lean-faced
    and shrunken
    little Jews...
    Humbly they come
    and knock at the door of the Holy Man...
(*with pain*) Freezing little souls,
    faint-hearted.
    They come,
    stretch out their hands
    to the Holy Ark:
    A spark! A spark!
    A gift, a small grant,
    a miracle, something –
    a hint and a sign from the Other Side!
    And everyone wants it for himself,
    for him only,
    for wife and child,
    for his own kith and kin...
(*Pause*) ... And here,
    tottering between death and life,
    a world sinks into darkness and fear,
    a world!
MIRYAM (*wife of Moishe, near the window*):
    The cloud is closing darkly in...
    Its shadow, like a bird,
    spreads out its wings...
RABBI: Clad in black
    as in a shroud,
    the Soul of the World –
    the Present Divine
    is crying aloud,
    mourning and moaning.
    In its own blood drowning,
    the Heart of the World
    is struggling to breathe!
(*rising, and raising his hands*):
    Redeemed from horror and pain
    must be –
    the world!
    ... I shall not make *Havdolah*, no!

MIRYAM: Angrily the cloud grows brown.
   Brown with rage the sky looks down.
   And they, the children over there, they smile –
   they do not see, they do not know!
RABBI (*bitter*):   So the Heavens are raging!
   Why does he not end,
   why does Shloime not end the Sabbath? . . .
   They have foregathered,
   the poor little souls,
   they have come back, the called-up pawns . . .
   Have the little doves not been soiled
   while on earth, released for a while?
   Haven't they lost a wing of a kind?
   Haven't they left a feather behind?
   We must look at them close and see!
   And for trial prepared
   is in Heavenly Court . . .
   In their golden gowns
   and flashing crowns,
   they are ready to sit
   in judgment . . .
   (*merciful*) And the little souls
   are fluttering
   and trembling with fear
   of Judgment Day!
   (*changing*) Don't tremble,
   don't fear!
   Reb Shloime will not make *Havdolah* . . .
   And Judgment there will not be!
(*Tense pause broken by wind outside.*)
MIRYAM: Winds are blowing,
   driving, drifting
   round the house, around the house . . .
   How they whistle, how they howl . . .
RABBI: So Hell is raging, too!
   It's sending out its messengers!
   Black-boding birds carries the wind.
   The Black Dog up there
   is rattling its chain!
   Holy Sabbath has gone,

yet Shloime insists
not to make the *Havdolah*.
Hell is being heated,
it is boiling,
it is seething ...
Smoking flames go up and wind their way
into the mists and clouds thickened with fog ...
'Come back, you sinners!
'To horror and pain,
'to evil and suffering,
'to heavy punishment ...
'why don't you come back?'
And the poor little souls,
soiled with sins,
they know
when the Sabbath is dimming away ...
and they tremble
and they pick
and beat their blackened wings
and stroke their flattened feathers
and press them to their skins;
and with trembling hearts
they hold on and cling
to the little clouds,
trembling ...
trembling!
(*changed voice*) Do not tremble,
  do not fear!
  Fly on freely
  at your will
  and where the wind will carry you –
  Sabbath shall not end!
VOICES (*in horror*): And what will be?
RABBI: There shall be Sabbath – Sabbath!
  I'll hold on to it, I'll not let it go!
  There shall be no trial or judgment!
(*Pause*) Up in Heavens, before His Mercy Seat,
  there a balance is placed.
  And the scales, they swing and sway
  unsteady, uneasy ...

The good deeds are laid
against the bad ones, and weighed ...
Guilty not fully,
nor guiltless completely ...
the beam does not rest in its place.
God in His Mercy and Grace
looks on and even He cannot help ... (*Pause*)
And the Messiah,
at the gates of Rome,
is waiting, wounded,
awaiting his time.
Undressing them now, now dressing them up,
his wounds do not heal.
And he cannot rise to redeem the world.
Yet, there is no strength to wait any longer ...
Into darkness and horror is sinking the world ...
(*with force*) THE WORLD, IT MUST BE REDEEMED!
VOICES (*quietly*):   But how, but how?
RABBI: Let there be Sabbath!
Sabbath lasting! Sabbath eternal!
None shall plough,
none shall sow,
none shall build or mend,
none shall sell or spend!
VOICE: But that will be the world's end!
RABBI: Let it be!
And we,
the Sabbath-inspired,
in festive mood,
our souls enchanted –
we'll walk over its ruins!
VOICES: Whereto, Rabbi, whereto?
RABBI: To Him, to Him!
Singing and dancing we'll go
to Him!
Sing with me,
dance with me!
... And so we go!
Singing and dancing we rise and grow!

We, the great – the great Jews we are,
Sabbath-inspired and festive Jews.
Our souls aflame, we reach out far.
The clouds are dwindling in our path,
the Heavens are opening up for us ...
... And we do not ask favours,
nor charity!
Great and proud people – Jews are we!
Our forebears before us have planted the seed,
we could wait no longer for the day to be freed!
The Song of Songs we recite and sing,
singing and dancing we close the ring ...

YISROEL (*enters the prayer-house from where a broad strip of light is cutting through the darkness*):
 ... Good Week to you, Jews, the Sabbath has gone!
RABBI (*sinks back into his high chair*):
SO IT WAS NOT TO BE!
ABRAHAM: Who has revolted against the throne?
YISROEL: Pinchas pronounced the *Havdolah*, the Rabbi's son. *Rabbi* Pinchas he is from now on!
RABBI: My son, my black son ...

1 *Havdolah* ('Separation') – ceremonial prayer, usually pronounced over a cup of wine, at the end of the Sabbath day to indicate the termination of the Sabbath (or of Festival) and the beginning of the new week (or of the week-day following the Festival).

Translated from the Yiddish, 1953

Two Poems by
Y. L. PERETZ

Brothers

Whites and Browns and Blacks and Yellows –
mix the colours with each other!
All are brothers, men and fellows,
of one father, of one mother.

Fellow men they are and brothers,
different only by their name,
different only by their colour,
nature made them all the same.

Fellow men they are and brothers,
whether white or black or pale.
Different faces, natives, races –
it is but a fairy tale.

The World is No No-Man's Land

Don't think that the world is a no-man's land, made
for wolves and for foxes to rob and to raid;
the heavens – put there to hide from God's view;
the mists – to conceal the criminal few;
the soil – to soak in the blood that is spilled.
Don't think that the world is a free-for-all place.

No no-man's land – no! No jungle, no waste!
For measured and weighed are all things on this earth.
No tear and no blood-drop is shed unaccounted.
No spark in an eye is put out unrecorded.
Of tears will grow rivers, of rivers an ocean,
of oceans a flood and of sparks will spring thunder.
Don't think there is no justice, nor judge!

'Peretzism' and Yiddish

JOSEF HERMAN

'Peretz summarizes a dream, and thus his leadership was never questioned.'

I detested the Yiddish I heard as a child and wanted nothing of it... It was all utility words which had little feeling, no lyricism and no music. Even in rages it sounded flat, without muscular vigour or suggestion of mood... As for tenderness the vocabulary seemed so poor that Peretz had to admit that 'it is impossible to love in Yiddish...' There were only basic words and these lacked sensuality, elasticity, variety, intensity of tone which could blend the emotional quality of the situation with the longing for loving articulation...

At seventeen or thereabout I met some young men my age or older men who spoke a different kind of Yiddish than the one I heard around me. They spoke Yiddish with a sense of pride, and one could recognize that they trained their minds in Yiddish and their Yiddish suggested a refinement and force I never thought Yiddish was capable of... Some of them were students from the Vilno Teachers' Seminary, some were members of the student organizations linked with the *Bund*... They all had one thing in common: they all loved Yiddish and worked for its enrichment... There may have been an element of youthful posturing but one thing was certain: their Yiddish was fluent and precise, inventive and natural, it had beauty and music... Above all theirs was an urban Yiddish free from village suggestions, village narrowness and village 'wit' ... Their Yiddish had a graver tone and an obvious serenity ... It was in every sense of the word a different Yiddish, and to be a revelation. Their love for Yiddish became my love, their feelings my feelings, their enthusiasm my enthusiasm ... One of them, Abe Gurfinkel if my memory serves me right, had much to do with my re-education. He said: 'Leave the classics for later ... For the present read our contemporary poets and prose writers, read Markish, Kwitko, Brodersohn; they are Europeans in Yiddish ... They are the true inheritors of Peretzism...'

'Inheritors of Peretzism' – this obviously has the sound of something important ... We can leave the 'inheritors' for the time being and concentrate on 'Peretzism'. It is about the nature of Peretzism and its significance for Yiddish that I intend first to comment on.

The European nature of the modern Jew found little expression until Peretz and his generation came on the scene of Jewish life. Hitherto, our separateness, our old age and the dim provincialism of our life, a life not altogether without depth, but certainly limited in its range, has found expression ... Mendele scorned that life ... Sholem Aleichem abhorred its pettiness ... But both remained within its enclosure ... Peretz synthesized what lay ahead. Hence Peretzism acquired a special significance; it meant something bigger than a person of genius, or a style in literature; and although it gave immense authority to Yiddish as a language it was a source of ideas, as a call to dignify our everyday, as an expression of our humanity, that Peretzism became symbolic of ... And like all symbols it had its own attraction but it was also an imperishable core of idealism and newness. Perhaps it promised more than could be achieved within the context of history; however, it shaped the consciousness of my contemporaries and later reached the deeper layers of our collective subconscience, so that decade after decade it continued to live and act upon us without our being aware of it ...

As a writer Peretz may not have had all the things expected of a great artist ... The very scrappiness of his literary output leaves one disheartened at times ... Professor Roback, in an appendix to a collection of Peretz's stories, may well be right when he says that neither Peretz's verse, nor his plays, nor even stories were the highest peak of our national achievement in literature... Peretz may have been surpassed in one field or another of creative writing... But David Frishman significantly says that more than a writer Peretz wanted to be SOMEBODY; at once the calibre of Peretz's quest, his very greatness becomes clear. It lies in a different direction. It has a Leonardoesque scale... The fragmentariness of Leonardo's output leaves us in a state of uncertainty: there were greater painters than Leonardo, there were greater sculptors, there were greater thinkers than Leonardo... Yet each generation for the last four hundred years was quite satisfied in thinking of Leonardo as SOMEBODY... The comparison with Leonardo should not suggest a similar quality of genius. But in art as in culture generally there appear personalities who cannot be understood in terms of professional achievement alone.

From the Jewish point of view, history was ready for a Peretz ... Peretz wanted to be SOMEBODY, and the NOBODY-Jew wanted to be SOMEBODY. This is why so many of his readers found his ideas so familiar... Peretz did not shock them with his newness; they were ready for it... Peretz summarized a dream and thus his leadership was never questioned. When Peretz wrote his famous lines:

> ... and so we stride!
> We proud Jews!...
>
> Sabbath-inspired and festive Jews.
> Our souls aflame, we reach out far.
> The clouds are lifting from our path.
> Our souls aflame, we reach out far.
> The heavens are opening up for us...
> ... Great and proud people – Jews we are!

his readers recognized their own striving to command all sloppiness out of their lives; they felt their backs straighten and their heads lift up high and as never before thought this earth their rightful place...

Thus being SOMEBODY meant very much.

When Peretz tells a story about two Rabbis of different schools of Chassidic thought, the very title *BETWEEN TWO MOUNTAINS* opens not only the immensity of our traditional sources but points at the exemplariness of the new idealism . . . The climax of the story is an image of Dionysian loveliness; two Jews larger than life in an ecstatic dance against a falling sun. The space is wide open and sparkles with all the luxury of eventide. The air is warm and friendly. It no longer mattered whether Peretz made his point about the kind of Chassidism he found more desirable . . . The mountainous monumentality of the Jew was established and this mattered most . . .

In the story, IF NOT HIGHER, the notion of love having precedence over ritual and prayer is of secondary importance. Peretz's are not moralistic tales to lift up momentarily the spirit. His stories are of a risen spirit. This new spirit meant, to concern oneself with Jews is to concern oneself with humanity at large. In this it revealed its European character. Not Judaism but *WELTLICHKEIT* – worldliness is the underlying current of his stories, whether thematically drawn from Chassidic life or not. This *Worldliness* is the desire to link up with the broader traditions of European ideas, with HUMANISM which, since the Greeks, has united European peoples and was largely responsible for the variety of forms in life and art of which archaic ages had no notion . . .

The Rabbi chopping up wood, on the night preceding the Day of Atonement, to kindle the fire in the sick widow's shack, this image and not some abstract 'first principle' establishes the humanity of the Jew, and once again it is this that mattered most.

It was the Jewish working class which became the vanguard of Peretzism . . . They carried the new spirit of initiative and action and to them Peretzism and its ideas became a mutual flame.

Thus Peretz was not taken at his word value, though his language was beautiful and precise; he was looked up to, I repeat, as a concentrated source of ideas . . . Although in the richness of his poetic imagination they were seldom more than pale diagrams, but they were recognizable enough for decades of creative men to work on . . .

The Yiddish-speaking Jew still thinks alongside the lines of Peretz, though for the time being his field of action is a lost horizon. It was very much a partnership of a generation; today it is a monument to that generation. Peretz's perception remained a burning oracle and Peretzism a national source . . . It reminds us that Yiddish was the language of a Jewish Renaissance; an everyday language which in time became a language of one of the most original literatures, perhaps the last of European literatures not to be alienated from the masses ... Viewed in this light the totality of Peretz's writing amounts to a book of basic truths: his purpose was didactic with an emphasis on the socio-moral norm. His dialogue was with the whole of the Jewish people in the language of their newly acquired creative energies ... Thus Yiddish was not a language of repression and downheartedness; it was, on the contrary, a language of hope and of dignity ... It was a language of self-respect and self-discovery in the national sense of the word ... It was a European language, not as rich and varied as French, German or English, not as subtle as Italian, but being, as languages go, a young language, it had all the potentials of languages with rich traditions ...

After the death of the millions of European Jews one cannot help being worried about the future of Yiddish ... No university faculty for Yiddish can replace the living sources of the Yiddish speaking masses ... Where is their concentration now? Even if we can point to the United States, Soviet Russia, and Israel, the question remains whether Yiddish is still the language of their quest for the Jewish identity ...

1974

The Trial: a Chassidic Folktale

SH. ANSKI

In 1963 the Jewish literary world celebrated the centenary of Anski's birth. His name is most closely linked with The Dybbuk, *a mystery play of deep symbolical significance, which was made famous by the* Vilna Troupe (*in the original Yiddish*) *and* Habimah (*in the Hebrew translation by Bialik*). *Shlomo Zanwill Rappaport, the author's real name, wrote many other poems, stories and plays, in addition to being a collector and interpreter of Yiddish folklore, and translator from other languages. His Collected Works comprise fifteen volumes. He died in 1920.*

> ... And it came to pass
> in the days not long ago
> when the world resounded
> with the wonders which Reb Elimelech,
> the Righteous one performed.
> In an ill-fated hour for Jews
> the Romanian King decreed
> that after three weeks from the day
> not a single Jew should be allowed
> to remain within his empire.
> Naturally, the Jews when faced
> with a disaster great as this,
> proclaimed a public fast.
> They wept, lamented, cried.

They stormed the ancient graves,
praying and protesting —
all in vain.
For those evil spirits
hunting Jews
ever since the Holy Temple
was destroyed,
did all they could,
with a kind of wild obsession,
to prevent both tears and prayers
from reaching the High Heavens.
Only one Jew in all Romania
did neither fast nor cry.
It was Reb Feivel, well-known
for his age and wisdom.
All his life he'd spent
in the House of Learning,
studying the Talmud
and the Commentaries.
When Reb Feivel heard the news,
he was terrified at first
and near to tears, like everyone.
But suddenly his mind was struck
by a thought profound.
With trembling hands he grasped
one of the holy books, the Chumash,
to find his thought confirmed
and printed black on white.

— Why? — he instantly exclaimed —
What is all this about?
This Emperor's decree?
According to our Holy Scripture
it is null and void!
And quickly, with an arrow's speed,
he hurried to the Rabbi.
(The Rabbi in those days,
who reigned throughout the land,
was Baal Shem Tov's great disciple,
the famous Rabbi Elimelech.)

It was late at night when Feivel
reached the Rabbi's house.
He woke him from his slumber,
and at once began with heat:
'Pronounce your Judgment, Rabbi!
It is written in our Torah –
clear as daylight, is it not? –
that as Jews we are the servants
of the Creator of the World.
Now then, how dares an emperor
to issue decrees against the Jews?
And, in particular, I ask you, Rabbi,
how on earth does God permit
such gross and strange injustice?'
– Listen, my son –
said Elimelech quietly –
I must tell you frankly,
I consider it
as sheer impudence on your part
to accuse Almighty God
of breaking His own Law.
Besides, to put God to the test of a Torah Trial
smacks of many dangers.
But on the other hand, I'm well aware
that for the sake of Jews,
a great and holy congregation,
you are prepared for risks.
Therefore, I accept your challenge
to arrange the trial.
But, of course, this time of day
is unsuited for the purpose.
Come back tomorow, after dawn.

*   *   *

That very night, quite unexpected,
three Rabbis, wise and saintly men,
came to visit Rabbi Elimelech,
and among them was the world-renowned
Rav of Apta, the Baal Shem's beloved

pupil. Elimelech promptly asked them
to join him and to act as Judges.

Next morning, when Reb Feivel
arrived at the appointed time,
the Rabbis donned their prayer shawls
and the Holy Tribunal
proceeded with the Trial.
The Apter was the first to speak.
'Reb Feivel!' – he called out –
'Four Rabbis solemnly command you
to state your case against the One on High,
the Nameless One, Creator of All Things.'

But Reb Feivel stood there, pale,
confused and full of fear.
'No, my Lords, I can't!' – he mumbled –
'Nothing's left of last night's passion,
and all my courage's gone!'
Whereupon the Rav of Apta, sternly,
stressing every word, made this reply:
'I, the Apter, do hereby restore
your strength, with wisdom, knowledge, passion.
You can be certain of the justice of this court!'

And Reb Feivel, seized with passion
Once again, began his plea:
First he quoted from the Scripture,
then presented passages from the Gemarah,
proving irrefutably that God Almighty
was absolutely bound not to allow
the emperor's decree.
At this point one of the Judges
intervened reproachfully:
'Perhaps, Reb Feivel, you'll concede
to blame the emperor, instead of God?'
'Why the Emperor?' Reb Feivel shouted
angrily. 'What is he to me?
What business have I got
with the Romanian king? Who is he,

anyway? A man, a human being!
My dispute is with the One on High!'

At this the Apter rose
from his Judge's throne,
and calmly and with pride
proclaimed:
Let God Almighty, the Creator,
give us a clear answer
to Reb Feivel's clear complaints!
Said Rabbi Elimelech:
The answer I will give you.
There is no doubt, Reb Feivel's right
in saying that the Jews, our brothers,
are the Creator's servants,
and that none except Himself
may rightly punish them.
This being so, however, may He not
cause punishment to be delivered
by a stranger's hands?

'No! He may not!' Reb Feivel
interrupted heatedly.
'Are we then servants only?
Did you forget that it is also written:
'For you who are my children.'
That is to say, we are God's children, too.
Now then, a father, if he wants
to punish his own children,
does so himself, not with the help of others.'

– If so, how come that Titus
was made to burn the Holy Temple?
– persisted Elimelech.
'Well said! The Holy Temple – was it not
God's dwelling place, His Own? If so,
He could destroy it at His Will.
And don't we know that since that day
the One on High regrets what He has done?
"Woe to me" – thus He laments –

"with my own hands I have destroyed
my dwelling place, and laid it waste and bare!" '

— Let it be! — replied Reb Elimelech —
I'll grant you the Destruction
of the Holy Temple. But can you deny,
for instance, that the Jews are sinning?
How often has Almighty God admonished them,
both by persuasion and by threats,
to give up their evil doings and repent?
And did it help? It was of no avail!
In the end Almighty God grew angry with His Jews
and lost His temper ...

'What does it mean: "He lost His temper"?
What kind of talk is this?
If we should allow it,
He could one day,
today or any other day,
in His boundless rage,
destroy the world —
this and all the worlds He has created —
and exterminate the Jews ...'

— He could, you know —
Reb Elimelech put in calmly.

'No! He could not and He mustn't!
— Reb Feivel staunchly demanded.
'Is there no Judge nor Justice?
Have we not our Law, our Torah?
Listen, my Lords, I say,
I shall not move from here
until you will pronounce your Judgment,
binding the Creator to fulfil
and follow all the Laws
of our Torah, equally with us!'
But the Apter put a stop
to further arguments.

Rising from his seat,
he stroked his beard
and spoke up with great force:
'The case is clear! Enough of talk!'
And then he added:
'It is customary in a court
for both parties in the case,
after it has been presented,
to leave the court room.
If one of them refuses,
he must pay a penalty
and then is dragged away
by the court's official
in disgrace...
Therefore, Reb Feivel,
do you mind...
Lord of the Universe, you too
must remove yourself from here...'

Jumped up Elimelech:
'How is that? Is it not written
clearly – "His Glory fills the World"?
How can God, I ask you,
take His leave from us,
even for a moment?'
After a brief silence,
the Apter raised an angry,
grey and bushy eye-brow
and then murmured quietly:
'Since it's written clearly,
"Your Glory fills the world",
we give You our permission
to stay on for a while.
But I must warn You strictly
that our holy verdict
will not be affected by Your presence.
You must remember that the Torah
is no longer in the Heavens,
since You gave it up to us...'

For three full days and three full nights
the court remained in session.
Arguments were tossed about
like thunder bolts and lightning.
Proofs and counter-proofs
flew through the air,
with precedents and quotes
from the Cabalah and the Zohar,
interspersed with secret hints
and sacred words,
derived from hidden sources,
and with sparks of wisdom
from the sayings, few in number,
of the Great Baal Shem Tov.
For three full days
the great debate continued.
The learned Rabbis
shouted, quarrelled,
sparing neither threats nor spite,
calling each other names such as
'ignoramus', 'fool' and 'scoundrel'.
But in the end they did arrive
at a compromise
and the following conclusions:
that it was by sheer mistake
that God Almighty did permit
the Romanian king's decree.
(He translated wrongly the related verse
and did not fully understand
the deeper meaning of a phrase
in the Holy Zohar.)
Therefore, the decree
was null and void
and was to be revoked at once.
A scribe wrote down the verdict
on a piece of parchment,
and the holy Rabbis
signed it, one by one.
And the parchment with the verdict

was placed among the Torah Scrolls
in the Holy Ark.

Before another day had passed,
the emperor's decree
was null and void,
and by order of the king
revoked at once. AMEN!

Translated from the Yiddish, 1964

JACOB GLATSTEIN

Silent Unrest

Jacob Glatstein, who died in New York on 19 November 1971, aged 75, was prominent both as poet and essayist. As one of the leaders of the group of *In-zikhistn* ('in-zikh' = 'within') or 'introspectives' he exerted a considerable influence on the development of modern Yiddish poetry in the U.S.A. in the twenties. In later years he returned to more traditional forms, giving moving expression to the tragedy of Europe and Jewry during the Second World War. Glatstein's poetry ranges from quiet lyricism to harsh rhetoric, of which the following two poems are good examples. He also made effective use of folkloristic and biblical motifs in quite a unique way.

> The city lies with half-open eyes
> in the broad arms of the dark at dusk.
> In its eye-balls still hover the shadows
> of a tree and a pond, of a roof-top, a man,
> and of windows alight with longing,
> lit up by the colours of the setting sun.
> The diamonds of the tiring pond sparkle
> with sleepy songs that are filled with old and cold wisdom
> against the tranquil stretch of sky.
> The stamping of man, dog and child gets lost

in the gracefully silent soft sand,
as silent and graceful as the gliding
of black fish in the waters of the pond.
Man, dog, and child move softly
on a carpet of silent unrest,
humming the song of silent passing.

>From the cycle *Fraye Fersen* ('Free Verse'), 1926

Translated from the Yiddish

Without Jews

Without Jews there will be no Jewish God.
If we should depart from the world in the end,
the light will go out in your tattered tent.
Since Abraham has first discovered you,
you shone in the face of every Jew.
You radiated from Jewish eyes.
We formed your image in that of our own.
Wherever we went, in each country and town,
our Jewish God went, too, a stranger like us.
Each fallen head of a Jewish dead
is a broken vessel empty of sound.
For we were the carriers of your light,
the living sign of your miraculous sight.
Our dead are counted in millions now.
The stars that surround you grow dim and low,
and with them recedes the memory of you.
Soon your kingdom will vanish, too.
That which was planted and sown by Jews
lies burned on the ground.
On dead grass weeps the morning dew.

The Jewish dream and the Jewish truth
are desecrated both
and die together.
Whole congregations,
small children and women,

young and old folk,
even your Pillars and Rocks,
the saintly and nameless 'Thirty-Six' —
they all sleep a deadly eternal sleep.

Who will dream you up again?
Who will recall you?
Who will defy you?
Who will long for you?
Who will, bridging his pain,
turn away from you, to return again?

The night is eternal for a people that's dead.
Heaven and earth disappear.
The light goes out from your tattered tent,
it flickers away, it's the Jew's last hour.
Jewish God, you'll soon be no more!

From the cycle *Shtralendike Yidn* ('Radiant Jews'), 1946

AVRAM N. STENCIL

MOSES ON MOUNT HOREB

Avram Nokhem Stencil, that colourful stalwart of Yiddish, author of volumes of poetry and prose, editor and distributor of his own 'little magazine', *Loshn Un Lebn* ('Language and Life'), he carries on the Eastern European cultural tradition, blending deep-seated religiosity with modern thinking, in the only language he knows and loves – Yiddish. When he left his distant *shtetl* in deepest Poland, as a young man, he took with him on his wanderings across Germany and Holland, before arriving in London in the mid-thirties, not only the shadows of the *Yeshiva* but also the smell of freshly ploughed fields and of apple trees in blossoming orchards planted on the foot of black coal mines not far away.

They live with him to this day, and follow him to the darkest corners of Whitechapel.

The following poem is one of his earliest, taken from a cycle on biblical motifs, written around 1927.

> Below in the shadow of the deep-dark valley
> in the goats' tent amidst the dried-up palm trees,
> there Tsiporah rests, heavy and full,
> a ripened and rounded pomegranate.
>
> Her pregnant body tense at the seams,
> flowing over its folds,
> her hands holding on to the tent's rope,
> curling around and clinging to it,
> she calls out: Moses! Moses!
>
> His head leaning heavily over his staff,
> amidst his tired-out flock on the mountain,
> Moses beholds the Egyptian's dead head
> cut off and buried in the sand.
>
> His fingers gripping the weathered staff,
> his feet feeling a bleeding cold head,
> he calls out: Tsiporah...
> His head turned downwards, he reads,
> inscribed in big letters across the sand:
> *Thou shalt not kill!*

Translated from the Yiddish, 1967

On My 80th Birthday

I am no Dante and don't know his 'Hell'.
Everyone goes through his own paradise.
The only thing left to me is my hope eternal
that human suffering will end one day.

Yes, that 'mine' and 'his' will cease.

Will it happen in our day, in front of our eyes,
or only when we'll be dead and gone?
I don't know Milton and his 'paradise',
but I know our Jewish tune, only the one.

Each tune, in turn, is genuine and true.

Of the one sound '*oi*' and the silence thereafter
I made up my poems and rhymes all those years.
And the joy in them, the tears and the laughter,
I learned in *cheder*, by my rabbi inspired.

The 'oi' in my joy – it grows more and more tired.

Translated from the Yiddish, 1977

To Josef Herman

Where if not here, the miner's dwelling place,
could you, the stranger, feel at home again?
Here, black on black, with sweating brow, each man
– a cloudy pillar – bears your father's face.

The cobbler's hammer in his hand held tight;
of thousand suns the halo on his head;
His purple apron black from tarried thread,
and you, his son, the youngest, at his side.

The man with hoe and headlamp, down the mine –
is it your father's image you have drawn,
strong-faced and wiry in grey wash and line?

God's glory is reflected in your grey.
But where's the 'blue and rose' of early dawn?
Like charring coal it glimmers in your eye.

Translated from the Yiddish, 1960

MOISHE TEYF (1904-1966)

Six Million

I am bone – a bone of yours: I am part – a part of you.
Hey, arise from your pits, my song calls to you.
And it flutters and flows,
and breathes and grows,
for my name is: the Iron Jew.

I am joy – the joy of yours; I am song – I sing of you.
And it blossoms and blooms in springtime anew.
And it flutters and flows,
and breathes and grows,
for my name is: the Iron Jew.

I am wound – the wound of yours, six millionfold in one.
Hey, you hangman, remember! Don't touch that wound, for it
  is not yet gone.
It's still hot in me, in the beat of my heart,
and in the beat of my song it is, too.
For my name is: the Iron Jew!

Translated from the Yiddish, 1954